VOID

Library of
Davidson College

THE LEGAL PROFESSION IN COLONIAL SOUTH INDIA

THE
LEGAL PROFESSION
IN COLONIAL
SOUTH INDIA

JOHN J. PAUL

BOMBAY
OXFORD UNIVERSITY PRESS
DELHI CALCUTTA MADRAS
1991

Oxford University Press, Walton Street, Oxford OX2 6DP
NEW YORK TORONTO
DELHI BOMBAY CALCUTTA MADRAS KARACHI
PETALING JAYA SINGAPORE HONG KONG TOKYO
NAIROBI DAR ES SALAAM
and associates in
BERLIN IBADAN

© Oxford University Press 1991

ISBN 0 19 562558 7

Typeset by Aurelec Data Processing Systems, Pondicherry,
Printed by All India Press, Kennedy Nagar, Pondicherry-605001
and published by S. K. Mookerjee, Oxford University Press,
Oxford House, Apollo Bunder, Bombay-400 039

IN MEMORY OF
MY MOTHER

PREFACE

This book focuses on the development of the legal profession in South India, between 1802 and 1928, from the perspective of social or institutional history. It asks why and how the British introduced the legal profession and how it has transformed itself over time. The success of Indian lawyers, generally known as *vakils* or pleaders, is a story yet to be systematically told. Although scholars have conceded the role that lawyers played in the political and social transformation of the country during British rule, many are unaware of the acute struggles within which lawyers were involved during the fight to achieve equality of opportunity and treatment in a profession that generally espoused constitutional rights. This study offers insights into how the authorities exercised control over the Indian legal profession and how the profession grew—despite stiff competition among members of the bar—especially between English barristers and Indian vakils.

The book is based on a dissertation completed in 1986 at the University of Wisconsin-Madison under Professors R. E. Frykenberg and Marc Galanter. I was fortunate to have known Professor Frykenberg as my guru, 'big' brother, and friend; not only did he spend many hours with me at different stages of this project— offering new ideas, encouragement, and pruning the written drafts—he also often interceded on my behalf to facilitate progress on my work. Professor Galanter provided the kind of intellectual direction without which this study would not have been possible. Frequent discussions over the years about the Madras bar helped extend this investigation far beyond a prosopography of a few eminent lawyers.

Many in India and elsewhere contributed equally to the progress of this work. Foremost among them were the Honourable Judges of the High Court at Madras, the Secretaries of the Advocates and the Bar Associations, and the Secretary of the Tamil Nadu Legal Aid Board. By their sympathetic understanding of my project and timely intervention, Justice P. R. Gokulakrishnan (then Acting Chief Justice), Justice G. Ramanujam and Justice V. Ratnam enabled me to consult and microfilm the High Court administrative records. Further encouragement came from Judge Ramalingam of the City Civil Court, Madras. Both R. Gandhi and P. R. Selvaraj, Secretaries of the Advocates Association (formerly the Vakils' Association) and S. Masilamani, Secretary of the Bar Association, allowed me to consult the records of their organizations. They gave free use of whatever I needed from their archives and libraries. M. Raja, Secretary of the Tamil Nadu Legal Aid Board, served as liaison between these individuals and myself, and also provided several introductions to others. His interest in my study remained constant as did his encouragement throughout my stay in Madras. My personal acknowledgement of kindness must go to all these individuals and their staff members. Without such help, this study would not have developed beyond its preliminary chapters.

The Tamil Nadu Archives and Library at Madras furnished valuable documents. Despite periodic inconveniences on account of limited staff and facilities, I received support from the Commissioner, the Assistant Commissioners, the Research Officer, the Librarian and members of the staff. Their general readiness to help locate, obtain and microfilm the documents was extremely useful. Other institutions, such as the Adyar Research Library (formerly the Theosophical Society), Connemara Library, Law College Library, Madras Literary Society Library, Madras University Library, Maraimalai Adigal Library and the Servants of India Society Library provided further materials. The librarians of these institutions, together with their willing staff, were helpful in locating numerous biographies and rare books on Madras lawyers.

In addition to individuals mentioned in the bibliography, I must also acknowledge the generosity of many I interviewed. They willingly shared their personal experiences at the bar or told me about their contacts with members of the bar. Among them were Justice R. Ramaprasada Rao (former Chief Justice of Madras High Court), P. N. Appuswamy (advocate-writer), M. Bhaktavatchalam (former Chief Minister), T. Chengalvaroyan (advocate), M. A. Manickavelu Naicker (former Congress Minister), T. R. Ramachandra Iyer (advocate), A. Ranganathan, K. S. Sankara Raman (retired judicial officer), P. N. Sivaraman (journalist), V. N. Venkata Varadachariar (son-in-law of Sir T. Rangachariar) and M. S. Venkatarama Iyer. A number of friends—such as Professor S. Ambirajan, Dolly Simon, V. O. C. Subramanian and V. Krishnamachari—provided help at various times and in varying degrees. The time I spent in their company makes me nostalgically long to return to Madras. In Delhi, Professor N. R. Madhava Menon and A. Mariarputham and S. Rangarajan (senior advocate) extended their warm friendship and assistance.

The Memorial Library of the University of Wisconsin-Madison, especially the Microforms Center and the Inter-Library Loan Department, served my needs beyond description. Individuals like Jack Wells, Ed Duesterhoeft and Judy Tuohy continuously provided help in locating books and other information. The Langdell Law Library of Harvard University also was useful for consulting numerous law journals and reports.

Support for my research in India mainly came from the American Institute of Indian Studies, in the form of a junior fellowship. Additional travel grants came from the Graduate School and from the History Department of the University of Wisconsin-Madison. Services rendered towards a Norwegian microfilming project brought remuneration from the Instituttet for Sammenlignende Kulturforskning through the efforts of Pamela Price (University of Oslo, Norway), although the project itself never materialized. Funds from my sister and brother and from personal savings enabled me to stay in Tamil Nadu longer than I had originally anticipated. A Summer Teaching Assistantship in Tamil (in the South Asian Studies Department), a History Department Fellowship, and a Domestic Travel Grant from the Graduate School further sustained my continuing study at the University of Wisconsin-Madison, and facilitated my subsequent scholarly activities. Participation in the 1988 NEH Summer Seminar on 'The End of the British Empire' at the University of Texas at Austin served as an ideal occasion to commence the revision of the manuscript. I received much encouragement and Professor W. Roger Louis' critical comments were beneficial.

Amidst their teaching schedules and committee responsibilities, Bill Pemberton and Marty Zanger, colleagues at the University of Wisconsin-La Crosse, meticulously read through the revised chapters and offered many suggestions in condensing the manuscript. I consider myself fortunate to have the friendship of scholars of their calibre.

The physical help of N. Muthu Durai in microfilming hundreds of documents at the High Court, at very short notice, can never be forgotten. His unswerving willingness to stay with me for nearly a month far exceeded the usual courtesy of a 'family-friend'. The stimulating companionship and encouragement of W. A. Sambasivam and N. Marimuthu, my friends of over two decades, sunk me even deeper in debt; they rendered comfort and relief during my final days in Madras, amidst their own responsibilities.

Finally, I must render acknowledgement, and thanks, to members of my family. My late mother Kamakshi Ammal, my sister Kamala Srinivasan, and my brother V. Raman, each in their own way, contributed much to the progress of my research in India. Their extraordinary support and sacrifices on my behalf can never be reciprocated. To know that the sentiments expressed by Tiruvalluvar (*Tirukkural* 69) had a personal application for my late mother and that her joy over my completing this study had redoubled gives me deep satisfaction. To her, I dedicate this work.

CONTENTS

Preface   vii
List of Tables   xiii
List of Abbreviations   xiv
Introduction   1

PART I: LAW PRACTICE IN THE COMPANY COURTS, 1802–1860

1 Beginnings of a Profession   17
   Legal Profession in the Company Courts / 17
   Legal Education of Pleaders / 31
   The 'Pamphlet Controversy' / 37
   The Role of Pleaders in Madras Society / 40

PART II: LAW PRACTICE IN THE HIGH COURT, 1860–1928

2 Rules of the High Court   45
   Admission of Barristers and Vakils / 48
   Admission of non-Madras Vakils / 55

3 The Barrister-Attorney Coalition   59
   Position of Barristers / 59
   Attorneys-at-Law / 73

4 Vakils' Preparation, Practice and Growth   82
   Preparing to Practise / 82
   Vakils' Practice / 87
   Anandacharlu's Pamphlet / 94
   Vakils' Growth / 96

5 The Limitations in Vakils' Practice   102
   Restrictions in Insolvency Court / 103
   Restrictions on Trade or Business / 108

PART III: THE VAKILS' ASSOCIATION, 1889–1920

6 The Association's Leaders and Privileges   119
   Officers of the Association / 120
   Duties of Officers / 122

xii *The Legal Profession in Colonial South India*

    Election of Officers / 123
    Resolutions of the Association / 125
    Privileges of Members / 130

7 Competing Voices in the Association   137
    Functions of the Association / 137
    Dissent and Unity / 146

PART IV: PROTEST AND REFORM, 1921–1928

8 Winds of Change   157
    Removal of Sex Discrimination / 158
    Debates on the Indian Bar Councils / 164
    The First Madras Bar Council / 174

Conclusion   182

Appendices
    I: Revised Rules of the Madras Bar, 1882 / 193
    II: Rules of the Attorneys Association / 196
    III: Rules of the Vakils' Association, 1889 / 201

Glossary   203

Notes   205

Bibliography   245

Index   259

TABLES

1	Enrolment of Practitioners between 1879 and 1908	99
2	Indian Graduates and Their Career Choices	100
3	Communal Representation of Graduates (in Arts and Law) in the Legal Profession	101
4	Presidents of the Vakils' Association, 1889–1931	120
5	Secretaries and Joint-Secretaries, 1889–1921	121
6	Some Members of the Managing Committee	121
7	Members of the First Madras Bar Council	180

ABBREVIATIONS

GOM	Government of Madras
HCAR	High Court Administrative Records
ILR-AS	*Indian Law Report-Allahabad Series*
ILR-CS	*Indian Law Reports-Calcutta Series*
ILR-MS	*Indian Law Reports-Madras Series*
ILR-PS	*Indian Law Reports-Patna Series*
LW-JS	*Law Weekly-Journal Section*
LW-RS	*Law Weekly-Reports Section*
MLJ-JS	*Madras Law Journal-Journal Section*
MLJ-RS	*Madras Law Journal-Reports Section*
MWN-JS	*Madras Weekly Notes-Journal Section*
RNP	*Reports on Native Newspapers*
TMLT	*The Madras Law Times*
VAM	*Vakils' Association Minutes*

INTRODUCTION

The modern Indian legal system is one of the most enduring legacies of the British Raj. Its growth over several centuries has yet to be adequately explored. How the British administrators of India, whether under the East India Company or under the Crown, went about introducing elaborate structures of courts, codes, functionaries, regulations and rules of procedure raises many questions that hold enormous significance for scholars. Does this system represent, as Professor Marc Galanter suggests, a striking instance of total displacement of one dominant intellectual tradition by one of foreign origin?[1] Or does it represent a more subtle blending of indigenous and alien institutions, a strange amalgam of local substances and foreign (Anglo-Saxon) procedures, and a curious composite of Indian and European inspiration and talent? Any study attempting to understand the development of various legal institutions must necessarily take into account the interplay between the socio-economic and political forces that shaped these institutions, on the one hand, and the roles played by various individuals—government executives, lawmakers, judges, lawyers or clerks—on the other. Only then would such analyses enable scholars to appreciate what the 'Indianization of law'[2] meant and how it gradually gained a firm footing in the subcontinent.

The complexities of social structure in India—with manifold fissures along lines of caste and community, language, religion and region—and the differential rates of impact in the spread of the legal system, both within and between the three Presidencies of British India, impose certain restrictions upon any investigation. It is for these reasons that this study is limited to the origins, growth and accomplishments of the legal profession in the Madras Presidency, focusing especially on those Indian lawyers who provided counsel and who served as the agents (*vakils*), brokers, or go-betweens (*dubashis*) in almost every conflict which came before a court of law.[3]

The purpose of this book is neither legal nor theoretical, but empirical and historical.[4] First in a series of projected studies on the emergence of modern professions in the nineteenth century,[5] it explains how the British in India scrupulously controlled each phase in the development of the legal profession. It explores the manner in which both pleaders and vakils responded to the opportunities that the rulers created, their interaction with other practitioners such as barristers and attorneys, and their resoluteness in creating a body responsible for establishing professional qualifications and ethical standards.

It would be useful to bear in mind some of the characteristics of the legal profession in India, which were absent either in England or America. The foundations of the modern legal profession in India can be traced to the nineteenth century, when the British in India developed the present judicial and political structure. From the beginning, a legal practitioner was 'an officer of the court' and, hence, the government frequently subjected him to innumerable rules of admission and practice. Even after the establishment of High Courts in Bombay, Calcutta and Madras, vakils and pleaders had little power or influence in charting the direction or growth of their profession. While law makers, both central and provincial, passed laws prescribing what privileges and procedures would be appropriate for vakils and pleaders, the High Court in each Presidency formulated the precise rules for their qualification and admission; judges also defined the rules of practice, whether at the highest judicial tribunal or at the lowest court in the Presidency. The local government's control of legal education, the budget, and appointments to judicial offices, clearly prevented vakils from contributing anything towards raising the standards of the profession. Only after the inauguration of the Bar Councils' Act in 1926 did lawyers themselves begin to play a significant role in moulding their profession. The profession obtained still more autonomy after the passing of the Indian Advocates' Act in 1961.[6]

The decision of hundreds of college graduates to choose a career in law was concomitant with fluctuations in the employment market during the second half of the nineteenth century. The growing impossibility of finding positions in government and a conservative outlook forced many graduates from higher castes, especially brahmans, to choose the legal profession as an alternative. As a result, for a long time professionals lacked the notion of public service or what is known as 'the Nightingale syndrome'.[7] Some of the most influential and successful vakils certainly spearheaded numerous social reforms and political activities, but their participation in such movements was subordinated to their professional interests. For example, throughout the period of Gandhian agitation politics, which swept the country during the 1920s and '30s, lawyers were unwilling either to boycott the courts or to give up their practices and undertake constructive programmes in the rural areas.[8]

The rigid requirements of the High Court, which did not allow for much latitude in what practitioners could do, led to less imaginative modes of settling disputes. Formal litigation, as distinct from out-of-court settlement, counselling or planning, became standard. Most clients from the rural areas were ignorant of court procedures, and their interests in litigation often ran counter to those of a lawyer. At times, suitors distrusted their lawyers, feeling that they were mainly concerned about their income. Judges, therefore, stipulated that prior sanction should be obtained from clients before practitioners could decide whether or not to pursue alternative legal strategies. So long as the specificities of such prior permission were not spelled out in the *vakalat* (or authorization), a lawyer had no authority to go against the wishes of his client and would have to confine his activities to courtroom performances. Thus, courtroom advocacy became a dominant feature of lawyers' practice. Indeed, it had been so ever since the days of the *Adalat* system of the Company in the eighteenth century.

While lawyers in Africa were able to secure positions and representation within the judiciary and bureaucracy only after their countries became fully independent during the 1960s, lawyers in India held such positions almost from the start. Members of the profession were co-opted into every level of the administration and into the judicial system during the nineteenth century. The waxing and waning process of 'Indianization' of services had been well on its way at least a century before 'Africanization' was set in motion. The experiences of Indian lawyers in developing, testing, and implementing constitutional means for the gaining and using of power, and the subsequent political dividends that they had reaped therefrom, placed them much farther along than their counterparts in other Asian and African countries.

HISTORIOGRAPHY

Apart from scattered accounts and anecdotes of lawyers in numerous law journals, biographies and autobiographies, no systematic study of the origins, growth, composition and achievements of the bar in

India has ever been made. A number of sociological or anthropological studies are now available on district court bars as they exist today. But historical treatments are very few and far between.[9] Only a few works, like those of Schmitthener,[10] Buckee[11] and Srinivasa Rao,[12] are of any consequence. These portray the development of the Indian bar in broad strokes, showing that the legal profession grew from 'low status and disrepute' and developed 'into the most highly respected and influential' profession of pre-Independence India.[13]

Written 18 years ago when research on legal history in India was still in its infancy, Schmitthener's lucid exposition was intended as a 'sketch'. His essay highlights broad trends in the 'national' character of the profession with little concern for detail or for differentiating regional variations, whether in quality or in types of practice. The sources consulted for his article represent a wide selection of published materials: government reports, historical accounts of the British legal system and biographies, including autobiographies. Since he did not have access to any primary documents, Schmitthener included no data from the government archives, High Court, or professional associations.

Buckee's dissertation, completed nearly 15 years ago, focuses on the growth of the bar in Allahabad High Court over a period of 70 years. In six separate chapters, she discusses the constitution of courts and judiciary, the beginnings of legal education, the social background of the High Court lawyers and their law practice, and the role of lawyers in politics. She uses information gathered from private and official manuscripts, printed government documents, published works and oral data. Her study reflects the use of rich source materials, a logical presentation of facts, followed by sound analysis and carefully drawn conclusions. She admits that she chose the Allahabad bar because it provided her with 'a relatively less complicated situation',[14] and hence her study proved an easier undertaking than a study of the other High Courts (in Bombay, Calcutta or Madras) might have been.

Two different kinds of law practice existed in these courts: the Original and the Appellate Sides. Whereas barristers and attorneys claimed audience on both, for many decades vakils were permitted only in the latter. Had Buckee chosen any other High Court bar than the one at Allahabad, her study would have been more valuable. She would have been able to expose certain inherent 'disabilities' under which vakils were obliged to pursue their duties. Impressive sources notwithstanding, Buckee has not consulted the records of professional organizations—namely, those of barristers and vakils. Mutual rivalry and separation between these groups obviously led to the formation of at least two separate associations. It would be useful to know who provided leadership, what facilities these bodies offered for members, and how barristers and vakils manipulated their respective organizations in strengthening their own private claims to official 'loaves and fishes'.

An essay by Srinivasa Rao, included in a collection of articles on the Tamil Nadu Bar, is important because it is written by a lawyer who as an amateur historian possesses a fund of personal information and knowledge; his essay deals with the profession in Madras, which is the focus of this study. Yet his approach is more descriptive, intended to serve the needs of his own profession rather than analysing the history of the development of modern professions; he does not deal with certain issues addressed in this study. The use of primary documents is also conspicuously absent from his article.

FINDINGS

Two different kinds of sources have been used in this study: archival materials and information gathered from special questionnaires and personal interviews. Records come from the Tamil Nadu Archives, the Madras High Court, the Advocates' Association (formerly the Madras High Court Vakils' Association), and the Bar Association. The High Court Administrative Records and the original minutes of the two professional associations have never before been made available to scholars. Other published materials in the Madras High Court Library, the Tamil Nadu Archives Library, the Theosophical Society Library, the Connemara Library, the Servants of India Society Library, and the Maraimalai Adigal Library have also been useful. To supplement the archival data, I prepared a questionnaire and distributed it among a number of senior advocates. The biographical information they provided served as a catalyst for questions raised during personal interviews with lawyers or their descendants, retired or acting judges in the High Court and subordinate courts, former politicians, administrators and journalists.

Part I of this book sets forth the historical background from 1802, when the Company introduced the judicial system, to 1860, when Sir C. E. Trevelyan, Governor of Madras, appointed a special committee to study judicial reform. From its very beginning, the legal profession was under the control of the Government of Madras and the Government of India. Known as 'pleader' or 'vakil', the emergent lawyer knew little about either law or procedure. Regulations, according to B. B. Misra, 'provided no definite qualifications . . . no precise mode of proceedings, [and] no rules of evidence'.[15] Therefore, as early as 1816, the government took measures to institute some form of legal education at the College of Fort St. George; the college received support from the government. Later, during the 1830s, George Norton contributed his share. Yet neither effort succeeded, presumably because of limited resources or lack of interest. Only with the introduction of law lectures at the Presidency College in 1855 and with the establishment of a separate university in Madras did legal education finally become part of the curriculum.

The admission of English barristers in the Company courts in 1846 was a major turning point in the development of the profession in India. For many years, barristers had been practising in the Supreme Court, established in 1800 under the Royal Charter. After 1846, the two strands of the legal profession—English and Indian—began to interact closely with each other. Pleaders learned the art of cross-examination from barristers, gained the ability to sift through a mass of evidence to bring about a logical and artistic construction of cases, and learned to present their arguments in the English language. However, pleaders never commanded the respect usually accorded to barristers. Indeed, they often displayed a servile attitude towards judicial officers who, in turn, treated them with contempt.

In the early 1850s, an open war of words between protagonists of reform and defenders of the 'Madras system' in the judicial administration drew considerable attention from the press and from those who had a personal knowledge of the situation. Even though no one claimed ultimate victory, further developments on the political horizon convinced authorities of the need to revamp the entire judicial structure by amalgamating the courts of the Crown and the Company. As a result, the High Court of Madras was established in 1862 under its Letters Patent; the new judicial tribunal possessed enormous powers to regulate the entire judicial machinery throughout the Presidency as well as to control the growth of the legal profession.

Part II deals with the rules of practice that the High Court had framed regarding the three classes of 'lawyers': advocates (who generally were barristers), vakils and attorneys. It also highlights the nature of rivalry among the three groups and the peculiar problems that each group was faced with. The rules that the judges had framed in 1862, but subsequently amended in 1863, generated a good deal of controversy: the respective rights and privileges of advocates (or barristers) and vakils became important issues. The rules permitted the former to practise both on the Original and the Appellate Sides, but restricted vakils to the Appellate Side only. When the judges later decided to throw open the Original Side to vakils, advocates became outraged and criticized the judges for their overt partiality and patronage of the 'natives'. The attorneys joined the advocates in this campaign.

The period between 1862 and 1890 witnessed the barrister-attorney coalition, which vehemently opposed the concessions granted to vakils. Barristers took the initiative to restrict the advances of vakils on the Original Side. In 1865, they first assembled under the banner of a professional organization, known as 'the Madras Bar'; it became a powerful institution whose opinions could not be ignored, either by the government or by the judges. The Madras Bar provided a meeting place and served as a medium to express the concerns of barristers; it also passed resolutions on various subjects such as obtaining briefs from vakils, giving commission to law agents, enforcing discipline and representing the interests of its members. The advocate-attorney coalition continued to display hostility towards vakils, even after a Full Bench decision in 1876, formally recognizing the measures that the judges had taken some 14 years earlier. That in Madras alone vakils had been permitted to conduct cases under both jurisdictions of the High Court, and that vakils exclusively performed all three functions—acting, appearing and pleading—placed them far ahead of their counterparts in other High Courts, both in the legal profession and in subsequent achievements.

If some judges showed an interest in the opportunities of vakils, others were critical of the way they conducted their business. The absence of a professional body responsible for regulating the conduct of lawyers and for dealing with allegations of misconduct had cast additional burden upon judges. Whereas both barristers and attorneys, for a while, had generally managed to escape the punitive actions of the High Court by appealing to the jurisdiction of their parent organizations in England—either the Inns of Court or the Law Society—vakils had no such recourse; they were, as a result, often brought to book by judicial officers. Often sharp but unwarranted criticisms from the bench eventually persuaded P. Anandacharlu, a vakil, to publish a pamphlet exposing the strengths and weaknesses of all three groups of lawyers. In his view, each possessed certain merits even though a number of black-sheep brought dishonour to their fellow lawyers and no group was perfect in its attainments or immune from abuses of its position in the High Court. Yet the vakils grew in strength and talent, vigorously competing for business with their rivals.

Part III discusses the rebirth of the Madras High Court Vakils' Association. A qualitative difference seems to have existed between vakils who had practised during the first 25 years of the High Court and those who followed later. The younger generation had more potential for leadership and vision; they brought much respect and dignity to the profession. By reviving the almost defunct Association and by shouldering much of the responsibilities requisite for efficient management of the organization, emerging vakils like V. Krishnaswami Iyer, P. S. Sivaswami Iyer, M. Venkataramiah Chetty, and P. R. Sundara Iyer steered the Association through many storms. A few 'legal luminaries' among vakils—such as V. Bhashyam Iyengar and S. Subramania Iyer—by their erudition and skill enhanced the reputation of Madras vakils throughout the country and, at times, even as far away as England. Leadership remained in the hands of a small number of vakils, who slowly built up lucrative businesses for themselves. Except for a few, leaders came from the two major categories of Tamil brahmans: Iyer and Iyengar. This brahman concentration within the professional body made it look like a caste association. As one informant put it, the Vakils' Association, for all practical purposes, was a small *agraharam* (or brahman enclave) that catered to its own interest. Whether by accident or by design, South India was increasingly dominated by brahmans.[16]

The Association nevertheless sought to improve the status of vakils in general. Resolutions passed by the Association dealt with such matters as professional dress, rules for the enrolment of apprentices, elevation of vakils as advocates, and admission of vakils from other parts of the country. The Association also offered special facilities for members, especially for those who were either beginners or mediocre practitioners. Since poor vakils found it hardly possible to maintain their own offices or libraries, the Association provided these essentials for them.

Membership as well as leadership in the Association increased one's chances for judicial appointments because the local government often looked to that body as a nursery for rising bureaucratic talent; this caused resentment on the part of non-members who practised in the districts. When leaders of the Association decided to inaugurate the annual gathering of vakils in 1904, a social event hosted by leading vakils, members found a common forum to grapple with such crucial issues as overcrowding, disparities of business between seniors and juniors, reforms in legal education, and improvements in the apprenticeship examination system. The Association played three major roles. First, as a professional watchdog, it regulated the conduct of members and participated in all proceedings instituted in the High Court against vakils. Second, it submitted memorials and made representations to the authorities regarding appointments in the judicial service. Access to such appointments had been the exclusive preserve of barristers during the nineteenth century, but, at the turn of this century, vakils began to dominate the profession and to carry away most of the prizes. Third, as an advisory body, the Association gave opinions on several matters: economic, legislative, political, professional and social.

The Secretary of State for India introduced a series of reforms in 1919, in the wake of widespread discontent, mounting violence and growing clamour for more political concessions. Political conflicts in Madras during this time became increasingly communal. The ascendancy of brahmans in both the political and professional spheres had aroused resentment in the City and the influence of the non-brahman movement spread in every section of society, including the legal profession. Non-brahman vakils banded together and organized a rival association in hopes of reaping greater rewards from patronage and positions within the judicial service. Although it is not clear how the brahman-dominated Vakils' Association responded to the challenges of this rival organization, S. Srinivasa

Iyengar, the president of the Vakils' Association and the advocate general in Madras, took certain steps to bring about greater harmony, unity and solidarity among vakils and pleaders. His efforts, however, proved to be a failure.

Part IV shifts the focus from the personalities and events in Madras to those in Delhi. Many vakils from all over the country were elected to the Legislative Assembly, constituted under the Montagu-Chelmsford Reforms of 1919. They wanted to use their new positions as 'law makers' to reorganize the profession, by creating an 'Indian' Bar and by removing all distinctions between barristers and vakils. The legislators showed enthusiasm in removing the bar against women by permitting them to become lawyers, but they strongly disagreed over questions relating to the unification of the legal profession at a national level. In 1923, the Government of India appointed a committee, headed by E. M. D. Chamier, to study the question of creation of an Indian Bar; in 1924, the committee published its report, suggesting the founding of provincial bar councils instead of a centralized body and the gradual elimination of all distinctions which divided barristers from vakils. In spite of the subsequent altercations which arose between these two groups in the Assembly, and in spite of the 'stone-walling' tactics of barristers, the legislature passed a bill to create the Bar Councils, which became law in 1926. After two years, the Madras High Court introduced the act. Under the new law, judges had power to frame rules for the operation of the first Bar Council, to supervise the election of officers, and to appoint a number of individuals to that body. Subsequent election results clearly showed that city advocates dominated the Council. Moreover, brahmans constituted two-thirds of this body just as they had previously held dominant positions in the Vakils' Association. Thus, the Madras Bar Council, for all practical purposes, became an adjunct of the Vakils' Association.

SOUTH INDIAN SOCIAL HISTORY

In November 1983, at a conference of the Society for South Indian Studies, Professor G. A. Oddie presented an overview of historiography on modern South Indian society.[17] He observed that a recent trend was a shift from caste, but that there still was a paucity of studies on the rise of the Western-educated professional elites.[18] Many years ago, R. Suntharalingam correctly identified the pre-eminence of the legal profession in the late nineteenth century in initiating protests against unpopular policies of the government, but his pioneering study ended in 1891, just a few years after the vakils had really begun to assert their strength by reviving the defunct Madras High Court Vakils' Association.[19] This study in some respects picks up the story where Suntharalingam has left off. Leadership that vakils subsequently provided, either in securing their own position in the profession or in disseminating democratic ideals and in rejuvenating the local political and cultural institutions, reached its zenith during the period between 1890 and 1930. There is yet another dimension to this study: it expands the horizons of South Indian social history. The growth and the achievements of Indian lawyers during the period under study were so phenomenal that a proper understanding of the influence exerted by the profession as a whole and by its key actors in particular augments our appraisals of the impact of the modern education within South Indian society.

As Oddie has shown, we know a great deal about the upward mobility of castes (or caste organizations), about their inter-caste and intra-caste conflicts and about various forms of religious conversion during the late nineteenth and early twentieth centuries. In this period, many South Indian communities also went through some fundamental structural or institutional transformations in response to various cultural movements, economic opportunities and social conflicts generated by the rapid integration of the subcontinent. Furthermore, the introduction of modern education, new forms of employment and rising political consciousness throughout this period accelerated the rates of internal transformation within some of these castes. However, very little is known about how these factors contributed to the emergence of modern professions, especially the legal profession, or about how vakils ultimately succeeded in replacing the social and intellectual dominance of both the administrative and the commercial elites between 1880 and 1928.

DEFINITIONS

This study employs certain specific terms related to the legal profession and even though their meanings are restricted by context, they need some clarification. Generic or less technical terms (as lawyer, law practitioner, legal practitioner and professional) are also used throughout the study.

Between 1640 and 1727, individuals who practised law in different Company courts styled themselves 'solicitors' or 'attorneys'. Their only requirement consisted of a 'capacity to read, write and speak that type of English current in legal circles'.[20] Therefore, 'any Englishman who could establish his acquaintance with the formalism of law' got himself enrolled. Given the preoccupation of the city of Madras with commerce and trade, these practitioners had numerous opportunities for conveyancing or for drafting contracts. Though they had no formal training in law, they represented clients in court. When Charles Lockyer recorded his impressions of judicial life in Madras (in 1711), he referred to these individuals as 'lawyers'. This term had a functional reference: someone who prepared the necessary papers in a commercial transaction and made representations in court. That is why Lockyer wrote, 'Lawyers are plenty, and as knowing as can be expected from broken linen drapers and other crack'd tradesmen who seek their fortunes here by their wits.'[21]

In 1727, the Mayors Court was established by the Royal Charter. Attorneys in the Company courts were permitted to practise in the new court without any of the formal restrictions that came into effect 75 years later, at the turn of the century. These practitioners now styled themselves 'advocates, attorneys and proctors' but still had no clearly defined functions. They seem to have performed all three functions—acting, appearing and pleading. In 1830, when Sir Thomas Strange testified before the Select Committee of Parliament in London, he informed its members that, with the founding of the Supreme Court in Madras, a division of labour between advocates and attorneys had been established. Ever since, they had retained their distinct functions: advocates only appeared and pleaded in court, while attorneys acted and appeared.[22] In other words, an advocate participated in all proceedings of the court and argued on behalf of clients. An attorney, in contrast, received instructions from clients, prepared briefs and advised the counsel. An attorney also participated in the proceedings of the court but did not argue a case.

In 1802, the government introduced the Adalat system in the Madras Presidency. Regulation X allowed aspirants to a career in law to enrol themselves as 'vakils' or 'pleaders'. The term 'vakil' in Persian meant an 'agent', 'ambassador', 'representative' or 'counsellor'. The office of vakil under the Mughals was one of much honour and exaltation.[23] V. N. Srinivasa Rao has observed that 'The Vakil of the eighteenth century had been beyond the reach of the common man. When the helper of a litigant in court proudly called himself a Vakil, this imaginative step aided the dignified development of the mofussil Bar.'[24] It is difficult to see why the terms 'pleader' and 'vakil' were used side-by-side. In Regulation X of 1802 both are found and what factors distinguished one from the other are not clear. When advocates who appeared in the Supreme Court of Madras were finally permitted to plead in the company courts in 1846 and when attorneys were allowed to do the same in 1855, no such distinctions were maintained in the *Sadr Adalat* or Chief Court of Appeal. Everyone—whether advocate, pleader or attorney—was simply treated as 'pleader' or 'vakil'. This imprecise use of terminology led to much confusion later.

The High Court, constituted in 1862 under Letters Patent, permitted three separate groups of practitioners: advocates who were barristers, vakils and attorneys. For many decades, both advocates and attorneys had their training outside of India, and almost all of them were Europeans. In contrast, vakils were the products of local institutions. The term 'vakil' acquired three distinct meanings during the High Court era. First, it referred to a type of practitioner who, by background and ethnicity, was a 'native'. Second, it distinguished a class or group of practitioners from barristers or attorneys, whenever authorities had to make decisions regarding promotion to higher ranks in the judicial service.[25] While most Indians came under this category, a few Europeans also styled themselves vakils (or even pleaders) in the districts where the distinctions were less precise. Third, it represented an institution known as 'the vakil system' as distinct from the dual-system or double-agency.[26] Whereas the former permitted all vakils to act, appear and plead in the High Court, the dual-system divided these functions between barrister and attorney.

From the outset, the privileges granted to barristers and vakils varied considerably. Advocates, because of their 'superior' education and training, received favourable treatment both in terms of admission and practice. They could practise under any jurisdiction of the High Court, as well as in the subordinate courts. But vakils were often subjected to changes in rules of admission and were excluded from conducting original cases as opposed to appeals on insolvency. Moreover, the judges severely dealt with vakils who got involved in any activities outside of their profession without the prior sanction of the High Court.

Unlike their European colleagues, most Indian attorneys during the nineteenth century were only matriculates and, therefore, they were required to complete a five-year pupilage or apprenticeship. Yet attorneys, as a group, were unable to compete with vakils. With a degree in law, vakils had the privilege of acting, appearing and pleading, whereas attorneys could only act and appear. The increasing number of fresh vakils each year and the comparatively lower fees that they charged made attorneys unpopular among clients.

When the Indian Bar Council's Act of 1926 was introduced in 1928, all previous distinctions that had existed for well over 65 years between these three groups were obliterated in Madras. Every High Court practitioner was henceforth given the option to enrol himself as an 'advocate'.

Part I

LAW PRACTICE IN THE COMPANY COURTS, 1802–1860

Chapter 1

BEGINNINGS OF A PROFESSION

> Lawyers are plenty, and as knowing as can be expected from broken linen drapers and other crack'd tradesmen who seek their fortunes here by their wits.
> —Charles Lockyer[1]

> The native courts have no learned bar, which helps to make a learned bench. They have nothing of the kind; and, in some respects, so much the better for the poor natives.
> —Sir Thomas Strange[2]

With gradual expansion and acquisition of large territory in southern India, the East India Company in 1802 assumed increasing political and judicial responsibilities. The rulers introduced an elaborate and rationally based judicial system, which had been in existence within the environs of the city of Madras, to ensure systematic and peaceful collection of revenue. They also passed numerous regulations safeguarding people's rights and the efficiency of the government. People could sue and settle their disputes with others or with the government through legal processes which included an elaborate apparatus of courts, judges and legal practitioners.

LEGAL PROFESSION IN THE COMPANY COURTS

Regulations of Fort St. George

The men who practised law in the Company courts served as intermediaries and stood between the courts and the suitors; they were in one sense purely a by-product of British rule. The term vakil—which meant an 'agent', 'ambassador', 'representative', or 'counsellor'[3] of a nobleman, *zamindar* or a *raja*—acquired a new meaning when applied to someone familiar with the laws and local government regulations, and with the constitution and proceedings of the courts. The preamble of Regulation X of 1802 of the Madras government said, 'It becomes indispensably necessary for enabling the courts duly to administer, and the suitors to obtain justice, that the pleading of causes should be made a distinct profession.'[4]

1. *Regulation X of 1802.* The government periodically passed regulations and set guidelines for the recruitment of 'qualified' pleaders. Regulation X of 1802, the first of such measures to be introduced, empowered the Sadr Adalat or the Chief Court of Appeal to appoint and license as many pleaders as might be necessary for the functioning of a multi-tier court system. Every pleader had to take an oath and affirm that he would faithfully execute the duties of his office, and Muslim pleaders, in particular, were to renew their oaths every six months.[5] On his engagement, a pleader took a retainer's fee of four *annas* and issued a 'written acknowledgment' which bound him to fulfil his obligations to his client. If a pleader had accepted a fee but subsequently refused to transact the business of his client, he was dismissed and lost his licence. Upon receipt of his written acknowledgment, however, the party engaging him should execute a vakalat or power of attorney, authorizing him to 'prosecute or defend the plaint or appeal . . . and binding himself (the client) to be able to abide and confirm all acts, which such pleader may do or undertake in his behalf in the cause.'[6]

Regulation X of 1802 stipulated that a pleader's fee should be based on the total value of the suit filed for money, personal property, or real property. Thus, each litigant deposited a security, which was part of the sum he owed a pleader, in the court where the suit had been originally filed. This fee would be payable after the decree had been passed.[7] When, in special circumstances, more than one pleader conducted a suit, the fee should be divided between them in proportions specified in the vakalat.[8] Each time a pleader submitted a petition or made a motion on behalf of his client, he received a fee of additional four annas.[9] The courts also had the power to award further compensation on the merit of any 'extra' labour that a pleader might have performed. Pleaders must give written receipts for all accounts and documents delivered to them by their clients.[10]

Regulation X also prescribed rules for disciplinary action against pleaders, who were guilty of disrespect or irregular in attending the court. Promoting litigation, employing dilatory tactics, or engaging in any forms of fraud, incapacity and misconduct resulted in the suspension of pleaders from office. Except for indisposition, in which case one must submit a written notification to the court, chronic absenteeism could also result in dismissal.[11] Subject to the approval of the court, however, a pleader could appoint a substitute to conduct cases during his temporary absences. Finally, pleaders should practise only at the court to which they had originally been appointed unless they had permission from the Sadr Adalat to plead elsewhere;[12] pleaders who represented the government in court—whether in the *zillah* courts, in the provincial courts or in the Sadr Adalat—should abstain from advising or getting involved in any way with the opposite party; in other circumstances they were at liberty to carry on their business in the same manner as did the other pleaders.[13]

Although it is difficult to identify the original appointees to the situation of pleaders, only 'men of character and education, versed in the Mahomedan or Hindu Law and in the regulations passed by the British Government,'[14] became eligible for appointment during the first two decades. A small group of men representing the learned traditions of these two communities and possessing some ability in reading and writing in the vernaculars must have responded to the opportunities afforded by the regulation. Apart from inferences one can draw from this regulation, one knows very little about the pleaders' actual competency to conduct cases, about their mastery of laws, both personal and statutory, or about their personal deportment in transactions with clients. The descriptions given by Professor B. B. Misra about how pleaders in Bengal practised their profession at this time might very well be applicable to their contemporaries in Madras. Misra writes:

> The vakils themselves hardly possessed a fair knowledge of their cases. ... The regulations had provided no definite qualifications for a vakil, no precise mode of proceedings, no rules of evidence. The parties or their vakils pleaded cases by a simultaneous exchange of questions and answers. These led to altercations in the open court.[15]

Divided in their opinion about the usefulness of pleaders in Bengal, judicial officers thought that pleaders had not contributed to the efficient administration of justice but that, at the same time, the institution had proved its utility by enabling individuals to have access to legal remedy in courts.[16] The Government of Bengal, aware of the usefulness of pleaders in establishing the rule of law, passed a more comprehensive and systematic legislation in 1814, Regulation XXVII, incorporating all previously enacted provisions.[17]

2. *Regulation XIV of 1816*. The Government of Fort St. George followed suit by passing its own Regulation XIV in 1816. Except for some modifications to accommodate local conventions, the regulation was exactly the same as that of Bengal. Its purpose was to involve the provincial courts in the selection of pleaders and in the exercise of authority over them. While the new legislation repealed most of the provisions of Regulation X of 1802, it also assimilated certain features from the latter. The intent of Regulation XIV of 1816 was to improve upon the existing rules for the enrolment and practice of pleaders.

The regulation permitted the judges of the provincial courts to have a major role in the appointment of pleaders. They issued a *sanad* or licence to the new appointees, with the stipulation that they must practise exclusively in those courts to which they were originally appointed. Pleaders must carefully ascertain the *real name* and the identity of persons wishing to engage them;[18] if a pleader filed a *vakalatnamah* under a fictitious name, he was liable to immediate dismissal.[19] Pleadings must be prepared in conformity with the law and should contain neither repetitions nor personal abuse of the opposite party or officers of the court.[20] Failure to abide by these stipulations would lead to unconditional removal from one's position. Vakils could not conduct criminal cases without previous permission from their own courts, but this prohibition did not apply to those appearing for the government.[21] If a pleader were to die, become incapacitated or be dismissed, a client should find a substitute within the time specified. The original pleader, whether dead or alive, was allowed an equitable remuneration for any services he had already provided.[22] Pleaders could arbitrate in suits pending before the courts and could claim fees for their opinion.[23] Finally, although the regulation abolished the retainer's fee, litigants still had to execute the vakalatnamah on stamped paper, authorizing pleaders to act on their behalf.[24]

Closer analysis of these provisions reveals certain difficulties that the courts had faced during the formative stages of the profession. Pleaders seemed to have been either ignorant of or somewhat indifferent to the rules of procedure, but tended to bring into pleadings all sorts of extraneous details and numerous irrelevant points. The severe tone in which the Sadr Adalat expressed disapproval against any kind of misconduct, absenteeism and dilatory tactics among pleaders seems to indicate that such practices were common. Although the government at this time clearly foresaw the need to develop an elaborate system of procedures for the proper functioning of courts and for overseeing the conduct of judges, pleaders and suitors, little did it realize the value of formal study of law or provide any facilities for it. Devoid of any training in law, pleaders were permitted to go through the motions of law practice each day, while clients resigned themselves to the arbitrary decisions of judicial officers who equally lacked a theoretical understanding of law. It is clear, therefore, why judges often complained that there had been much perjury, forgery and subornation among the litigants and witnesses.[25]

3. *Regulation IV of 1832.* Since the previous enactments permitted only Hindus and Muslims to become pleaders between 1802 and 1832, neither Eurasians nor Indian Christians had any such opportunity. Some argued that no positive provision for them had ever been made in the enactments and that the absence of any reference to their inclusion precluded them from such opportunities. The Eurasian community made many representations to the Government of India and later to Parliament soliciting patronage in public appointments.[26] Finding that the authorities in London were sympathetic, the rulers in Madras enacted additional legislation. Regulation IV of 1832 declared that, henceforth, 'no Native of India shall be ineligible . . . on account of . . . religious belief or persuasion,'[27] for any of the inferior judicial positions or for situation as pleaders.

4. *Personal Account of Richard Clarke.* When, in 1832, Clarke, a civilian, gave evidence before the Parliamentary Committee, he provided the members with more information on the qualification, practice and status of pleaders in the Madras Presidency. He said that pleaders were trained in the College of Fort St. George and were given a sanad by the Sadr Adalat. The sanad entitled them to practise in any court they wished. The emphasis at the College was not so much on acquiring a thorough knowledge of the law, Hindu or Muslim, as on possessing an acquaintance with the regulations. Clarke continued, 'the object of these arrangements was . . . to assimilate the natives to the European Bar, leaving it to the clients to make their own selection of their law advisors.'[28]

The duties of pleaders, according to Clarke, consisted of conducting suits, drawing pleadings and examining witnesses. A pleader could neither plead nor address the court orally, except in subordinate courts below a district court; and every pleading, motion or petition or whatever a pleader submitted before the court was rendered in writing. The reasons for this arrangement were twofold: first, the judges had not acquired competency in the local languages in spite of their many years of experience in the districts as collectors or subcollectors; and second, the pleaders had only limited proficiency in English—inadequate to make any formal address in court. To relieve the judges from boredom and disgust caused by the droning of pleaders, who were arguing in a language with which they were unfamiliar, it was customary to limit oral pleadings as far as possible; the judges put a few questions at the end of the trial and the pleaders answered them mechanically.

Notwithstanding such limitations, Clarke observed that many pleaders were 'acute reasoners' and that some were even 'good lawyers'. Obviously, the utility of such 'lawyers' in the administration of justice largely depended upon their knowledge of law, their accumulated skills and their years of courtroom experience. In comparison to those who had practised law at an earlier time, the pleaders who entered the profession during the 1820s were markedly superior.[29] Further evidence before the Parliamentary Committee from Bengal and the North-West Provinces revealed the existence of similar conditions in other parts of India.

Regulations of the Government of India

Parallel to the development of the legal profession in the Company courts, a totally different group of men emerged. Styling themselves advocates, they practised law at the Supreme Court (which had been established in Madras under the Royal Charter, in 1801). In 1799, Sir Thomas A. Strange, the Chief Justice, compiled a list of advocates and attorneys who had originally practised in the Mayor's Court (an institution chartered by the Crown in 1726). Thirteen different individuals figured in the list. Among them, eight were practising as 'advocates, attorneys and proctors', while five were 'advocates and attorneys'. There was only one barrister, Alexander Anstruther, who had any legitimate claim to formal legal training.[30] Testifying before the Select Committee of the House of Lords in 1830 on the occasion of the renewal of the East India Company's Charter, Sir Thomas declared:

> In the Mayor's Court there was but one description of practitioners; they practised both as barristers and solicitors; and the Court of the

Recorder adopted them in that compound character. They continued to practise . . . till the establishment of the Supreme Court. Then the profession was divided, and an option was given to those gentlemen to elect to be barristers and solicitors.[31]

The Supreme Court had jurisdiction over the British-born subjects both in the city of Madras and scattered throughout southern India. Contrary to the generally held notions that barristers had a lucrative practice, by the 1800s, the number of English lawyers in Madras had begun to dwindle. Indeed, some such men did not even possess the means to return home.[32] Legislative measures taken by the Government of India during the 1840s provided barristers with greater opportunities to plead in the Company's courts and thereby increase their income.[33] After the 1840s, therefore, the two distinct strands of legal profession—barristers and pleaders—had numerous encounters, opposing, interacting and competing with each other for large emoluments derived from *zamindari* and other commercial suits arising from the *mufassal*.[34]

1. *Act I of 1846*. This Act allowed English barristers to practise both in the Sadr Court and the district courts. The legislators in Calcutta had hoped that barristers, through their legal training, experience and tradition, would help render justice speedily and also elevate the dignity of the courts.[35] While the Act forever removed the restrictions on barristers' practice in the Company courts, it also introduced certain modifications in the existing rules of practice. First, barristers must 'abide by the same rules applicable to pleaders, whether relating to the language used in the court or to any other matter'.[36] Second, all practitioners now had the freedom to settle fees by private arrangements with their clients. Third, no one had to enter in the contract (vakalatnamah) the amount a pleader received for his services. Finally, in case of default, no longer did the court intervene between a pleader and his client and the former sought redress through civil litigation.

This legislation proved a mixed blessing. Insofar as it enabled barristers practising in the Supreme Court to frequent the Sadr Court and other subordinate courts, the Act provided a common forum for the two different kinds of legal practitioners: barristers and pleaders. In many ways, barristers introduced their knowledge, individual skills and traditions in the Company courts; the rulers had hoped that these qualities would increase the efficiency of courts. As John P. Willoughby, a civil servant from Bengal, later testified:

A highly educated Barrister will expound better law, secure more attention to the law of evidence, act as a salutary check upon the *inexperience* and *ignorance* sometimes manifested by the Judges, and will at the same time ensure more regularity of procedure.[37]

Nevertheless, the disadvantages that accrued from the enactment far outweighed the intended improvements in the legal profession. The legal procedures, which governed the actions of practitioners and judges became more complex. Despite the permission accorded to barristers to appear in the Sadr Courts, they were subjected to the same rules which applied to pleaders, especially the rule related to the use of language in addressing the court.

For many years, Persian and regional Indian languages had been the medium of proceedings in court. After 1840, English gradually replaced these languages. If a presiding judge was in favour of hearing arguments in English, he permitted practitioners on either side to argue in that language. But clients perceived the issue differently. The use of English in court provided an opportunity for one party to humiliate an opponent. In his testimony before the Select Parliamentary Committee, John F. Leith, a barrister from Bengal, observed:

> If one party knows that there is to be an English barrister employed, and he had intended to employ a vakeel who understood English, he [the client] will not avail himself of his services, but will employ a native for the purpose of shutting out the English barrister on the other side . . . no barrister . . . has been yet able satisfactorily to address the court in the vernacular language of the country.[38]

Although a barrister had a rather limited facility in the vernacular, he did not desist from the defensive use of his mastery of the procedure and expertise in the technicalities of English law. The mufassal civilian judges by and large lacked such training and skill, and their ignorance of the technicalities of law gave barristers an advantage. The judges attempted to conceal their ignorance by leaning towards the arguments of barristers.[39] Except for those who had been practising at Sadr Courts in different Presidency towns, the mufassal pleaders were inadequately prepared to accept the challenge of a barrister and often succumbed to the latter's browbeating tactics. Being nervous, they performed poorly and often lost their cases. This evil was brought to the attention of the members of the Parliamentary Committee by Willoughby when he attested:

> Under the present system . . . we occasionally see a Barrister from Westminster Hall appearing in Court on one side, and a poor illiterate

uneducated Native Vakeel on the other. I think that may very often lead to a denial of justice and wrong decisions.[40]

Pleaders' transactions were not without reproach. If a pleader possessed a tolerably sufficient knowledge of English and had been in practice for some years, he emulated the style of barristers and even demanded similar fees. Cases in which pleaders exacted high fees were far from infrequent,[41] as was underbidding or entering into conditional arrangements with clients.[42]

In spite of such unforeseen and, perhaps, unavoidable results, the Act was yet another step in the development of the legal profession in India. Never before had pleaders been challenged and motivated to study the English language in order to offset the potential of a 'threat' or of a monopoly of control by a handful of barristers who had been slowly but methodically making inroads into the mufassal. The pleaders, moreover, realized that in order to weather the changes in the rules of admission or procedures in court and in order to prosper under these circumstances, they would need better legal training. Superficial familiarity or rote memory of the regulations would no longer be enough. That a few pleaders eventually became leaders of the 'Native Bar', that they received approval and encouragement even from barristers for their rise in the profession, and that they began to participate in other local civic activities showed their burgeoning ability and talent.[43] Such, however, could not be said of those pleaders who continued to practise in the mufassal courts.

2. *Act XXXVIII of 1850.* A few years after the passing of Act I of 1846, the Government of India permitted pleaders and barristers in criminal courts. Not only did Act XXXVIII of 1850 enable them to have access to criminal courts, but it also brought additional income for many, who otherwise had no means of livelihood. Many mufassal pleaders profited from this provision, especially as petty criminal cases were more frequently taken to court. The Madras government willingly gave effect to the legislation because of its potential benefits both to the public and the courts.[44]

3. *Act XX of 1853.* For the first time, attorneys of the Supreme Court also had the privilege of pleading in any of the Company courts provided that they abided by the same rules that applied to barristers and pleaders. Circular Orders by the Sadr Adalat during the late 1850s stipulated that unless the candidates, who wished to become *munsifs* or pleaders, passed the written and oral

examinations conducted at various centres, they would neither be appointed nor given a sanad to practise.

Evaluations of Baillie

Despite the rulers' intentions in bringing together both the European and local men of law to improve the status and the quality of law practice, the general conditions of the profession in the interior reflected little development. Judges continued to exercise constant surveillance over pleaders, who neither had any independence nor any immunity from the arbitrary fines. The treatment of pleaders by judicial officers was anything but cordial or respectful. Moreover, pleaders themselves often behaved in a way that merited such treatment. Their own obsequiousness and lack of self-esteem and pride brought them to grief. Clients commonly distrusted the motives of pleaders; some even discredited them as being inefficient and tactless in court performance, especially when adverse decisions were passed against them. At times, clients withheld fees legally due to pleaders on the ground that they had failed to win cases in court. The only possible way to recover the fees was by recourse to litigation, which most pleaders were not prepared to take because of inconvenience and unpredictable court decisions.

Correspondence between London and India between 1848 and 1853 illustrates the changing state of the profession in India. In February 1848 N. B. E. Baillie wrote to the Court of Directors, describing the lowly position of Indian pleaders in the Company courts and suggesting ways to improve their character and dignity. His letter eventually reached the Government of India, which in turn sent it to the three local governments inviting their responses. His views were explicit:

> For the due administration of justice according to any regular system . . . competent pleaders are just as necessary as efficient judges. I have come to this conclusion not from any prepossession in favour of the English system . . . [but] I believe it to be radically good, well calculated for the great end of all judicial procedure . . . to elicit facts, and law principle, and place them in a convenient form before the Judges. At the same time I think it has fallen short of those objects and chiefly for want of a proper subordinate agency to work the system.[45]

Elaborating his thesis point by point with convincing logic, Baillie showed how pleaders had very little in common with the law practice of barristers. The majority of Hindu and Muslim pleaders had neither the legal training nor the status comparable to that possessed by European judges, nor did they attain anything like the independence of the English Bar.[46] Coming out of institutions and traditions of royal or imperial courts in India—where their position had been that of humble supplicants presenting petitions (*arzis*) on behalf of their clients—their style of addressing the court had long been much like that of menial servants to their masters.

Baillie said that pleaders were not only accustomed to 'exalting the person addressed' but also to 'unnecessarily lowering themselves'; this practice had added 'to their degradation in the eyes of Judges'. The Company's judicial officers had responded by treating pleaders with little or no respect, and, at times, did not even allow pleaders to sit in the presence of European judges in the mufassal. On many occasions, these judges subjected pleaders to arbitrary fines as passion or caprice might dictate. By their mingling ignorance with unpreparedness, pleaders tended to bring abuse if not open insult upon themselves from the bench. However, the responsibility for such mistreatment did not lie with the pleaders. Baillie added:

> There is usually action and reaction in such cases and if the native pleader has continued for nearly sixty years in his present abject state almost useless in the administration of justice, *some blame* must be ascribed to the Judges. There [could] be no doubt that the Company's Judges [had] been too careless of the condition and character of . . . pleaders and . . . in a great measure from imperfect notions of the important part which they might [have been] made to perform.[47]

Pleaders in India played a dual role: of barrister and attorney. They provided the only medium of communication between judges and suitors. Unlike practitioners in England, who were often successful in settling disputes outside of courts and thereby reducing the volume of cases litigated, pleaders had little influence over their clients. Their inability to settle disputes out of court naturally led to an increase in the volume of formal suits. In the absence of any fixed code of law, furthermore, the litigiousness of the local people grew rampant. When a case was brought to court, a competent pleader would quickly reduce the issues to a few succinct statements of facts, citing the applicable law. The more common practice, however, was to make matters unnecessarily complicated. The plaints were so voluminous that a judge had to spend hours trying to ascertain what was at issue.[48] Frustrated and puzzled in such cases, judges often remanded suits for reinvestigation by lower courts. Thus, several other factors tended to adversely affect the cheap and efficient administration of justice: protracted delays, catechistic or unsuitable modes of pleading, unreliable forms of evidence, and hasty decisions of irascible or less sympathetic judges who were more concerned in the quick and easy disposal of cases than in adhering to principles of law or equity. The inevitable outcome of such injudicious pronouncements was 'in a great measure the barrenness of Indian decisions'.[49]

Baillie thought that the remedy lay in removing the limitations imposed upon pleaders and in introducing incentives for their professional aspiration, efficiency and success. Removal of fines, he suggested, was the foremost and fundamental change to be introduced. Failure to attend the court every day, especially on a day when a pleader's case was not heard, did not constitute an offence and the imposition of fines for such actions meant that his actions deserved public 'disgrace'. While graver offences or violations of trust deserved outright suspension or dismissal, petty faults or oversights should be dealt with by a 'dignified rebuke' from the bench. The judges must also alter the rules for awarding fees to pleaders so as to reduce the number of cases and the implausible grounds on which they were sometimes filed.[50] To accomplish this, the courts needed to reassess the value of lands or other properties in dispute and set a minimum value for cases admissible in court. There were instances in which a pleader had been awarded a paltry sum of just a few rupees in a case, a wasteful use of judicial machinery.

Moreover, even the more competent and experienced pleaders had hitherto systematically been excluded from such subordinate judicial offices as district munsifs, sadr amins and principal sadr amins.[51] Future appointments to these positions should be thrown open to eligible pleaders who had the same educational qualifications as those law officers under the government, with an additional requirement of five years' experience in a mufassal bar. Such an arrangement would enhance the status of the profession in public opinion, and would enable the members of the bar to increase their self-respect as they conducted their business more carefully before the native judiciary with whom they might have an opportunity to compete as rivals in the 'same honourable race for promotion'.[52] The offices of the superintendent and the government pleader in the Sadr Adalat, which had been the preserve of civilians, should also be open to pleaders. Increasing their salary and conferring rank on them as officers of the court would also induce them to accept these appointments when offered. Finally, English should be introduced in the proceedings of every court with appellate jurisdiction. It should be incumbent upon judges as well as pleaders to learn the language of the other, that is, judges should learn the local language, and pleaders, English. The advantage from such requirement would be twofold: it would totally eliminate the cost of translation of documents and would enable the judges to consult the records in the original as they heard the cases.

The Government of Ft. St. George forwarded Baillie's communication to the judges of the Sadr Adalat, eliciting information on the allegations that Baillie had made. A year later, the Registrar, John Davidson, wrote that 'the Pleaders who practise ordinarily in the courts in the Province are without exception Hindoos and Mahomedans', but in the Sadr Adalat, four Europeans and one Armenian had been allowed to practise. 'Barristers,' Davidson said, 'have likewise been admitted to plead under Act I of 1846, but hitherto their pleadings have been exclusively written.'[53] With regard to the practice of frequently fining pleaders, the Registrar said the mufassal judges exercised this power rather 'sparingly' and 'the Sudder Court have no reason to think that the power was abused'. The judges viewed that the power to fine pleaders must be retained as a wholesome measure of 'check and restraint' since the character of pleaders as portrayed by Baillie had unfortunately been made 'applicable to this Presidency as to that of Bengal'. With the passing of Act I of 1846, pleaders in Madras already had the liberty to demand their own fees and, unlike Bengal, they had been selected to the office of district munsif by judges whenever the latter deemed it necessary. The Registrar concluded:

> The Judges concur generally with Mr Baillie in thinking that considerable advantage would accrue from the introduction of a number of highly educated men as pleaders in the Sudder Adalut; but this has in part been effected already and the increase of their number would seem to depend upon whether the business coming before the Court be sufficiently extensive and lucrative to attract others.[54]

The extensive correspondence between the Sadr Courts, various provincial governments, and the Government of India resulted in the enactment of yet another legislation. Act XX of 1853 abrogated the existing rules requiring compulsory attendance of pleaders in court or subjecting them to arbitrary fines.[55] However, the practice continued for many years after 1853 as is borne out by a pleader in the Salem District Court:

> Nobody knows when any of the three judge would come to Court. Sometimes they would come 10 o'clock, sometimes 2 o'clock, one Judge sometimes come 6 o'clock morning, another 5 o'clock evening, and Vakils must attend to all. If Vakil not present when Judge gentleman call, he will fine. Therefore we sometimes must go Court at 5 o'clock morning and remains till 5 o'clock evening. Still as Court was close we find time to make ablution and perform ceremony and eat rice. When Judge not come early morning we attend 10 o'clock, and talk to one another, and with clients, and take little sleep, and such kind thing to pass time.[Sic].[56]

Despite Baillie's diagnosis of the problems of the profession and his proposals to alleviate them, he made no reference to the importance of legal training for pleaders or judges. Neither had any training in jurisprudence apart from their insufficient acquaintance with the regulations and procedures of court. Occasionally a judge or a pleader might teach himself the principles of jurisprudence, equity and law of evidence, but this was always more the exception than the rule. The subject of legal training continued to arise in discussions and correspondence between the authorities of Madras, Calcutta and London, but no immediate result was forthcoming. Only with the eruption of a public debate and 'pamphlet controversy' in 1853, and the discussion of charter renewal, did matters progress any further.

At that time the Sadr Adalat also came to terms with the problem of untrained pleaders. The judges sensed 'an urgent need' for educating pleaders in the 'rules of procedure and the doctrines upon which ordinances rested'.[57] When the 'pamphlet controversy' broke out, bringing to the notice of several individuals of Madras the 'crying evils' in judicial administration, many in India urged for the legal education of pleaders in the ensuing reform proposals. Some individuals with experience in India voiced the same concerns before the Parliamentary Committee in London. Among the numerous pressing demands of the time was the need for a thorough reorganization of the judicial system, including the establishment of law colleges in all three Presidencies. A complete unanimity prevailed on this topic among those who testified before the Committee.[58]

LEGAL EDUCATION OF PLEADERS
College of Fort St. George

Ten years after the legal profession had been instituted in the Company courts in Madras, the government thought that pleaders ought to be given some formal training, if not in abstract principles of law, at least in regulations which might equip them to plead before the courts. When, in 1812, the government founded the College of Fort St. George, it provided instruction on local conditions, both administrative and social, and taught various South Indian vernaculars to junior civil servants arriving from England. The rulers hoped that a civilian who had received training from the college for two years in any particular language would be able to converse with the local people, learn local customs and become a competent administrator.[59] Later, when the college threw open its doors to individuals selected for positions of native law officers, who could aid the judges in deciding cases of Hindu or Muslim law, arrangements were also made to establish a separate class for pleaders. Whereas the 'law officers' received financial support from the government, depending on the number of years they studied at the college and their subsequent achievements, the pleaders enjoyed no such privileges. They endured hardship, economic or otherwise, in order to acquire the prescribed qualifications. The annual report prepared by the College Board for 1816 sheds some curious sidelights on the training of individuals as 'law officers' and 'pleaders':

> Each individual was examined separately in grammar, logic and law; the result was highly satisfactory, evincing in the examined zealous application to study, honourable emulation to be distinguished by the success of their labours, and confidence that talent and assiduity would receive their merited reward.[60]

The same year the College Board put an ingenious suggestion before the government. Since the candidates for law officership were trained with government support, the Board thought that those candidates who had passed with distinction should be declared equally eligible for the office of pleader. 'The experience,' the Board added, 'which would thus be gained by the natives to be hereafter appointed Law Officers would be of very great advantage to them in their performance of their duties. We would suggest that in consideration of the pay which the candidates will receive, they should be considered Vakeels of Government.'[61]

Candidates, who wished to become qualified pleaders, obtained the pleadership certificate in two ways: either by studying in the government institution and taking the examination conducted by the Board, or by passing the same examination given by the zillah courts. The law officers and government vakils in the districts examined the candidates and then forwarded the results to the College Board. The Board then issued licences to successful candidates. Neither the college nor the government offered any assistance to students enrolled on their own, except for admitting them in the lowest or beginners' class. All 'Moosulmans and Hindus of pure cast [sic]' could seek admission and there were no restrictions on the number of candidates.[62] Training at the college brought higher status to a pleader over his counterpart in the mufassal, even though a Madras pleader stood far beneath the law officers both in formal knowledge and in public recognition, and also possibly in his earnings. Those in the district and *taluq* towns studied the regulations only in the vernacular and had almost no contacts in the city. Nor could they afford to undertake visits to Madras: distance, lack of means, unfamiliarity with its urban culture, and other factors inhibited such mobility. Thus in the decades to follow there emerged a gulf between these two groups of pleaders: those who had received training at the college and those who had studied law privately in the districts. Such differences were to create an even more striking contrast in life-style, attitudes and interests between these groups.

The College Board, in concluding its report of 1816, strongly urged the government to pass a law defining the policies of appointment of law officers and vakils, and declaring that a certificate from the college was essential to practise law.[63] The government adopted this proposal and in the following year made into law Regulation V of 1817. The Regulation also removed the restrictions on government pleaders and allowed them to offer opinions to litigants who opposed the government in any civil suit or proceeding.[64] The report for 1821 reveals that three candidates appeared for the examination and 'acquitted themselves with much credit, upon being examined in the Regulations'.[65] Occasionally the college dismissed one or two students because of their 'hopeless incapacity' to absorb the information or to perform well under the stress of examinations, which lasted for several days.⁶⁶ In 1827, thirteen persons took the examination, but it is unclear how many successfully passed and received certificates. From the pragmatic view expressed in a letter from the secretary of the College Board to the government, it is possible to infer that most, if not all of them must have received certificates. The letter said:

> Though their [the pleaders'] knowledge of the Code, either in spirit or letter, was but *limited*, the Board in consideration of the *demands of the service*, thought it advisable to grant certificates to those among them, whose knowledge of it approached that degree which it is requisite that they should possess.⁶⁷

Those who had completed the examination received either the B or the C certificate, which authorized them to commence legal practice at any district court or provincial court, as also at other inferior courts below the district. Comparing the accomplishments of pleaders possessing certificates B and C, the secretary of the College Board observed:

> Although the pleaders to whom the certificate C was granted possessed, to a certain degree, a knowledge of the Regulations, and were conversant with the forms of the Courts, and the details of the duties of the pleader, their knowledge of Law was but superficial.⁶⁸

No wonder that many complained against pleaders, alleging that they were inept and that they constantly fomented petty litigation. A vivid but somewhat impressionistic description of personnel attached to one district court has been recorded. In a series of letters written from Madras 'by a Lady', presumably Julia Maitland, one catches a glimpse of her visit with the district judge of Vizagapatam:

> I am very much amused with all the natives who come to pay their respects to the 'Judge Doory'. (Doory means gentleman.) My favourite, hitherto, is the Moofti, or principal Mahometan law expounder. He is one of the handsomest and most elegant creatures I ever saw—somewhat dirty perhaps—with beautiful cashmere shawls worn threadbare, and in his shabby magnificence looking like a beggarly king. Then there is the Pundit, or principal Hindoo law expounder—a Brahmin, very much of a mountebank, and something of a cheat, I should guess, by his face and manner. There are plenty of underlings, but these are the principal men. They always come accompanied by their Vakeels, a kind of secretaries, or interpreters, or flappers—their muddles, in short: everybody here has a muddle, high or low. The Vakeels stand behind their masters during all the visit, and discuss with them all that A— says. Sometimes they tell him some bare-faced lie, and when they

find he does not believe, they turn to me grinning, and say, 'Maem, the Doory plenty cunning gentleman'.[69]

Correspondence between the Madras government, judges of the Sadr Adalat, and the College Board shows that several changes were imminent in the operation of the college. One change was the decision to discontinue the law classes altogether. Available records do not reveal why the authorities had decided to take that step but a few explanations are possible. In spite of stringent rules and rigorous examination procedures, approximately eight to ten individuals had completed their studies at the college each year; these graduates were entitled to function as law officers but as long as these men had remained unemployed, the government felt obliged to pay them each a monthly allowance.[70] This surplus of law officers was more than sufficient to fill up any future vacancies; the sums spent for the law classes could be put to other uses. Furthermore, the establishment of a government-sponsored educational institution as opposed to those run by missionaries seems to have been a subject of much deliberation, correspondence and planning; part of the original considerations was to introduce law courses for those who opted for a career in law.[71] With the enactment of Act XXVII of 1836, passed by the Governor General-in-Council of India, came the termination of law classes. This law repealed the Madras Regulation V of 1817. Henceforth, pleaders were appointed by the provincial courts on the recommendations of district judges under the provisions of Section III, Regulation XIV of 1816.[72] The question of legal education of pleaders and judges had not surfaced in official discussions until the 1850s when controversies over the alleged inefficiency of judicial administration split European society in Madras.

George Norton and Legal Education

After the termination of law classes in 1836, no one showed an interest in the education of pleaders until the arrival of George Norton, the Advocate General, in 1840. He delivered law lectures to a small group of interested students, who understood English, and his lectures consisted of dialogues rather than formal presentations of legal concepts and ideas. Even so, one of the listeners confided to Norton privately: 'Master may talk. Now and then I look in just to see other people there, and then I make slumber.'[73] There is no evidence that suggests that his law lectures continued for a long time, but, until his return to England in 1853, Norton remained an influential person in Madras, whose views on higher education reflected a progressive outlook. President of the University Board, constituted in 1840, Norton had the task of formulating the rules and policies for the proposed university. As he later testified to the members of the Parliament in 1853:

> By the fundamental rules, there were to be two departments; one . . . the Collegiate Department, was more specifically for substantive knowledge in the sciences and the professions. The Scholastic Department was rather more for the exercise of the powers of the mind, strengthening them, elevating the moral feelings of the scholars and forming their tastes.[74]

Committed as he was to the intellectual and moral development of young people through education, when Norton saw that the University Board had not adopted his recommendations he became, understandably, extremely bitter. According to his original proposal, the first batch of proficients (or graduates) from the Madras University High School (established in 1841) would have entered the collegiate wing, attending classes in engineering, medicine and law.[75] Not until the arrival of approval from London (known as 'Wood's Dispatch') in 1854 were Norton's original schemes put into effect: resulting in the conversion of University High School into Presidency College.

Introduction of Formal Law Lectures

In 1855, after twenty years of striving for legal education, law classes began in Presidency College. None other than John Bruce Norton,[76] a fearless spokesman for public causes and an incessant critic of government policies, became the first professor of law. In his inaugural lecture, he observed that the impact of study of law was 'likely to be attended with a widespread influence reaching to the very door and roof tree of every individual of the entire nation'.[77] The goal of the appointment of a law professor, he added, was 'something more elevated and elevating than the mere delivery of a dry course of Lectures'. It was rather 'to train up a completely instructed body of pleaders who [might] spread themselves through the Mofussil Courts, and introduce a *total revolution* in the present practice of the administration of law'.[78] He admonished the candidates against encouraging litigation, forgery, avarice, and such abuse of freedom of speech as hurling insults at opponents' lawyers, clients or witnesses. The attitude of a pleader towards the bench, Norton admonished, should be one of deference and respect. He said:

> Bear in mind the almost sacred dignity of the Judge, and never let your manner or your tone, any more than your words themselves, convey to him . . . an impression that you have even for a moment forgotten the courtesy and deference which should ever make the intercourse between Judge and Counsel.[79]

A sympathizer with, as well as an ardent promoter of education among the Indians, Norton hoped that the ties between himself and the students could be forged on the basis of friendship rather than that of mentor and student. While he promised his utmost to 'labour [with] assiduity and patience and a sincere desire to be useful',[80] he expected his students to pay attention in the classroom, to reflect upon the lectures, and to consult available books on a given subject. Useful though the lectures delivered in classes might be, he cautioned the students against supposing that what they had heard would qualify them for the their professional duties. 'The proper Study of Law,' he said, 'itself covers an immense space; but for practitioner, there is no science, no art, no branch of human knowledge, an acquaintance of which may not at some period or other become useful or even necessary to him.'[81] Norton subsequently delivered lectures on Law of Evidence, Hindu and Muslim Law, Mercantile Law, Commercial Law, Civil Procedure, Pleading and Jurisprudence. Since no suitable books were available to supplement his lectures, as a remedy he published them. Only his lectures on the Law of Evidence have survived.[82]

Although no records are available on the number of students who originally attended or on their social backgrounds or origins, the report on Public Instruction for the year 1857–8 contains some information on law lectures. In 1857, John D. Mayne, a barrister who had succeeded Norton, delivered lectures on the Law of Contract and Torts, and conducted examinations at the end of the term. He reported that the students were 'adults, passed students of the Presidency College and others whose performance was creditable'. The average attendance, however, was disappointing. No more than 15 students attended the law classes because the university rules stipulated that a candidate must obtain a degree in arts prior to his admission to the law course.[83] Commenting on this rule, *The Madras Daily Times* observed:

As the rules stand now, the degree of B.A. is an essential preliminary to that of B.L. This policy partakes too much of the protective spirit, and as a necessary consequence it discourages the manufacture of native lawyers. Why should not the examination for a degree in Law be put on a similar footing to that for a degree in medicine? It is out of the question to expect that young Hindoos will, for some time to come at least, be prepared to expend so many years of their life . . . before sitting down for the real business of the study of law, if they have fixed upon that as their vocation . . . something has to be done by one body or another towards the removal of obvious discouragements to the study of law by the natives of this Presidency.[84]

At the end of 1850s, an individual could follow one of two routes to a career in law. On the one hand, he could read the few prescribed texts privately and undergo the examinations conducted at four designated centres—Bellary, Trichinopoly, Mangalore or Rajamundry—and receive the sanad after successful completion.[85] He could, on the other hand, attend classes at Presidency College, obtain a Bachelor of Law (B.L.) degree from the university and then begin his career at the top, at the Sadr Adalat.[86] Distinctions in education would ultimately result in two different strands of the legal profession in India: pleaders and vakils. A third group, whose origins and training were somewhat obscure, also emerged. Known as 'private vakils', these frequently appeared in criminal proceedings of inferior courts.

The statistical table provided by Suntharalingam indicates that only 16 students graduated with degrees in law between 1857 and 1866. Graduates from other professions such as engineering and medicine were even fewer in number (five and one respectively for the same period).[87] Factors like travel distance, tuition cost, lack of support from relatives, the bewildering life-style of metropolitan Madras, and a lack of evidence or conviction that struggle to obtain professional status would pay off in actual elevation in socio-economic status, might have been partly responsible for this low enrolment.

THE 'PAMPHLET CONTROVERSY'

Reference has already been made to the 'pamphlet controversy' and to the subsequent debates, occasioned by the publication of a leaflet by J. B. Norton. In scathing language, he recorded his observations on the maladministration of justice in the Madras

Presidency. Since a majority of judges presiding over the Company courts in the districts had no legal training, he argued, they were unable to appreciate the complexities of disputes brought before them. As a result, the decisions often betrayed inability to sift through masses of recorded and oral evidence, to apply the right principles of law to the issues, or to pass verdicts in a calm and methodical manner. He wrote: '[S]o long as the present system continues there is not only no hope of any amelioration, but on the contrary this must go on ever from bad to worse, until in the lowest depth, there is at last no lower bottom still.'[88] He left no aspect or facet of the judicial administration untouched, reminding the Madras government of its commitment to safeguard the rights of people and to make justice available to all. When in 1853 he wrote to Robert Lowe, President of the Court of Directors, he pointed out how the government had deviated from its original commitments:

> If the people, so far as our experience of them in our Courts of Justice is a safe criterion, are desperately deceitful, forgers, perjurers, and suborners of perjury, assuredly we have not only our sins of omission, what we have not done for them, to answer for; but I much fear that our rule has in no mean degree contributed to make them what they are.[89]

Others in India confirmed Norton's pointed analysis of the condition and quality of judicial administration.[90] A few judges, especially William Holloway, Charles R. Baynes and Thomas A. Anstruther, took exception to his views.[91] Each independently published a pamphlet refuting Norton's allegations and vindicating the Madras system. They carefully demonstrated circumstances peculiar to India, which in some measure affected the manner of judicial administration. These circumstances, according to them, were the unpleasant and enervating climate, the language barrier, the moral depravity and litigiousness of the people, the craftiness of pleaders and witnesses, and the added administrative burden. The civilian judges argued that both the integrity and the performance of European judges were eminently superior to those of the local subordinate judges, who had not always been able to resist various outside influences. The proponents of reform, especially *The Madras Daily Times*, responded by stating that 'more . . . [was] needed of a Judge than the simple possession of moral qualities. A legal education was indispensable.'[92] The defenders of the existing system, in contrast, believed that it was best left alone, as it had potential for self-correction and improvement from any inadvertent errors. A civilian with the pen name 'White Brahmin' even went a step further than the defenders of the system, and criticized the role of the Supreme Court at that time. He wrote:

> What, however, has been the actual result, as to its working, of our own Barrister guided and governed Supreme Court? It has . . . with the united assistance of Judges and Barristers, succeeded in passing decisions, which the most enlightened English lawyer in existence, has, in his place . . . called the worst in the world, and might . . . be abolished.[93]

The English public and press, however, knew that Norton had opened up a controversy about the quality of the judicial system, which could not be ignored any longer.[94]

What were the consequences of this controversy? It captured public attention in London and Madras, urging the necessity for legal training as a prerequisite for anyone who desired to hold the office of a judge as well as for anyone who aspired to become a pleader.[95] If justice were to be meted out efficiently and impartially to the people in South India, the entire system would have to be overhauled, beginning at the top court of appeal, the Sadr Adalat, and trickling down to the lowest court, the district munsif's court. A body of uniform law governing both procedure and rules of evidence needed to be codified and introduced throughout the Presidency. The pamphlet controversy presaged that the time had come for an amalgamation of two different systems of judicial administration, the English Supreme Court and the East India Company Court. The grim and horrible events of the Mutiny of 1857 proved to be a blessing in disguise, at least for the Madras Presidency. The assumption of political control by the Crown (in 1858) paved the way for the unification of the judicial structure in 1862.[96] The controversy was one in the series which periodically raised questions about the legal training of civilians, and about the apparent wisdom of appointing them as district judges when numerous well-qualified and competent barristers and vakils were available for such positions. Maintaining a balance in the judiciary by appointing men who might represent different sections of the legal profession or different communities, therefore, became a persisting dilemma for the government, whose decisions in such matters were neither predictable nor consistent.

THE ROLE OF PLEADERS IN MADRAS SOCIETY

As vakils and pleaders gained status, recognition and achievement, they, along with commercial leaders and landholders, became more prominent during the 1850s and 1860s. Pleaders like V. Sadagopachari, P. Rangaiah Naidu and V. Ramanujachari supported the Madras Native Association, which had been brought into existence through the indefatigable efforts and pecuniary sacrifices of G. Lakshiminarasu Chetty. Of the first, John B. Norton once stated:

> Here is my learned friend Sadagopah Chari . . . who has had the manliness to trust to his own powers and attainments. He has boldly preferred to rely on his own abilities as a Pleader, to taking service under Government . . . His emoluments are equal to his success . . . I hope to see the day when the highest judgment seat shall be open to his abilities and his integrity.[97]

M. Venkatroyalu Naidu, also a pleader, started his own newspaper, the *Rising Sun*, to focus on the social problems of the Hindu community.[98] He also founded the Hindu Reading Room and Hindu Debating Society for the purpose of evoking among people, students in particular, an awareness of the backward condition of the country and to discuss ways of improving society.[99] T. Rama Rao and S. Subramania Iyer, who later became leaders of the vakils in the High Court and champions of public service, commenced their practice during the early 1860s. In 1889, when the High Court vakils reorganized their defunct association, Rama Rao became their first president.[100]

It is misleading to assume that only the Madras Native Association and Hindu Debating Society served as vehicles for public discussion or agitation against government policies. On many occasions during the 1850s and 1860s, by taking part in various *ad hoc* meetings a small number of pleaders in Madras provided leadership.[101] They led the way so that their colleagues in the districts might emulate their roles and assume responsible positions in municipal governments. City lawyers also became models for future generations, instilling in younger vakils and pleaders a sense of duty to take up causes of public interest. Leaders of the Madras 'native bar' demonstrated, through their own efforts, what learned and economically independent members could achieve for the improvement of their own profession and for the social and political transformation of the country. But they had to learn to wait patiently for their turn in the corridors of power. Obediently and respectfully they had to follow their 'barons', the barristers, observing both the style and the procedures of doing legal business. In this alone lay their access to greater prominence, recognition and status. How they would gain confidence and how well they would fare in the execution of their professional duties in the midst of acute competition from Europeans and what conditions or events would lead to their transformation were still beyond the horizon.

Part II

LAW PRACTICE IN THE HIGH COURT, 1860–1928

Chapter 2

RULES OF THE HIGH COURT

> It is anomalous that [vakils who are] . . . allowed to practise in the appellate branch . . . should not be allowed also to practise in a Court from which there is by law an appeal to this branch. The anomaly, however, has been created in their favour. . . . I would simply say that in this matter we see no reason for modifying . . . the rules.
> —Justice William Holloway[1]

The general outcry during the 1850s rested in the reorganization of the judicial system by amalgamating the courts of the Crown and the East India Company. Although the subject had been under deliberation for some time by select committees in England and Calcutta, they 'recommended no change for the time being at Madras'.[2] However, during his remarkable but short-lived career as the Governor of Madras, Sir Charles E. Trevelyan appointed a special committee on 25 April 1859, to enquire into and report on 'the evils which . . . [existed] in the . . . system of judicature and on the means whereby they may be most effectually remedied'.[3] The committee consisted of four members: two civilians (William A. Morehead and Thomas L. Strange) and two barristers (T. Sydney Smyth and John B. Norton).

In January 1860 the committee submitted its report, signed by Morehead, Smyth and Norton, with Strange dissenting from the rest and publishing his own minute.[4] From these reports it is clear that not only had the committee failed to reach a consensus on the exact measures of reform to be introduced in the process of amalgamation, but that they also had disagreed on how quickly their recommendations should be implemented. More importantly, what role would the Indian practitioners play when the proposed High Court was constituted? Should they, as members of the 'Indian bar', be permitted to practise on the Appellate Side of the High Court as they had been doing for so many years in the Sadr Adalat? Or should they be totally excluded from such privileges since the High Court would be structurally somewhat different from any of its predecessors? If and when such an institution commenced its operation, what avenues of practice would be open to pleaders so that their minimum subsistence and professional aspirations might be safeguarded?

The committee, except for Strange, agreed that the system of double-agency (or the division of duties between barristers and attorneys), which had been in operation since the inception of the Supreme Court in Madras, would have to continue, at least on the original jurisdiction of the High Court.[5] They disagreed, however, on the nature of practice on the appellate jurisdiction and on the status of Indian practitioners. The question arose whether the double-agency should also be recommended for the Appellate Side or everyone who was a lawyer should be permitted to act, appear and plead on behalf of his own clients. Disagreement on this important question led the members to write their recommendations in separate minutes.[6] Morehead wrote that in deciding which of the two forms would best serve the interests of litigants on the Appellate Side, the question of double-agency became an unresolvable issue.[7]

Advocate General Smyth favoured introducing the double-agency on the appellate wing and completely excluding Indians from the High Court. He maintained that legal work would be done more efficiently through a division of labour, that the expenses involved in employing a barrister and an attorney would not be greater than the fees that some Sadr Court pleaders already charged, and that if no distinction were to be made between the different kinds of practitioners, such practice would tend to deter young and aspiring English barristers from coming to India. These barristers might not consider it proper to practise without being instructed by an attorney. Moreover, Smyth was apprehensive that by personal character, legal qualifications, or intellectual capacity, the local lawyers would tend to 'lower the tone of the [rest of the] practitioners' in the highest judicial tribunal, if they were allowed to practise there.[8]

Both Norton and Morehead refused to be swayed by such arguments. They contended that, by introducing the system of double-agency on the appellate jurisdiction, suitors would not have any option in the kind of practitioners they could choose to entrust with their cases. The services of two professional men would invariably tend to be more expensive than one. Except for the advocate general, members of the Supreme Court bar had already been practising before the Sadr Adalat with no such professional distinctions. However, if and when the Indians were to be excluded from practising before the High Court, what would happen to those individuals who had already achieved the distinction as practitioners of the Sadr Adalat, the highest appellate court in the Presidency? Most would be deprived of any legal work and would eventually disappear. 'Some consideration', therefore, was due to the members of the 'native bar'.[9] Norton even struck a note of optimism:

> We may certainly look forward to the time when the natives shall stand much more on par with the Europeans in respect of advocacy. Their natural intelligence is quite capable of this; and the opportunities now opening [in] obtaining a . . . legal education, and watching the method of the barristers, lead me to hope that such a consummation is not far distant.[10]

When the governor received the report, he recorded his own views on the recommendations of the committee. Commenting on the disagreement on the status and standing of Indian practitioners, he wrote:

> The commissioners are divided in opinion in regard to the eligibility of persons to be practitioners of the High Court. At present barristers, attorneys, and vakils plead before the Sadr Court, while barristers have exclusive audience before the Supreme Court . . . it would be hard to deprive the natives of the privilege which they have long enjoyed, of employing a cheap and rapidly improving, though still generally less efficient, description of agency; and I am confident that English barristers *do not* require exclusive privileges to enable them to maintain their position.[11]

The report of the committee, together with Trevelyan's minute, was dispatched to the Secretary of State for India in England and also to the Government of India. It took slightly over a year and a half for the British Parliament to act. On 6 August 1861 the Parliament passed the Indian High Court Act, empowering the Crown to issue Letters Patent 'to erect and establish High Courts of Judicature at Calcutta, Madras, and Bombay'.[12] The subsequent Letters Patent, dated 26 June 1862, was published in the *Fort St. George Gazette* on 19 August 1862.[13] Among other powers, the newly constituted High Court exercised all 'civil, criminal, admiralty and vice-admiralty, testamentary, intestate and matrimonial jurisdictions, original and appellate, in the Madras Presidency and beyond the limits of the Presidency town'.[14] Sections seven through ten of the Letters Patent authorized the High Court to admit advocates, vakils and attorneys according to the specific rules of qualification and admission to be formulated later.[15]

ADMISSION OF BARRISTERS AND VAKILS

The 1862 Rules

When on 18 August 1862 the new High Court assembled, Sir Colley H. Scotland, the Chief Justice, announced that 'a little time' was necessary to make rules concerning the business and practice on the Original and Appellate Sides of the courts, and to issue a table of fees.[16] In the meantime, he said, barristers and attorneys of the late Supreme Court and the pleaders of the Sadr Court would be admitted as advocates, attorneys and vakils. While the advocates would be

> entitled to appear and plead *in all* business before the Court, the Vakeels will be entitled to appear, and plead and act on behalf of the litigants in any appellate matters, which would be consistent with their former privileges in the Sadr court, *but not in any matter of ordinary original trials*. The attorneys will be admitted to appear and act for the suitors in all business before the court.[17]

The ten days that followed witnessed much confusion and chaos. Practitioners began to wonder how the new rules, though temporary, might affect the privileges, status and standing of barristers and vakils. That the same court now had original as well as appellate jurisdictions caused great consternation among barristers, especially those who had been practising as pleaders before the Sadr Court. They did not wish to jeopardize their former precedence over vakils. For instance, John D. Mayne, who commenced his practice in 1857, objected that the anticipated rules might treat him as a junior vakil in the High Court and consequently he might only be allowed to assist senior vakils in conducting appeals from the lower courts. The distinction between senior and junior vakils was based on two factors: the number of years that a practitioner had formally been enrolled in the Sadr Court and the extent of his practice.

Even though barristers had been admitted in the Sadr Court since 1846, the absence of evidence makes it difficult to ascertain whether their names had ever formally been entered on the rolls of that court. If this was the case, there were many uncertainties as to whether the High Court would retain this system or not. To treat a barrister, who was admitted on the Original Side of the High Court and who also wished to practise as a vakil on the Appellate Side, as a new entrant or as being equal to a local vakil would not be acceptable to barristers who had possessed considerable experience in India. Any such measures, which the High Court might propose, would be 'humiliating' to the English barristers. Mayne pointed out that many individuals who were practising as pleaders in the Sadr Court, and who subsequently signed the rolls as vakils of the High Court, had been his former law students in the Presidency College. He said, 'I would ask the Court to look [into this matter] in all its aspects, and I trust the Court will not offer us an opinion which can't be accepted without humiliation.'[18]

It appears that the judges themselves were not in complete agreement in formulating the requisite rules for the qualification and admission of practitioners. The distinction between the original and appellate jurisdictions which represented the previous jurisdictions of the Supreme and Sadr Courts, and the three different categories of practitioners allowed to appear before the High Court caused much jealousy and intense competition among members of the profession.[19] The High Court periodically made rather unsatisfactory efforts to revise the rules to ensure that the interests of these three groups were not violated, even though such rules initially were favourable to both barristers and attorneys.

The rules promulgated by the High Court on 28 August 1862 sought to ease the dilemma felt by Mayne and other barristers. These made allowances for their seniority and precedence over the new entrants. Otherwise, the standing of barrister-vakils would 'date *from* the time of their first admission to practice, in the same manner as pleaders in the late Suddar Court'.[20] The vakils retained their privileges in all civil and criminal appeals and in extraordinary original civil litigation, but they were prohibited from conducting any business in the ordinary original jurisdiction of the High Court. Occasionally, permission would be granted to some vakils to conduct appeals arising from original suits which involved questions on Hindu or Muslim law and custom.[21]

To the uninitiated in the technicalities of law practice, these provisions relating to the practice of barristers and vakils in the High Court might suggest that the judicial reforms did not bring much change in the existing position or status of vakils. They merely continued to handle appeals. Yet a closer look reveals something totally different. A list of officers of the Supreme Court shows that, on 17 August 1862, the last day of that court's existence, of the 27 official positions only three had been occupied by Indians. These had functioned as interpreters in Tamil, Telugu, Persian and Hindustani.[22] Being the Crown court and with powers to try original cases, the Supreme Court had hitherto excluded Indians from appearing before it. The High Court, in contrast, made it possible for the Sadr Court pleaders to be enrolled as vakils. As such, they freely moved about the court and fully observed the mode of practice, particularly on the Original Side.

This new opportunity enabled vakils to become familiar with the procedures of that legal maze. In other words, what had been denied to them previously was now available. On numerous occasions and with many opportunities vakils witnessed the proceedings in the new court, watching barristers examine witnesses and display their forensic skills. In time, vakils acquired a new confidence by assimilating these techniques. Within a few months after the High Court had come into operation, they petitioned the judges for permission to practise on the Original Side. Considering their past professional expertise and limited experience, this was a bold attempt on their part.

The 1863 Rules

The High Court framed further rules in 1863, 1866, 1870 and 1884 to deal with the qualifications and admission of vakils. Some minor modifications apart, these rules essentially reiterated the same prerequisites as embodied in the rules of 1863: a vakil candidate should have a bachelor's degree in law and should have completed his study or apprenticeship for a year under an advocate, vakil or an attorney. The rules also specified that vakils, who entered into contract with apprentice candidates, should have been eligible to practise on the original and appellate jurisdictions of the court. Alternatively, if he chose, a candidate could simply attend the court for two consecutive years, observe the proceedings daily, and obtain certificates from the Registrars on the Original and Appellate Sides, confirming his regular attendance. Candidates who had kept six terms at one of the Inns of Court in London and regularly attended the lectures and had passed one of the examinations were also eligible to become High Court vakils, provided that

Rules of the High Court   51

they also completed their apprenticeship for nine months under an authorized local practitioner. Testimonies of good character and conduct properly signed by the practitioner(s) under whom an apprentice had completed his course were also required from all candidates who wished to be enrolled as vakils.[23]

Despite the seemingly unlimited possibilities, not everyone with a degree in law found a sympathetic patron, who was willing to accept the fresh law graduate as his protégé. Nor did many choose to remain in Madras. Instead, they returned to their original towns in the mufassal or district headquarters to set up practice as pleaders. Should they ever wish to become High Court vakils, the rules enacted by the High Court in 1884 permitted such a course. Under this provision, an individual, who subsequent to his graduation had practised in any district or subordinate court for five years, was eligible to be admitted to the High Court, provided that he presented excellent credentials of good conduct.[24]

However, when the judges introduced a set of new rules in 1863, they permitted future vakils to practise on the Original Side, and this concession tended to divide vakils into two separate groups rather than uniting them as a single body: vakils enrolled in 1862, when the High Court first came into existence, had no privilege on the Original Side, while those who came later had that privilege immediately after the new rules came into effect. This anomaly resembled the similar experiences of barristers. The High Court permitted some to enrol themselves as barrister-vakils, but after 1863, newcomers could enrol only as advocates and not in that dual capacity even though they still had the privilege of appearing and pleading on the Appellate Side uninstructed by an attorney. This anomalous situation created by the High Court in order to maintain certain distinctions among barristers, attorneys and vakils naturally led to a sense of outrage among those vakils who had formerly been pleaders in the Sadr Court. They felt aggrieved at the concessions granted to barristers and attorneys to practise on the Appellate Side, while they were excluded from the Original Side. The judges justified their decision on the basis that both barristers and attorneys had been admitted to the late Sadr Adalat on equal terms with pleaders, while the latter were altogether excluded from the Supreme Court. Any attempt at precluding these two groups from appearing on the Appellate Side would engender much hardship to their professional aspirations and survival.

In late 1862, a correspondence took place between Clement Dale, the new appointee as the government pleader, the Madras government, and the High Court on the question of appointing barristers and attorneys as vakils.[25] Prior to the amalgamation, appointment to the government pleadership always went to Indian practitioners. Under the new system of judicial administration, the local government appointed Dale, a barrister, to that position, which provoked vakils who until now had been only quietly grumbling. They decided to petition the judges to reconsider their rules of 28 August 1862. The petition was sent on 14 October 1862. Prior to this, V. Sadagopachari, a prominent member of the late Sadr Court bar and a leader among the High Court vakils, communicated with the advocate general. He wrote that vakils were intending to seek permission from the High Court to practise on the Original Side as well as to raise objections against barristers and attorneys who had been permitted to practise as vakils. 'We have no objection,' Sadagopachari wrote, 'to Barristers and Attorneys electing to be . . . vakeels, but they should not be allowed indulgence in *both* capacities.'[26] The judges, however, refused to accede to the vakils' requests.

Although the vakils were reacting to the special position and opportunities of barristers and attorneys, conferred upon them by the judges in 1862, their real grievances involved a fundamental question on the interpretation of the High Court charter regarding the admission of different groups to practise law. Whereas both barristers and attorneys interpreted the charter as though it referred to three distinct functions, vakils strongly thought that the charter sanctioned the appointment of three separate groups, each with specific functions. In England, a barrister could only appear and plead, and an attorney could only act and appear. In contrast, a vakil could act, appear and plead before the High Court. That the High Court, particularly the Chief Justice and two other judges, also interpreted the charter in this manner lent even greater support to the vakils' contention. Moreover, Dale himself admitted that if the judges were to support the vakils' view as being consistent with the tenor of the charter, then he, as the newly appointed government pleader, would have to forfeit his status as a barrister. As such, technically he could not plead uninstructed by an attorney.[27] But since the judges denied the requests of the vakils, neither did Dale relinquish his office nor did barristers lose the privilege of practising unaided by attorneys on the Appellate Side.[28]

Undeterred by the adverse decision of the judges, vakils sent another petition on 10 November 1862, requesting that they be furnished with any minutes or opinions that the judges might have recorded on their previous petition. This boldness on the part of the vakils naturally offended the judges and they simply refused to divulge the reasons for their refusal. Despite the pains that the vakils took in observing the conventions and courtesies usually accorded to their 'Lordships', the judges haughtily but confidentially remarked that in requesting copies of the minutes, the vakils' behaviour had been highly 'irregular', 'unbecoming', and 'unprecedented'.[29] As a result, the late Sadr Court pleaders continued to argue on the Appellate Side and they never practised on the Original Side, despite their repeated petitioning to the High Court,[30] and the Governor-General in Calcutta.[31] Justice Holloway's comments reflected the prevailing attitude of the judges regarding the petitions of vakils, when he wrote:

> The petitioners have not passed any examination calculated to prove their fitness for the office of an advocate. Having been [members of] the Bar of the late Suddar Court, they have been permitted to continue practising in the appellate branch of the [High] Court. It is anomalous that those who are allowed to practise in the appellate branch . . . should not be allowed also to practice in a Court from which there is by law an appeal to this branch. The anomaly, however, has been created in their favour. . . . I would simply say that in this matter we see no reason for modifying . . . the rules.[32]

Confined to their practice on the Appellate Side, vakils of the previous era lingered on until they were outnumbered by young aspirants with superior legal education, talent and industry. By 1876, there were just two vakils left from the 'old school', who possessed no degree in law while others, about 33 in all, were graduates in law.[33] Thus, the Sadr Court practitioners gradually receded into the background while young luminaries emerged on the legal horizon. It is both imprecise and contrary to available evidence to maintain, as some scholars do, that vakils dominated on the Original Side of the High Court, and 'even began to encroach on the Appellate Side, long the preserve of the European barristers'.[34] In reality, it was the other way around. As the vakils themselves put it, practice on the Appellate Side was 'a matter of right' but entrance to the Original Side was granted 'under the new

Rules [of the High Court] . . . and . . . according to the words and spirit of the Letters Patent'.³⁵

Reasons for the 1863 Rules

The broader question of what factors or motives induced the judges to replace the 1862 rules within a short period requires some explanation. The most important feature of the new rules, passed in October 1863, was the granting of permission to vakils to argue on the Original Side. Never had vakils enjoyed such privileges before. Their admission to the Original Side generated a good deal of professional animosity and open competition between themselves and attorneys. No sooner had the 1862 rules come into force, than the judges realized that they had inadvertently created certain practical difficulties whereby a spate of suits for small amounts of money clogged the business of the court. To institute a case on the Original Side, the litigants had to employ the services of the double-agency or both a barrister and an attorney, each of whom charged clients an established fee for services provided. Sympathizing with suitors over the heavy expenses incurred by employing the double-agency, the judges sought a 'cheaper medium'. They found it in the body of vakils. They had hoped that vakils would readily avail themselves of the opportunity to represent clients in small suits.³⁶

Later, Chief Justice Scotland gave a different explanation. He said as the number of law graduates from the local university gradually increased it became apparent to the judges that the right to practice could not be generally withheld from those candidates who had been trained in higher liberal education and who had been subjected to strict examinations in law. He added, 'I look back to the concessions with satisfaction'.³⁷ These two explanations on why the High Court permitted vakils to practise on the Original Side do not seem to be antithetical. The proposition which Justice Holloway made shows the *immediate* and more pragmatic solution to the problem of making advocacy easily affordable by suitors in small claims, while the explanation by the Chief Justice alludes to the judges' favourable disposition towards those numerous Indian law graduates. In granting such concessions to vakils, the Madras High Court led the way because both in Calcutta and Bombay vakils were excluded from the Original Side for a long time.³⁸

ADMISSION OF NON-MADRAS VAKILS

Under powers conferred by the Letters Patent of 1865, the High Courts of Bombay, Calcutta and Madras formulated their own rules for the qualification and admission of lawyers. As autonomous institutions, the jurisdiction of each High Court was primarily limited to its own province and the rules of each High Court, therefore, varied. No two courts adopted the same rules. These rules dealt with different classes of practitioners, their academic qualifications and their professional privileges. For example, in the Madras High Court only three classes of practitioners were recognized, but in Calcutta there were five.[39] Whereas the Calcutta High Court allowed vakils, pleaders and *mukhtars* to appear only in appeals, in Madras vakils performed all three functions—acting, appearing and pleading on both sides of the court.[40] The Bombay High Court essentially followed the same rules as those in force at Calcutta.

Between 1865 and 1895, only Madras University graduates who had completed their apprenticeship under a local advocate, vakil or attorney were allowed to enrol as vakils of the High Court. In 1895, however, vakils practising in regions contiguous to the Madras Presidency and fresh law graduates from other universities began to inquire whether they as outsiders would be permitted to practise in the Madras High Court. The first to make such an inquiry was M. A. Swaminatha Iyer, who petitioned the judges that he be permitted to appear before the Madras High Court since vakils of that court had been permitted to appear before the High Court of Travancore.[41] He wondered whether the judges would be willing to vouchsafe the same concession 'under the principles of international law' to vakils from other areas, especially to conduct appeals of cases which he himself had argued before the lower courts in the Madras Presidency.[42] The judges did not give Swaminatha Iyer any clear answer, beyond a brief reference to the rules of the High Court which had no clear provision for the questions raised by him.

Subsequent enquiries and petitions from Trivandrum, Calcutta, Bombay and Allahabad, persuaded the judges to reconsider their rules of admission.[43] In November 1906 the High Court sent a circular to the Vakils' Association in Madras, which had been functioning since 1889, inviting their views on the question of admission of vakils from other provinces. On 15 November 1906 the members discussed the subject of permitting both practising vakils and law graduates from universities outside of Madras. The unanimous resolution of that body stated that it supported the idea of permitting law graduates from Bombay and Allahabad universities provided that the High Courts in these places reciprocated the arrangement of the Madras High Court.[44] The same resolution also recommended that such arrangements be made between Calcutta and Madras High Courts.

In view of this recommendation from the Association, the judges rescinded all previous restrictions and permitted other practitioners and law graduates to practise permanently in Madras.[45] Only in the case of Pudukkottai, a tiny princely state encircled by the Madras Presidency, did the Vakils' Association hesitate to lend support. In 1911, vakils from Pudukkottai petitioned the High Court through the local *durbar* and through the Government of Madras, expressing their desire to become High Court vakils. The judges, as usual, referred the petition to the Vakils' Association which gave 'an adverse opinion'.[46] As a result, the judges turned down their request.[47] Yet Pudukkottai vakils persisted and pointed out that the princely state enforced practically the same civil and criminal laws as those administered in British India and that the state had introduced all the British Indian enactments with their latest amendments.[48] The petitioners further stated that a third of the Chettinad lay within the state and that Nattukkottai Chettiars who lived outside of the state also owned lands and had extensive monetary transactions within the state. As a result, the Chettiars monopolized a considerable portion of the litigation and the vakils of the Chief Court in Pudukkottai had unique opportunities to become familiar with litigation bearing on the customs and practices peculiar to that very enterprising commercial community.[49]

Sir John E. P. Wallis, the Chief Justice, did not consult the Vakils' Association at this time. Instead, he wanted to find out the views of his colleagues who had been former vakils: Justices T. Sadasiva Iyer, T. V. Seshagiri Iyer, C. V. Kumaraswami Sastri, and K. Srinivasa Iyengar. These four judges agreed that the permission sought by the Pudukkottai vakils should be granted considering the nature of their practice and that their abilities were not inferior to other vakils practising either in Travancore or in any subordinate judge's court within the Madras Presidency. Justice K. Srinivasa Iyengar observed:[50]

> I agree that the petition may be granted. There is no question that the litigation in the Chief Court is at least as heavy and intricate as in any of the subordinate courts in the Presidency. . . . I believe the Chief Court Vakils want to get themselves enrolled as High Court Vakils for the *status* it gives and not with the object of practising regularly in the Madras Courts though occasionally they may go to Madras specially in an important case. The moffusil pleaders who enrol themselves as High Court Vakils do so with the same object and scarcely any of them with the object of practising in Madras. I think in the interest of the profession we must encourage local practitioners of inferior grades to the highest grade.[51]

Having read the minutes of four vakil-judges, Chief Justice Wallis was inclined to grant the petition. But first he wanted to have unanimous agreement in the matter and, to that end, he wanted to consult other barrister- and civilian-judges.[52] They agreed with the Chief Justice but suggested that, as a courtesy, the Vakils' Association should be consulted before issuing a final order. The brief reply from that body was favourable because the Association did not wish to disagree with its former leaders and friends, who had now become judges. Consequently, on 23 January 1918 the High Court amended Rule 1 of the General Rules of Qualification and Admissions, enabling practitioners from Pudukkottai, who had been in practice for five years, to enrol as vakils of the Madras High Court.[53]

Why did law practitioners from princely states and other provinces seek admission to the Madras High Court? The first and most obvious reason was the increase in the number of law graduates, who had begun to experience the pangs of unemployment throughout India at the turn of the century.[54] While many seniors or successful vakils opted to remain in their own cities and towns, new graduates were willing to settle down permanently in any locality. These individuals, especially those who lived in areas either between the Presidencies or between princely states and British India, desired to augment their income by obtaining permission from the judges to practise both in the High Court and in the subordinate courts of the Presidency. Second, the Madras High Court became an outlet for unemployed lawyers. During the second half of the nineteenth century, many barristers from Calcutta decided to move down to Madras where professional competition was not nearly as fierce as it was in Calcutta. By the early twentieth century, vakils from all over India migrated to and settled down in either Madras or other towns in the Presidency. When the judges perceived that the enrolment of vakils steadily increased each year, they decided to introduce a number of additional requirements directed at vakils as a group. Judges required that vakil candidates should undergo a period of apprenticeship and attend a series of lectures on professional conduct and advocacy prior to their enrolment.[55] Third, by the end of the second decade of the twentieth century, networks of nationwide transportation and communication had been so perfected that distances (and travel time) between major cities had shrunk remarkably. For many lawyers from other parts of India, therefore, practising in Madras was as challenging and rewarding as it would have been in Allahabad, Calcutta, Lahore or in Patna.[56]

Chapter 3

THE BARRISTER-ATTORNEY COALITION

> My English experience has given me a strong impression of the value of the class of young independent English and Irish Barristers and if the practice of the whole of India were thrown open to them . . . they would come out in greater numbers and would take more pains to qualify [for it].
>
> —Sir C. E. Trevelyan[1]

> It seems to me that the local Bar has virtually turned itself into a 'Trades Union'. It should take to rattaning and intimidation to complete the semblance.
>
> —Alfred Champion[2]

Barristers from England, Ireland and Scotland began to arrive in Madras in small numbers at the turn of the nineteenth century when the Supreme Court first came into existence. Although many dreamed of shaking the proverbial 'pagoda tree', most of them never gained even the wherewithal to return home.[3] Only the small minority that persevered during adverse conditions prospered, establishing practice not only in the Presidency town itself but in important mufassal areas as well. After the enactment of Act I of 1846, barristers also made inroads into the Sadr Adalat, representing the interests of many zamindaris, commercial firms, religious and communal institutions in innumerable appeals.[4] Individuals like George Norton, John B. Norton, Patrick O'Sullivan, Spring Branson, and John D. Mayne had formed a small coterie of barristers; their professional success and crusading zeal in public or social issues had received wide local acclaim from the press and individuals alike, in spite of the decided antagonism generally shown to the members of the legal profession.[5]

POSITION OF BARRISTERS

In 1862, the new High Court replaced the former Supreme Court and Sadr Court; it accorded most recognition and privileges to barristers. They appeared and pleaded before the Original and Appellate Sides of the court. In addition, barristers could also enrol as vakils since as pleaders they had previously practised in the Sadr Adalat. This concession, however, lasted only from August 1862 until July 1863 because of the strong protests from vakils, which ultimately led to the reformulation of admission rules. Rules passed by the High Court (in October 1863) prescribed mandatory academic qualifications for all those who had not been called to the bar in England, Ireland or Scotland but who wished to enrol as advocates. Such candidates had to produce a degree of Bachelor in Law (B.L.) from Madras University, with a certificate attesting that the applicant had also completed 18 months of apprenticeship under an already enrolled advocate; alternatively, a degree of Master of Law would be acceptable provided that a candidate also submitted with his application a certificate signed by the Registrars of the High Court, confirming his regular attendance in court for at least two years.[6] Advocates from Bombay and Calcutta also obtained permission to practise in Madras.

These admission procedures theoretically meant that the whole of British India could be thrown open to barristers arriving fresh from Britain and that unlimited opportunities would be available to them. This also meant that Madras was to become a 'dumpsite' for an already overcrowded legal profession in Calcutta, and barristers began to trickle down to Madras and enrol themselves as attorneys or vakils. *The Madras Times* observed, 'Whether they will all find practice or not is not the matter. . . . Calcutta is overcrowded with lawyers and attornies [*sic*], and our presidency seems to bid fair to be soon in the same predicament.'[7]

The admission rules that the High Court had sought to enforce in 1863 posed some nagging challenges to the judges; these rules quite clearly revealed their partiality towards barristers who had entered the profession before 15 August 1862. For example, Whitley Stokes, a barrister and law reporter of the High Court, petitioned the judges, requesting that he might be admitted as a vakil on the Appellate Side of the court. In support, he pointed out that the late Sadr Court had not made any distinction between barristers, attorneys and pleaders, that the terms 'advocate' and 'vakil' did not necessarily represent two different individuals but two distinct functions performed by one and the same individual, and that all barristers also had enrolled themselves as vakils when the High

Court was established. He informed the judges that rarely, if ever, had attorneys of the court instructed barristers on the Appellate Side. Stokes added:

> [U]nless barristers are admitted as vakils, the consequence will be that after the present barrister-vakils have ceased to practise, the business of the Appellate Side will fall altogether into the hands of attornies [sic] and of native and East Indian pleaders. Your Lordships can easily determine whether this result is likely . . . to [ensure] the satisfactory administration of justice on the appellate side or *to increase the inducement to a learned and able class of advocates* to join the bar of the High Court.[8]

Should the judges refuse to grant the prayers of his application, he requested the court to furnish him with the reasons for their refusal.

The High Court Registrar did not reply to Stokes directly. He instead sent a letter containing the decisions of the judges to T. Sydney Smyth, the advocate general and leader of the bar. This letter was explicit:

> The opinion of the Judges that an Advocate might practise on the Appellate Side of the Court uninstructed by an Attorney without acting in any way derogatory to his honourable position as a Barrister . . . has [already] been expressed from the Bench by the Chief Justice . . . [and] with reference to the rules enabling Advocates who were pleaders of the late Suddar Court to practise also as vakeels, [such rules] were made upon *special and peculiar grounds, to avoid all doubt and question as to the right of such advocates* . . . without being instructed either by a vakeel or an attorney.[9]

Although this letter apparently intended to give an appearance of concurrence on Stokes' petition, the minutes that the judges separately recorded give a totally different view on their behind-the-curtain discussions.

Briefly put, a heated discussion arose among the judges themselves. At issue was the question of whether the High Court charter dealt with three different classes of practitioners, each with specific roles, or only with three different functions any two of which could be combined in any individual. Chief Justice Scotland and Puisne Justices Adam Bittleston and Hatley Frere took the view that the charter expressly stated the exclusive roles or duties of three distinct and separate classes. But, Justices William Holloway and Henry D. Phillips contended that the charter did not forbid anyone from practising law in a dual capacity and that Stokes could be admitted either as an advocate or vakil, or both. Justice Holloway wrote, 'I think that we should be acting wrongly . . . in introducing such exclusion.'[10] Justice Phillips described the situation as 'a difficulty of our [own] creation' and suggested that a compromise should be reached. The chief justice, however, was persistent. With support from two other judges and with some minor modifications of his original draft, he thrust his interpretation of the charter on the rest and sent the reply on Stokes' petition to the advocate general.

The dissension among the judges on the correct meaning of the charter had important implications. First, in spite of the judges' public response to Stokes' application, the controversy revealed their inability to agree on the provisions of the charter or to formulate new rules of practice consistent with its meaning and intent. Moreover, the controversy brought to the surface old antagonisms between barrister-judges of the Supreme Court and civilian-judges of the Sadr Adalat. Second, since all barristers who had been enrolled prior to 15 August 1863 were admitted in a dual capacity as barrister-vakils, they had an undue advantage over those who later enrolled; their dual capacity enabled them to monopolize both original and appeal cases.[11] This inequality in High Court provisions meant that junior barristers suffered from low incomes. Third, the discussions among the judges also typified discord that would later surface whenever they dealt with issues related to different classes of practitioners, attorneys and vakils in particular. As far as the actual rule relating to the enrolment of barristers went, the judges introduced no major changes during the next three decades. This implicit judicial support and freedom from any further official interference enabled barristers to carry on with their professional activities under the patronage of the government and to fend off the encroachment of vakils.[12]

The Madras Bar Association

The Madras Bar Association met in March 1865. It consisted of a small group of barristers who realized the utility of having a professional body. This unincorporated association formulated and enforced various rules of practice and made periodic representations to the High Court, safeguarding its interests. It was also meant to oversee the activities of junior members, especially newcomers, whose standards of professional conduct and etiquette in a far-away land might not have conformed with English norms. No record has survived describing the background of the general development of its formation. What is apparent, however, is that it remained a relatively loose-knit body. With a few individuals as members, its meetings were held occasionally and irregularly.[13]

1. *Resolution against Vakils.* Resolutions passed during the first meeting show that the members decided not to accept any briefs from vakils or hold briefs jointly with them. This decision, as a professional tactic, discouraged the vakils from accepting original cases. Since vakils were neither totally familiar with the technicalities of pleading on the Original Side nor generally competent to oppose barristers, the latter sought to discourage them from making any undue gain on the Original Side. Being unable to instruct barristers who would argue cases in court, or to plead jointly with them, vakils had to refuse cases on the Original Side. This situation cleared the way for barristers to have the lion's share of the important criminal, civil, insolvency, admiralty and intestate cases coming to the court from the city. Repeated motions made by some junior members in subsequent meetings to rescind or alter this rule met with strong opposition from senior members.[14]

2. *Resolution on Fees.* The second most important issue that the Madras Bar frequently dealt with related to the difficulties in enforcing fee rules for services barristers rendered.[15] While some enjoyed an enviable position as members of a profession of long-standing traditions and reputation and even dominated on the Original Side as uncontestable cross-examiners, orators and jurists, such qualities could not be ascribed indiscriminately to all members of the bar. Some had recourse through means other than knowledge and skill to a steady and regular flow of cases, which alone guaranteed a standard monthly income. From time to time the association passed resolutions prescribing specific fees for the legal services barristers provided. Yet the records show that some recalcitrant members never did follow these guidelines.[16] Paying commissions to law agents (or touts) who brought cases, receiving less than the stipulated fee for appeals, and accepting briefs unaccompanied by fees (but alleging that such fees had already been paid) were common practices.[17]

The career of F. H. Lascelles was typical of a nonconformist. He came to Madras sometime around March 1877 to practise before the High Court. On 2 April the bar sent him a letter with a copy of the recently framed rules on fees. At first, he seemed to have accepted the rules indifferently and vaguely expressed consent to adhere to them. But between April 1877 and March 1878 he had second thoughts. He wrote to the association that 'he would agree to anything the members of the Bar might arrange not incompatible with the English Bar rules'.[18] Other members thought his reply unsatisfactory; they insisted he be required to give an unequivocal answer as to whether he was or was not prepared to abide by the rules. This correspondence between the Madras Bar and Lascelles set the stage for Alfred Champion, a leading attorney, to expose the whole 'commotion' caused, he alleged, by a 'free lance' in the bar:

> I hear that the Bar intends to hold a meeting, and if possible, doubtless, to 'air upon' this refractory member. Mr Lascelles' offence appears to be his refusal to consider himself bound by the rules of the Bar passed in his absence, or rather when he was not a member of the local Bar. As the matter is of public interest, as affecting the fees to be paid by suitors in the High Court for the services of counsel, I think it will be of interest if the case is openly and freely stated.[19]

Champion retraced various developments of several rules relating to fees since February 1870. One of the rules, he said, stipulated that a sum of rupees 87.8.0 per day had to be paid by clients for any services a counsel might provide, no matter how long it took to complete them. If a junior's assistance was necessary he too was to be paid the same amount. The bar modified this rule later: a senior should receive rupees 87.8.0 and a junior 52.8.0. 'But this alteration,' Champion observed, 'left the old grievance untouched, viz., that in the simplest case a fee of Rs 87–8 must be paid, and naturally clients insisted on the services of the seniors to the prejudice of the juniors.'[20] Champion pointed out that although a fee of Rs 87.8.0 paid on confirmation of certificate, for example, was unjustifiable, the rules of the bar were so 'inexorable' that juniors had no power to oppose or depart from them. Lascelles had brought upon himself the wrath of his associates by refusing to be bound by any such rules and by accepting whatever fee he thought adequate. Champion wrote:

> The big-wigs stroke their beards and say 'are we not generous? We allow, nay we insist, on the juniors taking senior fees.' 'Yes, yes,' says the client, 'but if a dose of castor oil costs as much as the amputation of my leg, I may as well have the castor oil administered by the hands of a

Jenner.' . . . It seems to me that the local Bar has virtually turned itself into a 'Trades Union'. It should take to rattaning and intimidation to complete the semblance, for by no argument can the Bar convince the public that a client is bound to pay as much for a dose of castor oil as for the amputation of a leg.[21]

A correspondent, who had simply identified himself as 'C', not only agreed with Champion's views but also encouraged the members of the bar, seniors especially, to think back on those years when they were struggling to gain a foothold in the profession. He said, 'the wonder is not that Mr Lascelles should refuse to be bound by such a partial, one-sided, absurd rule, but that it should have been acquiesced in so long, or how indeed it ever came to be passed. It is, in short, an ingenious contrivance for faltering leaders, and starting juniors.'[22]

3. *Resolution against giving 'Commissions'*. Lascelles' troubles did not end with his breach of bar rules, nor was this the only incident in which he acted contrary to its expectations. Twenty-one months after his nonconformity became known, he found himself in the thick of yet another controversy: that of giving commissions to those who acted as agents or brokers for bringing briefs and of making certain allegations against his fellow members. His behaviour, once again, seemed to have created a stir among his colleagues and, as a result, he executed his duties in an unfriendly atmosphere of mutual rivalry, jealousy, exclusivism, and even self-righteousness.

In March 1879 some members proposed that 'steps be taken to enforce the rule' of 7 January 1877, which prohibited the practice of giving commission.[23] The original resolution was explicit: 'The Members of the Bar agree that under no circumstances and in no manner will they give commission or other payment, directly or indirectly, to law agents or other persons bringing business.'[24] Even though this resolution had been accepted unanimously, one cannot be certain why the bar discussed this issue or who introduced it in the meeting. All one can learn is that the proposal was 'negatived as impracticable'. Even more puzzling, however, is the question why the members rediscussed the subject of giving commission in December 1879.

At a meeting on 18 December 1879 the bar issued special notices of reprimand to three individuals—Johnson, Lascelles and Normandy—about their alleged practice of making payments for bringing briefs. Eardley Norton, secretary of the bar, sent the letter to Lascelles and charged:

> A law-broker has assured me that he has frequently received commission from you for work brought by him to you. I and some of my friends think this charge so serious . . . both as regards yourself and the profession . . . we are members of, that we are of opinion you should be offered the opportunity of prosecuting the broker . . . for defamation. I regret to have to add that more than one of the Members of this Bar will be compelled to construe a refusal to prosecute as an admission of the truth of the charge.[25]

Normandy was present at the meeting of 19 December 1879. Johnson was absent but sent a letter indignantly refuting the charges against him. Lascelles neither wrote a reply nor put in an appearance. After a 'good deal of desultory conversation', discussion centred upon the habit of some barristers, who employed more clerks (or *gomastahs*) exclusively for soliciting clients. Some of these clerks could not even utter a word of English! Expressing 'strong opinions' on such 'dishonourable' practices, members then dealt with Lascelles' attitude towards the bar. Some believed that he had made certain 'defamatory and unprofessional charges to the practitioners from the mofussil against the members of the Madras Bar, and behind their back'.[26] Since all of this information consisted of oral testimony, obtained from uninvolved reporters, the bar took no action. With respect to the charge of giving commissions, the bar unanimously resolved to postpone its decision for another week before doing anything definite.

Bar members had also resolved at this meeting to address the High Court on the uncontrollable evil of touting among some of their members. They recommended that relevant portions of the Act XVIII of 1879, the Legal Practitioners' Act, be extended to the Madras Presidency.[27] Records are silent as to whether or not any further measures were taken against Lascelles or whether the bar actually sent its address to the High Court. In spite of their loud talk and denunciation of touting, the practice seems to have persisted. Not until April 1882 did the High Court finally recognize the increasing number of touts and decide to enforce the Legal Practitioners' Act.[28]

4. *Conflicts between Members*. A final blow to Lascelles' reputation and professional aspirations came when Patrick O'Sullivan, the advocate general, filed a suit in the Egmore Magistrates' Court

on charges of libel. Before discussing the grounds for the suit and its outcome, a brief discussion on the nature and constitution of the bar would be useful: how the members were called to the bar at home and to what degree they were able to uphold standards of professional ethics, unity, propriety and etiquette in India.

Individuals who went to India to pursue a career in law generally came from the four Inns of England,[29] from the King's Inn of Ireland, or the universities of Scotland. Each candidate had passed the secondary school matriculation examination (or an entrance examination) prior to admission. For three years (or twelve terms) he attended the lectures delivered in any of the Inns and ate six dinners in each term. Before being called to the bar, a student had to be 21 and had to pass the examinations on Real and Personal Property, Roman Civil Law, and Common Law and Equity.[30] He was also expected to 'attend' the chamber of a barrister with a 'considerable' practice for about a year. At the end of this period, the fledgling barrister would be proposed for admission by his master or some other barrister before a judge. Such a process marked his entrance into the legal career.

On admission to the bar, the candidate was then left to survive by his own wits, talent and ability. In the generally overcrowded and competitive profession at home, this was not always easy. Not a few barristers, understandably, would set out for India in hopes that they would find a niche in one of the High Courts and could eventually emerge as one of the 'leading' local barristers. Their previous training and experience in courts were usually inadequate and hardly prepared them for conditions altogether different in India; differences in social backgrounds, nationalities and political ties at home did not help them to act as a homogeneous group on reaching Indian shores. Indeed, they could scarcely be considered equipped to maintain their professional standards in this new environment. The professional and social gaps which existed between a well-established local barrister and a newcomer, no matter how much law he might know, were such that the latter had to struggle for years to secure briefs. In such struggles for survival within the profession, fought on a foreign and unfamiliar soil, professional integrity and pride (which had allegedly been inculcated through lectures while eating scrumptious dinners at the Inns) did not receive much consideration. At best, newcomers tended to show only a halfhearted willingness to abide by the rules of their seniors in the bar.

Under these circumstances, Lascelles' contumacious and independent spirit conformed to the frustrations of juniors, although they might never have had the temerity to depart from established practices. Impetuous and non-conforming, he wrote a short article for *The Madras Mail*, exposing the inferior legal training of some barristers from Gray's Inn, who opted to practise exclusively in India. They had attended the Inn, he claimed, for only two of the usual three years. While the Calcutta and Bombay High Courts had refused to admit these 'eight-term' barristers, the Madras High Court seemed to have taken a lenient view in the matter.

Lascelles was not the first to point out such violation of admission rules by Gray's Inn authorities. Some 15 years earlier a *Madras Times* editorial had dealt with the same issue, pointing out the differences in admission policies pursued by Gray's Inn and the Middle Temple. Two men from Madras—a solicitor and a magistrate—had gone to England a few years before. Having completed two years of legal training, they then applied for the diploma. Whereas the solicitor had succeeded in obtaining the diploma and had been called to the bar in Gray's Inn, the Benchers of the Middle Temple refused to admit the magistrate. *The Madras Times* elaborated upon the evils that might result when a solicitor-turned-barrister from Gray's Inn returned to Madras to set up his practice as a barrister. It conjectured that he might eventually be promoted to the bench, 'in which the consequences of his inefficiency [could] possibly be disastrous to the interests of the community who [were] guided by his decisions'.[31] In 1869, another report had claimed that the Council of Legal Education for the Inns of Court had passed a rule permitting all applicants from India with sufficient knowledge of Hindu and Muslim law and of different Indian Codes and Acts then in force to complete their course in two years or eight terms.[32]

It is not clear whether Lascelles knew about these subsequent changes in the admission rules of the Council of Legal Education when he wrote his article for *The Madras Mail*. What is clear, however, is his hasty and tactless reference to the advocate general as an 'eight-term barrister'. He alleged that the advocate general, together with a few others practising in Madras from Gray's Inn, was unwilling to introduce any modifications into existing rules on fees. As he put it:

The Barrister-Attorney Coalition 69

Madras Bar is now becoming sufficiently large and numerous for its members to see if they have adopted, or are adopting the same sanctions, and regulations, which are found salutory and necessary in other places. It is of no use now to rely on a *protective tariff of fees* . . . this professional *espirit de corps* is said to exist in Calcutta and Bombay in a much greater degree than it does in Madras.[33]

Although he later apologized to the advocate general in public, acknowledging the error he had committed, the latter took Lascelles to court demanding that a fine should be inflicted on the defendant.[34] The court levied a fine of Rs 200 on Lascelles along with costs. Little wonder that Lascelles decided to represent Cadwallader Waddy, a barrister settled at Nagapatam in Tanjore District, when the Madras Bar indicted him for unprofessional conduct. Not only did Lascelles want to represent Waddy by protecting him from any possible loss of privilege, but he also wanted to use the occasion for vindicating himself before the Benchers of the Middle Temple.[35] Records do not show whether Lascelles ever returned to Madras to resume his practice.

Government Patronage of Barristers

Despite the severe hardships and struggles involved in the early years of a career in law, the profession also had its moments of glory, especially for barristers during the nineteenth century. Rewards came to a talented few in the form of patronage under the local government which recognized their professional skills and usefulness. The most coveted and the most rewarding of these appointments—in terms of prestige, political contact and handsome salary—were the offices of the Advocate General, the First Judge of the Court of Small Causes at Madras, the Registrar of the High Court—Original Side, the Clerk of the Crown, and the Crown Prosecutor. There were other important positions as well.[36] Barrister-judges of the High Court enjoyed even greater rewards and great prestige in society. With a salary of Rs 5000 for the chief justice and Rs 3750 for puisne judges, their positions were almost beyond any peer.[37] Some barristers also found opportunities elsewhere. Whitley Stokes, for example, who once had applied to the High Court for permission to be enrolled as a vakil, became a law reporter. He then moved to Calcutta, appointed by the Government of India as the administrator general, still later became Under Secretary in the Legislative Department, and finally the Secretary.[38] *The Madras Times*, alluding to such preferential treatment accorded to barristers in those days, commented: 'The Sun of patronage shines more pleasantly on the lawyers than on the Army.'[39]

If appointments under the patronage of government went to a few leading barristers, the bar as a special interest group also actively demanded greater representation for its members in the judicial administration. The Public Service Commission visited Madras in 1887 to collect information in order to augment the quality, training and character of men in national and provincial administrative service. Although the initial enthusiasm shown by the members of the bar on 28 January 1887 had later petered out, the Commission listened to their concerns and ambitions. The bar preferred that all legal appointments such as the 'Small Cause Court Judgeships, Registrarships, and Magistracies', and not just judicial positions alone, be filled by legally trained individuals, whether barristers or vakils.[40] The obvious reason for adopting that position was to limit the number of seats thrown open to civilians entering the judicial service, who also aspired to rise on the ladder of success.

Frequently the local press also supported barristers by pointing out to the High Court the 'injustice' of granting more privileges to attorneys and vakils.[41] Whenever official posts became vacant and whenever these positions were filled by non-members of the Madras Bar or by others who were not barristers, as in the case of Walter Morgan who was related to the then Chief Justice Sir Walter Morgan, the press would lead a crusade criticizing the policies adopted by the government and the High Court.[42] The press would interpret such actions as being discourteous and even insensitive to the interests of local bar members, especially juniors whose position was unenviable, being involved in vain fights for survival.[43] For example, defending the view that appointment to the office of Crown Prosecutor ought to be exclusively reserved for members of the local bar, *The Madras Times* wrote: 'The appointment by custom belongs to the High Court Bar; and the custom *becomes a right* unless there be no member of the Bar competent to perform the duties of the office satisfactorily.'[44]

Contributions of Barristers

1. *The Roles of Barristers*. Apart from enjoying a successful law practice or obtaining prestigious appointments, some barristers

devoted their time to the advancement of education and social reform. They periodically delivered lectures and addresses in local colleges, 'native' institutions and the university. Trained in Western classics and in law, men like John B. Norton and John D. Mayne earned a reputation for their 'admirable eloquence'.[45] Others wrote useful commentaries on different topics of law, edited law books, or compiled digests of cases decided by the Indian High Courts or by the Privy Council.[46] Moreover, by independently editing and circulating a few legal periodicals—whether for diffusing knowledge in points of law, educating the members of the 'Native Bar', or providing a forum for discussion on topics related to law—barristers took an early lead in publishing law reports. This enterprise blossomed in the hands of vakils a few decades later.[47] However, not every barrister got involved in such extra-professional activities, nor did barristers as a group show much interest in the educational or social improvement of the Indian people.

2. *Barristers and Public Opinion.* Barristers as a professional group were not without reproach. The local Anglo-Indian society and the press perceived them as devoid of any scruples, and as if the profession as a whole deserved 'to be reproached as [being] both dirty and dishonest'.[48] The reasons for such perceptions were obvious. For the average litigant, hiring the services of a barrister, whether experienced or a newcomer, was generally a very expensive and risky venture. The system of 'double-agency', and barristers' insistence on advance payment of stipulated fees for services to be rendered (a system unique in India), could cause considerable inconvenience to any suitor on the Original Side of the High Court. That vakils had neither the privilege of practising on the Original Side nor much experience in conducting trials, tended to contribute to barristers' greed. In the 1870s and 1880s the vakils began to successfully withstand the competition of others and offered substantial reductions in fees since each vakil himself combined the functions of attorney and barrister. Nevertheless, the original perceptions of barristers as being interested only in fleecing the litigants died hard.

Time and again, both prominent individuals and the press in Madras criticized barristers for taking fees from clients and then failing to appear in court when their cases were called for hearing. Editorials pointed out that if similar practices existed among members of other professions, such as doctors, they would have been sued for breach of contract and damages would have been assessed against them for neglect of duty. *The Madras Times* commented:

> That barristers who accept fees for services which they fail, intentionally or unintentionally, to render, ought to be required to restore what may under the circumstances be accurately enough described as their ill-gotten gains.[49]

The Bombay High Court, the paper went on, had to intervene in such circumstances by ordering barristers to return the fees they had taken from clients. It is difficult to gauge to what extent this practice prevailed among Madras barristers or exactly which barristers committed such acts. It is less difficult to see what the implications of such alleged misconduct might be. Such imputations seemed to underscore the fact that many leading barristers made extortionate demands of their clients while, at the same time, they showed little sympathy for their juniors who suffered from 'briefless inactivity'.[50]

The tactics which barristers pursued in eliciting information from witnesses also came under public castigation. Despite their forensic skills, quickness of mind and facility in the English language (occasionally in the vernaculars as well), a barrister's manner of cross-examination of witnesses was far from gentle or courteous. As *The Madras Times* put it, 'A barrister can, under the shelter of his gown, put the most insulting questions, insinuating the most unfounded charges, against an unfortunate witness, and the latter has no redress whatever.'[51] Every time a witness took the stand in court, he faced the most incriminating and morally debilitating questions put to him by a barrister. No matter how well a lawyer had coached his witnesses to meet the questions from the opposing lawyer, witnesses often collapsed, being unable to answer. Being unfamiliar with the technicalities of proceedings in law courts, a witness would tend to be worried, timid and perplexed, loathing every moment of his ordeal in the witness box. Little wonder that when the Central Assembly introduced a new Evidence Bill curtailing severely the privileges and immunities of counsel, barristers in Bombay, Calcutta and Madras immediately petitioned the Viceroy for redress. They protested against the setting aside of their long cherished privileges and traditions.[52] The local press tried to silence such protests; it defended the steps taken by the Government of India by stating that barristers 'like all other men, should exercise their profession at their own risk'.[53]

There were other factors that polluted the aura of barristers. Some seniors were haughty and unsympathetically demanded large sums from apprentices who would eventually become High Court vakils,[54] and some even obtained briefs unlawfully by paying commissions to touts. Moreover, the disparities between senior and junior barristers in the city, and between city and mufassal barristers—whether in government patronage, income or life-style—tended to lower their proverbial image. Without the co-operation of attorneys, who charged the clients for 'receiving and instructing' the counsel and who kept up a steady flow of briefs to barristers, many would have sunk into abject poverty.

ATTORNEYS-AT-LAW

The attorney, also known as solicitor, was an intermediary between client and counsel. Since both the traditions of their own profession and the rules of the High Court in Madras only permitted barristers to appear and plead in court, especially on the Original Side, an attorney did all the spade-work connected with a suit, *before* and *after* it was heard. As a distinct professional body, attorneys did not appear to have entered the legal picture in Madras until the Supreme Court was established in 1801. Prior to that, no distinction had been maintained between barristers and attorneys, either in the Mayor's Court or in the Court of the Recorder. Those who had practised in the early courts functioned in a 'double-capacity', as both barristers and attorneys.[55]

Attorneys in the Pre-High Court Era

When the Supreme Court commenced operation in 1801, those who practised law had the option to choose the functions of barristers or attorneys. Until 1853, attorneys transacted their business by making wills, drafting contracts and deeds, and instructing counsel. Then, for the first time, the Sadr Adalat permitted them to enter the portals of any of the sadr courts, but it did not retain the distinction between attorneys and barristers as had been the case in the Supreme Court. Barristers, attorneys and pleaders received the same kind of treatment and privileges to appear and act as well as plead.⁵⁶ In March 1859, however, the Sadr Adalat passed a rule, enabling barristers to have precedence over attorneys and pleaders; and attorneys themselves had precedence over pleaders. This rule created some mark of distinction and status among the various groups of lawyers.⁵⁷

No clear information has survived on the activities of attorneys during the pre-High Court era, except the information reported in local newspapers.⁵⁸ It is clear, however, that the division of labour between barristers and attorneys in the Supreme Court had become notorious for creating unprecedented expenses for litigants.⁵⁹ Just a few months before the amalgamation of the Supreme and Sadr Courts, the local society, particularly the press, decried the system of the attorney's Bill of Costs whereby the attorneys forced clients to pay for services which they might very well have provided for themselves. For example, when *The Madras Times* had to appear in court on charges of libel, the adverse verdict against it cost Rs 14,000. This the journal paid only after much protest. The *Times* called for 'radical reform', to be instituted by the chief justice. It exhorted: 'Let lawyers be paid fairly for work done, and all mere subterfuges and pretences be swept away.'⁶⁰ With the arrival of the new High Court Charter in 1862, conditions slowly began to improve. It empowered the judges to approve, admit and enrol attorneys who should be authorized to appear and act for suitors under the rules and directions of the court.⁶¹ Yet frequent changes in the rules of practice tended to arrest what few improvements had been made.

Attorneys of the High Court

1. *High Court Rules.* The judges passed the first set of rules on 28 August 1862 specifying the continuation of privileges that attorneys had enjoyed prior to the amalgamation of the judicial systems in the Madras Presidency. This meant that individuals, as 'attorney-vakils', were able to conduct business both on the Original and Appellate Sides of the High Court. On the Original Side, as intermediaries between clients and barristers, they performed several duties: receiving instructions from clients, preparing briefs and advising the counsel. On the Appellate Side, they represented clients and pleaded or argued in court. Although this facility was in no way different from what had also been accorded to 'barrister-vakils', attorneys slowly began to gain ground. As this happened,

barristers raised protests against granting such concessions to attorneys.[62]

A second set of rules stipulated that applicants outside of India must have proofs of previous enrolment 'in one of Her Majesty's courts at Westminster or Dublin' and proofs of good character and ability.[63] In contrast, candidates from within the Presidency, who were ordinarily high school matriculates, had to complete four years as articled clerks under some High Court attorneys and produce a certificate of good character and ability. They also had to pass an examination to display their competence in executing the duties of the profession.[64] Contemporary opinion shows that the examination was 'singularly inappropriate' and that a mufassal pleader possessed a far greater education than did a High Court attorney.[65] Despite their inferior academic preparation, in 1876 the High Court vouchsafed several privileges to attorneys: practising on the Appellate Side, appearing for cases heard in chambers, and pleading as counsel on the Original Side 'even at the final hearing of causes, if they [were] undefended causes'.[66] For many years, barristers had a clear monopoly over the last two privileges and it is understandable why they became so indignant when the High Court extended such privileges to attorneys.

2. *Attorneys' Backgrounds, Qualifications and Doings*. Unlike barristers, who were almost always Europeans, attorneys tended to be a mixture of Europeans, Eurasians and Indians. Although many competent European attorneys maintained their firms remarkably well, their Eurasian and Indian colleagues generally lacked sufficient preparation or training. Except for the high school matriculation certificate, as mentioned above, only a few had any higher qualifications; few of them possessed any long-standing traditions which could bring them the sort of esteem and recognition usually accorded to European attorneys. Labelled as 'legion' because of their preponderant numbers and inferior qualities, they tended to be severely criticized in the press. As one writer put it:

> [A] young and hopeful [would-be attorney] is allowed to enter the office of his patron, where he generally reads—nothing. He walks into the different courts while the cases are going on; takes the best seat to the exclusion of his elders, tries to look manly and fast, in which he woefully fails. . . . After this sort of life for four years, he passes some examination. I don't know what it is like; but it cannot be very hard, for I never heard of anyone being plucked . . . [then the] young legal takes a dingy little den in the neighbourhood of that delightful place,

Second Line Beach. . . . He then hunts up for clients and being a beginner he is willing to take less than the older hands, in fact what his clients may offer. . . . Having made a start, a little boasting and swagger enables him to get a few more clients, and so at last he is fairly launched on the sea legal. . . . In the course of time he however raises his charges till he equals the rest of his brethren; but he will always take a lower fee rather than lose the case. The young lawyer's mine of wealth is the Small Cause Court. These cases are the easiest to manage, for a very little law suffices.[67]

A fair amount of exaggeration may be allowed in the foregoing description, but it is clear that as these young attorneys or articled clerks, who were aspiring to become attorneys, went about their business in ways contrary to the norm or used devious methods in securing briefs, they earned ridicule and scorn. Touting for business, remunerating agents who brought briefs, and overcharging clients for services that took only a few minutes were common practices among attorneys.[68] But such abuses were not very uncommon among barristers or vakils, either. What was disturbing about attorneys, especially if an important case had been instituted on the Original Side, was the crippling 'Bill of Costs'. For many litigants, and more specifically for a losing party, the arrival of a Bill of Costs could presage financial doom. Such a bill often foreshadowed perennial indebtedness and perhaps even a 'bonded commitment' to engage the same attorney for future legal work.

The High Court set guidelines on fees that vakils and attorneys could demand for services rendered in original suits, but these guidelines never described exactly what could be legitimately construed as 'legal services'. The rules simply stated, 'In all bills of costs . . . every item of disbursement and the cause thereof shall be distinctly specified and credit shall be given therein for all advances.'[69] Without much scrutiny or objections, the Taxing Officer generally approved whatever was claimed in the bill, unless the attorney of the opposite party objected. Attorneys tended to take advantage of this ambiguous rule, and the result was detailed but cryptic bills of costs. The comments from *The Manchester Guardian* at this time in England were revealing:

> A great part of . . . bills [of attorneys was] made up of charges for drawing and copying documents of various kinds, and almost all these documents have been made longer than they need be in order that the solicitor may obtain indirectly remuneration for time, skill and thought bestowed upon his client's business which the law does not allow him to obtain directly.[70]

This practice seems to have been imported wholesale into India, especially into Madras, where it had gone out of control. C. V. Sundarum Sastri, a local attorney with nearly 25 years of experience, bore out this fact. He published a pamphlet exposing the different ways by which many attorneys increased the items of services they claimed to have provided. The real motive behind such actions, he contended, was to escalate the Bill of Costs. Sundarum Sastri pointed out that the High Court never kept a record showing when a bill had been approved. The only available record of a bill ever preserved was 'the affidavit of the service of the notice of Taxation Officer and the total amount of the Bill as taxed between the party and party'.[71] Nor did the High Court ever keep any diary; this would have preserved all the necessary information on any particular suit, showing in chronological order what new developments had taken place, how many times the case had been adjourned and reposted, and at whose insistence what had been charged. The administrative oversights (or loopholes) gave attorneys unlimited freedom to include items of services which could not be quickly or easily verified in the records. Under 18 different subheadings, Sundarum Sastri candidly and succinctly described the practices of some attorneys in their charges of fees.[72]

What was the outcome of such public unmasking of the unsuited system of double-agency? What reforms were introduced subsequently in the scale of costs? And, more importantly, how did attorneys as a group respond to such open and scathing criticisms by a member of their own profession? Answers to such questions are not readily forthcoming. But, as early as 1863, there was public disagreement over fees charged by attorneys. Such controversy reveals, at least in part, how attorneys then responded to these mounting criticisms.

On 6 March 1863, the *Atheaneum and Statesman* published an article showing that for a sum of three rupees and four annas, the services of an attorney could be secured to attend the court between eleven a.m. and seven p.m. The newspaper pointed that this amount was only sufficient for one's daily meals (excluding any alcoholic beverages), that if attorneys were not paid more it would be ruinous to their profession, and that many would undoubtedly incur considerable debts. The *Times* responded with indignation and sarcasm. A few years ago the *Times* had been involved in a libel suit which had ultimately cost it Rs 14,000, and which seems to have been the underlying reason for the editor's response. The *Times* remarked:

> We object most strongly to any increase in fees. If the orthodox 'three and four' is a small sum per se, it becomes inconveniently large by repetition. A resolute agglomeration of *three and four's*, *as we have seen*, may mount up to fourteen thousand rupees.[73]

Another correspondent also wrote in the *Times*:

> [T]he system in force here is objectionable in the highest degree when compared to those adopted in Calcutta and Bombay; and it is objectionable not only to suitors who are bled under it, but to all right thinking practitioners who have to charge pursuant to it.[74]

Meanwhile, a rumour had spread at this time that attorneys were thinking of taking a procession through the principal roads and streets of Madras, chanting the following verse:

> The Barristers swig a great deal of Port;
> The judges make champagne dear;
> But blow their hats they swallows [sic] likewise,
> We poor Attorneys' Beer, Beer,
> We poor Attorneys' Beer.[75]

While the rumoured procession never took place, an attorney did protest with a long poem titled 'The Attorneys Lament':

> Kyind Christian friend, for mercy's sake
> Give ear' to our complain't,
> We haven't got no Beer to drink
> And yet with heat we faint.
> The water in Madras is bad,
> And *eau de vie cusis* more
> Than poor Attorneys can afford
> With fees of 'three and four'.
>
> *Chorus*
>
> Oh! wretched fee, oh! paltry fee,
> Oh! fee of 'three and four'.
> Compelling us our beer to beg
> With tears from door to door.[76]

3. *Ad Hoc Meetings of Attorneys*. No professional organization of attorneys seems to have existed during the High Court's first 30 years, but they did occasionally meet to discuss various issues related to their professional interests. A report submitted by the attorneys and preserved among the minutes of the Madras Bar provides information on an *ad hoc* meeting which took place on

29 July 1882 at the request of the Madras Bar. Twelve persons in all, two of whom were Indians, attended. The meeting was presided over by E. Barclay, a leading attorney.[77] At this meeting, several issues were discussed: accepting cases from vakils after the vakils had already negotiated the fees with the clients, reducing the existing cost of Counsel's fees, requesting the barristers 'to bind themselves not to take briefs from Vakils in cases in the Original Suits of the High Court', and forming a Society of Attorneys.[78] The attorneys then sent a report of that meeting to the Bar Association. Their report brought out two basically related but important issues: the undercurrents of professional rivalry among attorneys themselves and rivalry between attorneys and vakils.

Because of professional success of a few, competition and jealousy increased. Several attorneys present at the 29 July 1882 meeting, urged the Madras Bar 'not to take briefs from any attorney who [was] reported to have acted contrary to the resolutions of the general body until such time as a Committee of the Attorneys shall report his adhesion thereto'.[79] Reasons for this request are self-evident. Of the 32 attorneys who were practising in Madras at this time,[80] only 12 members were present at the meeting. This small but influential clique tried to exert pressure over those 20 who were absent. They requested the members of the bar not to initiate or sustain any professional contracts with those uncomplying and 'wayward' attorneys. This resolution of the attorneys seems to echo the very similar kind of controversy which had already taken place between the Madras Bar and Lascelles over fees.

Rivalry between attorneys and vakils became even more sharply defined, especially after the decision of the High Court in 1876 when vakils had seriously threatened attorneys' business on the Original Side. Even though barristers, attorneys and vakils practised before the same High Court, no one group was responsible for nurturing jealousy and competition within the profession, because the task of defining the parameters of professional activities rested with the High Court. A combination of factors contributed to such professional animosity. Frequent changes in the rules of admission, the autonomous nature of each High Court, and the lack of any communication between them prevented the judges from consulting with each other. As a result, these courts failed to define the uniform roles and privileges of lawyers throughout India and the penalties for the violation of such roles. Had it been possible, the integration of all High Courts into a single all-India judicial system, or the creation of a body such as the All-India Bar Council, would have taken place at a much earlier stage than it actually did.

Whereas barristers had passed resolutions against accepting briefs from vakils or against jointly holding briefs with them and had consistently managed to thwart any moves that some of their own members made to undermine or alter this decision, the attorneys took even more drastic measures to stem the tide of vakil encroachment on the Original Side. A group of attorneys met in July 1874 and drew up a petition imploring the judges to rescind the rules formulated subsequent to the second charter of October 1865.[81] These rules permitted vakils to perform all three functions—acting, appearing and pleading—on the Original Side. The petition claimed:

> [T]hat this arrangement [has] already done *serious injury* both to the Bar and the attorneys, for it is obvious that it confers on a single class of the profession, and that the *least educated* and *least fenced* about with tests, privileges, which are enjoyed by neither Barrister nor Attorney, neither of whom can in the long run contend against a class of practitioners, who combine in themselves all the rights of other two classes, *who are bound by no rules*, and *do not profess to observe any professional etiquette*.[82]

The attorneys also 'prayed' that they might once again be permitted to practise on the Appellate Side, from which they had been excluded since 1866 when the High Court had passed a new set of rules for qualifications and admission.[83] In response, the judges conceded only the second request and permitted attorneys to resume practice on the Appellate Side.[84] Not satisfied with this partial gain, the attorneys determined to exclude vakils totally from practising on the Original Side. On 9 October 1875, several of them assembled and resolved to submit a formal petition; this time, the petition would be supported by the argument of counsel for an order that the rules permitting vakils to practise on the Original Side should be cancelled because the 1862 Charter did not authorize such rules and that the wording of the 1865 Charter was in contradiction with the provisions of the statute under which both had been issued.[85]

The Full Bench heard this petition on 14 January 1876.[86] A huge gathering of barristers, attorneys and vakils was present to witness the scintillating arguments from both sides, in spite of the *Pongal* holidays. Leading barristers, especially Patrick O'Sullivan, appeared on behalf of the petitioners. Both T. Rama Rao and P. Ananda-charlu represented the counter-petitioners. John Gould, after reading the attorneys' petition *in extenso* argued 'at some length' that the judges had acted 'beyond their power' under the High Court Act and the Charter of 1862. The admissions of vakils on the Original Side, he said, had 'inflicted a great hardship and wrong' on the attorneys.[87] Following the reasoning of his 'brother-barrister', O'Sullivan argued that the judges had 'exceeded their power'. In reply, the two vakils defended the actions of the judges, maintaining that such actions were not altogether outside the scope or the intent of the powers conferred upon the judges by the High Court Act and the Letters Patent. Rama Rao summed up his arguments:

> The High Court is *one* Court with *many* jurisdictions. It has the power to admit Vakils to appear, plead, and act. . . . It had by its rules admitted them to exercise their calling generally, and has not confined them to any special classes of cases, or to the description of work that the Vakils were allowed to undertake in the Sudder Court.[88]

Chief Justice Sir Walter Morgan read the judgement. He remarked that, on the one hand, there was no doubt among the judges on the question of law. The legality of permitting vakils on the Original Side was unquestionable. But, on the other, he acknowledged that the allegations of hardships or loss of business were legitimate because the High Court rules gave largest powers to one class of practitioners who were in no way superior to the rest in terms of professional skills and attainments.[89] However, the judges decided against the petition.

Although defeated in their efforts to curtail the concessions gained by vakils, the attorneys did not rest; they kept up their opposition to the privileges enjoyed by vakils on the Original Side and they continued to oppose them even until the second decade of the twentieth century. When in 1916, the same question was mooted before Justice Coutts-Trotter in the case of *T. Namberumal Chetty v. M. P. Narasimhachari*, he reaffirmed the position that the judges had taken in 1876,[90] and thus he permanently put to rest the question of legality of vakils practising on the Original Side. But by then the vakils had completely obscured the attorneys in terms of sheer numbers, ability and monopoly of original suits, and therefore the argument became irrelevant and lacked force.[91]

Chapter 4

VAKILS' PREPARATION, PRACTICE AND GROWTH

> A Native Bar will be gradually formed, but it will be *following* the lead and *imitating* the example of *our* English barristers.
> —Sir C. E. Trevelyan[1]

The British carefully controlled the development of the legal profession, and the absence of an independent law society or Inns of Court in India gave them great freedom to discourage any expression of self-regulation. During the adalat days the provincial and central governments alone had power to regulate the profession, but after the amalgamation of the judicial systems the High Court exercised that power; the judges periodically revised the requirements for enrolment, each time making a new demand on vakils: possessing a law degree, completing a year of apprenticeship under a High Court practitioner, and attending a series of lectures on professional conduct and advocacy. Failure to meet these requirements resulted in rejection of a candidate's application for enrolment or postponement of his enrolment.

PREPARING TO PRACTISE

Academic Preparation

With the establishment of the High Court in 1862, pleaders of the Sadr Adalat became vakils, whose only qualification consisted of possession of a pleader's certificate.[2] In 1863 the High Court modified the rules for admission, stipulating that new entrants should have a bachelor's degree in law. Among the many enrolled under this rule and who later became eminent practitioners were T. Rama Rao, R. Balaji Rao, P. Anandacharlu, V. Bhashyam Iyengar and S. Subramania Iyer.[3] In the late 1870s law students adopted a new strategy by first completing the degree in arts and then attending the law college for their second degree.[4] Although the reasons for this shift are not known, the younger generations pursued this path, as had been required of pleaders in the 1850s. Possession of two degrees became a custom for anyone who wished to become a vakil, even though the High Court did not require this until 1896.

A small fraction of practitioners pursued graduate studies in law after their enrolment as vakils. Such an undertaking brought them further recognition, though not necessarily much more business. Those who successfully completed the 'very difficult' examination received a Master of Law (M.L.) degree, which enabled them to become advocates of the High Court.[5] Advocates enjoyed pre-audience and also had special privilege in appearing in insolvency court. However, their supposedly superior position made them a sort of legal hybrid, fully accepted neither by barristers nor by vakils. As one vernacular paper put it:

> Those Advocates feel it beneath their dignity to practise, like vakils, in the Small Cause Court and City Civil Court. Being neither Vakils nor Barristers, they cannot become members of either the Vakils' Association or the Barristers' Association. The vakils keep aloof from those Advocates regarding them as their superiors while the Barristers do not allow them into their society, regarding them as inferiors.[6]

Records from the Madras Bar Association provide further evidence of the antagonism between English and Indian advocates. In 1898, Eardley Norton chaired a select committee, which met to discuss the low morale among the bar members. In responding to allegations by S. Vaidyanatha Iyer that the bar had become more exclusivistic, not only did Norton refute such accusations but also defended the admission policies that had been recommended to the bar. The reasons he adduced in the course of his speech resembled what Indian barristers would later say during the debates on the creation of an Indian Bar Council and on the removal of all distinctions between barristers and vakils. Norton remarked that:

> He had toiled on behalf of the natives of India and had fought in their cause for the last 18 years; and it would be ungrateful of them to regard him as a foe. There was no question of colour or race feelings in the Report of the Committee and he felt, that the European element welcomed the native Barrister in their midst and would welcome the local Advocate in the same manner on being called to the Bar. The Bar had traditions and codes of honour which the local Advocate could never understand and it was impossible for the two bodies to amalgamate in the least. . . . We were a separate creation and wish so to remain; by all means let the local Advocate form themselves into an Association and go on paying their one rupee subscription a month.[7]

Practical Training

The mere possession of a bachelor's or master's degree was not in itself a passport to a legal career. Other hurdles stood in the way of would-be vakils and advocates. High Court rules required that the candidates should undergo further practical training in the chambers of a senior practitioner, pass examinations on Civil and Criminal Procedures, and attend lectures on professional conduct and advocacy. When in 1863 the High Court formulated rules of admission, vakils had two options: either to complete a year of apprenticeship or to attend the court for two years and pass the examination on procedures.[8] The judges permitted the latter option because, during those earlier years, not many European barristers were willing to accept Indian candidates as apprentices; without fulfilling such requirements, law graduates found it impossible to commence practice on the Original Side. With a view to reduce the extent of burden on officials, perhaps, the High Court modified these rules and prescribed only one year of apprenticeship in 1870, dropping altogether the requirements of two-year attendance in court and the examination in the procedures. During the next two decades, this system had degenerated 'into a farce', since it provided for no supervision of the relationship between a candidate and a practitioner.[9]

Judges realized the degenerate state into which the institution of apprenticeship had fallen and deemed that the system required a thorough overhauling. Justice Horatio H. Shephard thought that 'as the vakil has greater privileges, so greater care ought to be taken to see that applicants are fit and proper persons'.[10] This observation finally led to an amplification of existing rules in 1891. The apprentice was obliged to regularly maintain a diary showing daily the work done by him.[11] Each month, his 'master' or senior inspected and initialled the diary; the candidate submitted the diary to the Registrar along with any additional information on his performance, before he was formally inducted into the profession.[12] A decade went by without any further alterations in the rules relating to apprentices until a change in the Madras Law College curriculum made the judges re-evaluate and alter their rules of admission. Law students had been studying the Civil and Criminal Procedure Codes as one of the subjects, but in 1900 the college introduced Criminal Law as a separate subject in lieu of the course on procedure.[13] As soon as judges got wind of these proposed changes in the curriculum, they also began to require apprentices to pass an examination on procedure.

Lectures on Professional Conduct

In addition to completing a year of apprenticeship and passing the examination in procedure, apprentices had to meet yet a third requirement. Suggested by Justice V. Krishnaswami Iyer, the judges decided to inaugurate a series of lectures on professional conduct and advocacy.[14] On 19 August 1910 the High Court announced that an apprentice should produce before his enrolment a certificate showing that he had attended not less than two-thirds of the lectures on professional conduct and advocacy.[15] This new regulation became effective from 1 January 1911.

The cumulative effect of these stringent rules on apprentices is not difficult to evaluate. From the viewpoint of the judges, acquisition of practical skills, as well as the improved moral tone of apprentices, loomed large. Since the High Court Charter of 1865 provided them unlimited powers, judges cared little for the opinions of vakils. Whether realistic or not, the judges expected apprentices to become acquainted with the structure and functions of the court in twelve months, while at the same time developing skills in drafting plaints, memoranda and other legal documents. Then, the apprentices literally had to cram for the examination in Civil and Criminal Procedure Codes. Furthermore, no means existed for objectively evaluating whether or not an apprentice derived any special benefit from attending lectures. Minimum attendance hardly improved the moral fibre of the younger generation of vakils who often led lives of briefless inactivity, ennui and anxiety.

Leaders among vakils agreed that keeping the apprentice system was necessary; they believed that this would ensure that candidates would be 'brought into the atmosphere of judicial administration and the presence of men who are engaged day by day in the actual work of the practice of the profession'.[16] The difficulty, however, lay in translating such lofty ideals into actual practice. Only too anxious to get through the hurdles, apprentices cared little whether they actually acquired any professional skills or imbibed any of the bar's noble traditions. Moreover, seniors who did take apprentices rarely had any time 'except to give the apprentice a licence to enter their chambers and now and then use him as an amenuensis'.[17]

When the Madras Lawyers' Conference met in 1920, it discussed the inherent defects of the institution of apprenticeship and recommended that the High Court should abolish the examination in procedure altogether since it served no practical purpose.[18]

To an apprentice, meeting the requirements of the High Court did not seem so insurmountable as finding a compassionate and yet reputed practitioner who would be willing to take a novice under his wing. Numerous tales circulated about apprentices who could neither find a 'master' nor afford the *dakshina* (the offering) for the privilege of being a pupil. Finding a patron who was not very prejudiced against Indian candidates was generally difficult. Not only did European barristers resent the intrusion of vakils on the Original Side but they often refused to admit Indian apprentices into their offices.[19] In exceptional cases barristers did take apprentices, but they usually demanded a fee of Rs 1000, no small amount in those days.[20] As the number of vakils increased at the High Court, the plight of apprentices gradually improved as the latter tended to rely on bonds forged out of regional, linguistic or communal affiliation, family ties and friendship.[21] Once the contract had been made between an apprentice and his master, the novice had to be at the beck and call of his leader. Seniors often commenced their routines even before the break of dawn. As one practitioner put it, 'The masters in those days were truly taskmasters whose unmitigated outbursts of temper and verbal abuse were notorious.'[22]

The Enrolment

Once the technicalities of the course of apprenticeship had been completed, the would-be vakil had to submit a formal application for admission. This was a relatively easier procedure to comply with, except for the stamp fee which had to accompany the application: by 1879 it was Rs 500.[23] This cost imposed a heavy burden on future vakils, especially since they also had to pay large sums to seniors at the commencement of their apprenticeships. Yet in their efforts at searching desperately for new sources of revenue in 1922, the government authorities solicited the opinions of the judges on a proposal to increase the enrolment fee from Rs 500 to 750. A majority of them did not hesitate to unequivocally disapprove.[24] Chief Justice Coutts-Trotter wrote:

> I am entirely opposed to the proposed increase of the enrolment fee.... The student and lawyer class are not as in England recruited from [the]

wealthy; they are mostly the sons of middle class people of (some) means, to whom the education and enrolment charges are already [a] heavy burden. The increased fee will probably induce many to borrow the money requisite to meet it—a most undesirable start of the career.[25]

The government, in consequence, decided to take a middle course and raised the fee to Rs 625.[26]

Motion in Court

When preparing to seek admission, a candidate had to give one month's notice to the Registrar and had to publish his intentions for four successive weeks in the *Fort St. George Gazette*.[27] A bench of three judges, including the chief justice, reviewed the application. On the appointed date the senior practitioner under whom an apprentice had completed his terms made the motion in court. More often than not, judges mechanically approved the enrolment with little or no scrutiny of the papers appended to the application; however, there were instances when a few candidates were refused admission on the grounds of personal character.[28] This ritual of 'moving' the court marked the formal beginning of a career in law. The new-born vakil, though still inexperienced, would then be left to fend for himself in the midst of stiff competition.

VAKILS' PRACTICE

The Junior

Upon admission, an emerging vakil had to decide both the nature and location of his practice. He had the choice of remaining in Madras or returning to his home district.[29] In the district courts, other practitioners, especially pleaders, would regard him as belonging to a superior class because he was a 'High Court vakil'; he would be treated with even more courtesy by others who might not have had the privilege of undergoing such a fashionable apprenticeship or of donning the professional black gown. Regardless of his decision, a junior vakil faced several years of hardship and difficulties. Building up a steady practice was no easy task, especially if a vakil decided to remain in the city. Some vakils sought family help to subsist in those earlier years.[30]

A small number of enterprising vakils managed to continue with their masters, who doled out small briefs as well as financial assistance. P. R. Sundara Iyer and P. S. Sivaswami Iyer were, for example, fortunate enough to receive assistance from their seniors, R. Balaji Rao and S. Subramania Iyer. As an apprentice under Horatio Shephard, C. Sankaran Nair enjoyed good treatment. He wrote:

> I . . . became an apprentice under Mr Shephard . . . I was for one year under him. I used to read all his cases, receive full instructions from the clients or Pleaders from the Lower Courts instructing him, and acted as his junior sitting by him in court. The result was that his clients generally paid me some fee, and I was able to earn my own living and the heavy stamp fee for enrolment. I became well-known and there was no one else from my District of Malabar then practising in the High Court; the result was on the day I was enrolled as a Vakil in 1880, I was engaged in 8 or 10 cases.[31]

Not every junior could boast about his first years of practice in this manner. Many a junior was left in the lurch. When in 1910 P. S. Sivaswami Iyer delivered his lecture on 'Law As a Vocation For Young Men', he painted a realistic but stark picture of the vicious cycle in which a junior found himself caught. In order to acquire practice, opportunity was essential; but the opportunity came only to those who were already known and established. One way of making oneself known was by joining some leading lawyer and doing his work for nothing. Regardless of any monetary compensation, some seniors believed, a junior should consider it a privilege to be allowed to do all the work related to a case without the pleasure of appearing in the case himself.[32]

In this respect, a junior's position was almost indistinguishable from that of an apprentice. Whereas the latter had to pay a fee in addition to his year-long free service to his master in order to learn the craft as well as the system, the former served even a longer period under his senior who might eventually condescend to give a small pittance or direct some of his clients to him. In both situations, long hours and tireless work were the order of the day. W. S. Krishnaswami Nayudu's career serves as an excellent example of the kind of ties that sometimes existed between a senior and a junior. Of his work under O. Thanikachalam Chettiar in 1924, he wrote:

> Mr Chettiar would not even turn around and see what I was doing in his chambers. When working up a case, I myself, however, used to intervene and pick up the caselaw from the Digest and give one or two cases to him. My Senior naturally felt that I am interesting myself in

the profession and now and then he used to ask me to work some points of law or others. The clients who came to him used to like me for the interest I have been taking in their cases. . . . I was a little popular not only with the staff but also with the clients. . . . On one of those days he said that he proposed to give me a small monthly allowance which I may accept. He said he proposed to pay me every month Rs 35 which I may use as my conveyance allowance. I thanked him for this and willingly accepted the same.[33]

Many juniors, however, became despondent over the prospects of ever establishing themselves in the profession. Some were unable to resist the temptation of employing touts even though they knew that such associations brought them reproach. Leaders in the profession generally described touts as 'the most poisonous fungus in the life of a young lawyer'.[34] While there was a lot of empty talk and expression of concern over the plight of juniors, it took a long time before either the seniors or the Vakils' Association accomplished anything that materially benefited the juniors.

Criticisms from the Bench

Despite gains on the Original Side, vakils during the early years of the High Court had no permanent organization to represent their interests. A somewhat loosely-knit organization functioned until 1885 but it neither recruited sufficient membership nor exercised enough authority to regulate its policies. Consequently, it became defunct.[35] Lack of any long-standing tradition and etiquette in the Indian legal profession contributed to several instances of unprofessional conduct among a few vakils. As examined in the preceding chapter, obtaining cases through touts, giving commission to law agents, employing clerks for the sole purpose of soliciting briefs, and underbidding were common to many practitioners. While vakils learned their professional skills from barristers, they also unwittingly inherited some unprofessional practices from them. For instance, during the mid-1870s when the Madras Bar passed a rule forbidding members to give commissions to touts, the bar invited vakils to pass a similar rule, but they refused to comply, citing the demeanour of some barristers 'as an apology and a precedent for their refusal'.[36] Occasionally, vakils came under judicial censure which generated a good deal of controversy, which embarrassed barristers, attorneys and vakils. On 6 December 1878, Justice Kernan expressed concern over the custom which prevailed among certain vakils who represented moneylenders (*saucars*) of discounting their clients a portion of the cost recovered from defendants.³⁷ He also said that in the future he would require vakils to certify that they had actually received the amount they sought to recover from the losing party. *The Madras Mail* reported this incident, adding a few comments:

> It does seem extraordinary that Vakeels should jump at once into all the privileges and emoluments of counsel, without being governed by any Laws or Rules, or by the etiquette of so responsible a profession. It really seems high time that the various branches of the legal profession were once more regulated.³⁸

No sooner had this article appeared in the *Mail* than an individual, who had signed as simply 'A Vakil', responded to the criticisms. He wrote that he had been present in court when the judge remarked on certain vakils' habits of 'taking a less fee from their *saucar* clients than what the Courts gave them, and allowing their clients to pocket the differences'.³⁹ No reporter was present, he stated, when the judge uttered his remarks. The writer traced the source of information to some attorney or barrister who had been wrongly motivated 'to attribute his want of success in his profession to other than the true cause'.⁴⁰ The judge's remarks, he added, did not apply wholesale to every vakil but only to a few individuals who were considered 'black sheep' in the flock. Otherwise, such remarks would have been a 'gross libel' against the entire profession. 'Vakil' referred to instances of attorneys accepting cases by taking little or no fee from clients with an understanding that if they won the case a vindictive Bill of Costs would be made against the opponent.⁴¹ Also, some barristers accepted fees which a 'respectable vakil' would have been ashamed to take. In conclusion, the writer asserted that as long as there were 'starving men with high pretensions' such unprofessional practices would continue, but one should not use such episodes to condemn the entire body of vakils. He was willing to offer proofs for his imputations against certain attorneys or barristers to anyone, especially to the informant of the *Mail*, interested in seeking reform.

Supporting the arguments of vakils, *The Madras Times* then took its turn. Always a trenchant critic of attorneys, the *Times* once again used the opportunity to lash out at English lawyers, particularly at attorneys. The newspaper indicated that the position of attorneys was so low that certain social clubs would never admit them.⁴² The *Mail* quickly responded. Not only did it disagree with the *Times*, showing that the latter had taken a prejudiced view on the role of attorneys, but it also pointed out that there were many respectable attorneys in England who were not black-balled in every social club, and that their professional organization, the Attorneys' Association, had the power to formulate the rules of discipline. The *Mail*'s leader asserted, 'That Association [had] undoubtedly been potent for good in purifying the profession.'[43]

But the situation was drastically different in India, especially in Madras. Not only did the High Court not maintain any distinction among lawyers, except perhaps between barristers and attorneys on the Original Side, but no uniformity existed in enforcing discipline over any of the practitioners. While the Madras attorneys had no association but merely some rules, the barristers had both an association and rules; but those rules lacked the 'living force' of the rules that existed in England. Vakils had neither an association nor rules. Every vakil acted individually and according to his own will. The *Mail* suggested that a body of new rules governing all three branches of the profession should be made and administered by some association or law society. The presiding officer of the society should be vested with power to make inquiries regarding complaints against unprofessional lawyers. Some systems to check upon the activities of lawyers would ensure their good conduct as well as the security of public interest.[44]

Despite the wisdom that the *Mail* displayed in dealing with the questions arising from Justice Kernan's remarks in court, R. Wilson, an advocate, took a different view. He did not deny the allegations made by 'A Vakil' that attorneys and barristers underbid, but claimed that the reasons for the prevalance of such practices lay not among attorneys and barristers but with the High Court. He blamed the judges for their partiality towards vakils and urged them to wake up 'from the somnolency induced by the enjoyment of *fat salaries* for doing nothing or next door to nothing, and revise in an equitable spirit their rules of practice, which at present are scandalous'.[45] The rules of practice Wilson referred to were those that the judges had promulgated in 1866, confirming the vakils' privileges in conducting original suits. He reiterated his scathing objections to these rules:

> They [the judges] allow[ed] a parcel of people called vakeels, unrestricted by the rules applying to barristers and attorneys, but combining the privilege of both, to practise in the Courts, with what result can [as]

well [be] imagined as described. What the motive of the Judges [was], nobody knows, unless it be to gain popularity with the *beloved natives*.[46]

An attorney, who signed his name 'J. S.', took his turn in adding fuel to the growing controversy.[47] His letter dwelt on four major issues: the organization of a law society to watch over and control the actions of practitioners, the truth about the alleged misconduct of certain lawyers, the rules of the High Court on claiming fees, and the apparent unrestricted movements of practitioners in other professions, namely, doctors, bankers and editors. In his judgment, there was no need for the establishment of a society because both the internal code of each profession and the laws of the court were sufficient to provide punitive measures in situations where lawyers were accused of cheating, negligence or breach of contract with clients.

The 'misconduct' or deviation from established practices, according to 'J. S.', essentially centred on fees. He objected to the prevailing custom of paying the same fee to an experienced senior as to a briefless junior. Instead, he felt the principle of supply and demand when applied to lawyers would bring about the desired end of complaints on fees. 'This principle,' he wrote, '[had been] observed everywhere except on the Original Side of the High Court.'[48] As far as the rules for deciding fees due were concerned there was a 'double-provision'. If a lawyer and his client had entered into a special arrangement of fees, usually higher than the stipulated rate, the court upheld such agreements. Otherwise, the court enforced what was considered a 'reasonable remuneration'. This inconsistency allowed serious malpractice. Whenever the court was suspicious of claims made upon a losing party, even if consistent within the meaning of a 'reasonable remuneration', the court required the winning lawyer to certify that he had actually received the amount claimed. Some practitioners who were 'black sheep' in the profession might falsely certify and 'share the spoils with their clients', because of loopholes in the rules of practice. Therefore, in making his remarks against certain practices of vakils, Justice Kernan ought not to have simply referred to such practices but ought to have taken some preventive measures in redefining the laws. 'J. S.' added that while lawyers received much public criticism for their malpractices, no one held the rod over doctors, bankers and journalists. If the Madras legal profession did not have an organization to enforce rules of discipline over different groups with varying privileges and protection, neither did the other professions. The journalists, especially, needed a similar association. 'There are matters [breaches] of etiquette among editors as well,' he wrote, 'but I never heard of an association of editors for enquiring into such breaches.'[49]

Only the High Court judges kept themselves aloof from this war of words since they ordinarily avoided involvement with socio-political issues. What had been uttered as an additional or incidental remark in chambers by Justice Kernan, however, had turned out to have ignited a public debate. A little spark had quickly flared up into an open fire, not only consuming much ink and paper but bringing out unmitigated anger and passion. Comments directed against one body of practitioners involved all members of that profession—barristers, attorneys and vakils—and no one group could claim immunity from these open criticisms.

Commenting on this 'duel', the *Civil and Military Gazette* tackled the issue differently. It pointed out that the legal profession as a whole was obligated to proving its innocence to the public. The profession ought to show that neither was it to be blamed for the defects that might have existed, nor did such defects exist on account of the members looking askance.[50] Although this public assailing of lawyers gradually died out, vakils as a group stood below barristers and attorneys in status; such inferior standing had been the characteristic in the previous adalat era. No wonder the judges constantly revised the requirements for enrolment of vakils and added something new each time.

Vakils received criticisms for various other unethical practices as well: taking fees from clients without issuing receipts, writing letters to clients about the progress of suits pending in court but not keeping copies of letters, and taking fees but failing to defend the clients, especially in criminal cases.[51] Both the English and vernacular newspapers carried articles on such questionable practices. Occasionally lawyers—both barristers and vakils—defended themselves against the indictments. As late as 1889, *The Hindu* devoted two long editorials to relations between vakils as a group and the High Court.[52] Chief Justice Sir Arthur Collins, who later came to be known as one of the most sympathetic towards vakils, took steps to enhance the dignity of the High Court.[53] To achieve this goal, he personally kept close surveillance on vakils during the early years of his career; and whenever charges were made against that body, the chief justice spared no pains in delivering admonitions in harsh language. Every time a dissatisfied client filed charges against his vakil, the charges would be presumed to be true and the 'seemingly offhanded manner in which complaints against [vakils were] dealt with . . . had an unfortunate tendency to multiply such complaints'.[54]

The Hindu exhorted Sir Arthur to take into consideration that, as 'officers of the court', vakils themselves were as committed to preserving the dignity of the court as was the chief justice himself. It also recommended that judges as well as the leaders of the bar should ensure that the special privileges of 'rubbing shoulders' with the judiciary outside of court should be extended to less glamorous members of the profession. Such encounters, the newspaper predicted, would provide opportunities 'to prize each other and reciprocate esteem in the manner and in the degree inaccessible to persons whose intercourse [is] limited to business relation only'. The Hindu added:

> We think that the manifest course is for the Judges and leaders of the profession periodically to organize occasions where they might unbend and come into genial contact with the bulk of the profession. . . . While the profession as a whole will undoubtedly gain by it in the way of acquiring a genuine sense of honour and respectability and see solid grounds for maintaining them inviolate and almost instinctively, the Judges too will soon become conscious of the unseemly lordliness and perverted aptitudes to judge in haste which, in not a few instances, mark some of them.[55]

Twenty-five years later, the leaders of the Vakils' Association implemented this recommendation by organizing the annual meetings for members to meet for social intercourse and conviviality.[56]

ANANDACHARLU'S PAMPHLET

In 1883, P. Anandacharlu, a High Court vakil, wrote a pamphlet entitled *The Madras Bar and How to Improve It*, and circulated it among select individuals attached to the local university, the government, members of the bench and the profession, and a 'discriminating' part of the public.[57] He intended it as an antidote to the persistence of a 'good deal of adverse comment' against vakils, based on invidious comparisons between the three branches of legal profession. In making such comparisons, Anandacharlu stated, one always used the 'worst specimen' of the vakils and the best of barristers and attorneys.[58]

Anandacharlu described the qualifications, skills and abilities of barristers, attorneys and vakils; he offered suggestions to improve the profession of law as a whole. He reviewed the linguistic, intellectual (or academic), technical (or lingual), legal and moral condition of lawyers who practised before the highest court of the Presidency. While no one group scored high in his tests of qualities, he saw no one group as totally deficient. For example, in the linguistic criterion, if vakils excelled because of their fluency in the vernaculars (many possessed facility in more than one local language), they failed miserably in their capacity to prepare a clear plaint and to apply the rules of practice. In both these qualities, attorneys outshone vakils. In the sphere of general or preparatory education, the barristers, vakils and some European attorneys normally received training beyond the high school level; but the Indian attorneys merely studied up to matriculation. Likewise, in their professional or vocational training, the barristers had gone through the portals of their own respective Inns, the vakils had their B.L.s, and the European attorneys had received 'some' training from the 'solicitor-making' authorities in England. But the Indian attorneys had no such training. Consequently, their comprehension of issues, logic and reasoning were far from comparable.

With respect to an understanding of Indian laws and of the myriads of customs revered by the people, both barristers and attorneys, the new entrants in particular, lagged far behind vakils, who demonstrated a keen intellectual superiority because of their facility in Sanskrit, in the vernaculars as well as in the customs peculiar to both Hindus and Muslims.[59] Anandacharlu maintained that all three groups generally possessed a high moral rectitude, with the exception of a few 'upstarts' who lacked the patience to persevere against the odds of competition; such individuals resorted to touts for business, gave commission to those who brought briefs, lengthened the volumes of pleading, shared a portion of their fees with clients, and the like.[60]

Anandacharlu suggested a few remedial steps which would ensure the quality of future practitioners. He recommended a more rigorous academic training for Indian attorneys. Every attorney should complete both his B.A. and B.L. degrees, as the vakils themselves had previously done. Barristers and attorneys ought to have as complete a knowledge of vernaculars as any district judge in the civil service. If they were unable to acquire such skills, they should then hire, at their own cost, authorized interpreters, who would honestly mediate between clients and lawyers and who would translate numerous documents into English. European barristers and attorneys should also be required to study Indian laws and customs, either during their preparation in England or subsequent to their arrival in India. The High Court must revise the rules of practice, especially those related to the selection and examination of apprentices, awarding costs to lawyers, and the scale of fees.[61] The judges took notice of Anandacharlu's suggestions and in 1885 passed a new set of rules for the qualification and admission of attorneys in the High Court.[62]

VAKILS' GROWTH

New Opportunities

Both the High Court and the government treated cordially the leaders of the bar, whether barristers or vakils. While barristers as a group received higher appointments that brought greater public esteem and material benefits, vakils only occasionally enjoyed such official 'loaves and fish'. Between 1860 and 1890, several vakils received appointments as clerks of the judges, while others became district munsifs, district judges or sub-judges.[63] A few served as government pleaders, assistant professors and lecturers in the Madras Law College, as assistant secretary to the Legislative Department, and as members of the Governor's Executive Council.[64] The most enviable appointment a vakil could receive at that time was as a member of the Indian Civil Service Commission. In 1886, Salem Ramaswami Mudaliar played an important part both in serving on the subcommittee and in drawing up the final report of the Commission.[65]

Apart from holding these appointments, vakils also had the privilege of being among the select few who could attend government balls or public social events. For the first time under the administration of Sir Charles Trevelyan, 'natives' were invited to attend such public 'durbars',[66] a practice later continued by other governors as well. Although their traditional upbringing and the social and cultural distance that existed between all elite communities must have created a certain amount of stiffness in such public events, it was an honour to have had the privilege of attending. Thus, in one way or another, vakils as a group not only began to establish themselves firmly in the professional arena but also made their presence felt more conspicuously in other areas of urban life and in other public institutions.

Politics and Leadership

After much discussion, between 1877 and 1881, leading individuals in the city decided to resuscitate the defunct Madras Native Association. As a result, this quasi-political organization once again began to play an active role under the leadership of individuals from the learned professions. C. V. Ranganatha Sastri (the first Indian judge of the City Small Cause Court), Salem Ramaswamy Mudaliar, V. Bhashyam Iyengar, P. Anandacharlu, G. Subramania Iyer and M. Veeraraghavachariar were among the members. Ranganatha Sastri and Ramaswamy Mudaliar were elected President and Secretary. When Ranganatha Sastri died in 1881, the mantle of leadership fell on V. Bhashyam Iyengar. By then he and S. Subramania Iyer had become the two Indian leaders of the High Court Bar. Public opinion at that time held that these two individuals divided most of the professional income from appeals between themselves.[67]

In 1883, when some of the local government officials withdrew their support from the Madras Native Association fearing that they might incur the wrath of their European masters, the Association once again became crippled and ultimately vanished. In 1884 a new organization, the Madras Mahajana Sabha, came into existence; most members were High Court vakils.[68] The very next year, 1885, the Indian National Congress was born in Bombay, where several vakils, pleaders and journalists from Madras attended the first session. In 1889 the same group of city vakils who had once been members of the Madras Native Association, and who joined the Mahajana Sabha and the Indian National Congress, decided to revive their professional organization, the Madras High Court Vakils' Association. Preoccupation with political and social organizations indicated an increasing belief among members of the legal profession in well-orchestrated group activities through which they could safeguard their interests. Their first symbolic gain was the approval of the High Court in 1889 to appear before the judges wearing black gowns, somewhat similar to those worn by English barristers. Wearing trousers and shoes was optional. Previously they had appeared in court wearing dhotis and in bare feet.[69] Consolidating every gain they had bargained for, vakils harnessed their talents. As a result, they emerged, at the end of the 1880s, as an influential body of men who belonged to a respectable profession.

Numerical Strength

An important feature in the development of the vakil element in the High Court was the ever increasing number of aspirants who kept entering the profession. Under such welcoming headlines as 'Still They Come', 'The New High Court Vakils', and 'More Vakils', local newspapers regularly reported the enrolment of barristers, attorneys and vakils, leaving it to the imagination of readers to figure out how they could all survive in this intractably competitive profession. Despite obvious contradictions in computations, and confusions in figures and nomenclature, the Census Returns provide useful data for gauging the general development of the profession in Madras City. The Returns for 1871 and 1881 classified individuals who practised law into five different categories: barristers, attorneys, lawyers, vakils and advocates. The figures show that the number of barristers rose from 7 in 1871 to 19 in 1881, while the number of attorneys increased from 10 to 27. Vakils had the largest representation during the same period: 21 and 59. The identity of 'lawyers' is somewhat unclear and a possible conjecture may be that it represented pleaders, who were not vakils of the High Court and who practised in the Small Cause Court. Only one advocate figures in the data.[70] The 1891 data is altogether unreliable because the tables do not break down the total number of practitioners except to state that 16,618 persons were barristers, advocates and pleaders, while 4119 were article clerks and lawyer's clerks.[71]

A better reconstruction of the growth of vakils, however, is possible from the annual reports on the administration of justice for the Presidency between 1879 and 1908.[72] These reports contain the actual numbers of practitioners entering the profession each year. Table 1 provides the figures for every five years from 1879 to 1908.

The establishment of a law college in 1891 contributed to the marked increase in the number of vakils; the college functioned almost like a factory, manufacturing law graduates year after year.

TABLE 1
Enrolment of Practitioners between 1879 and 1908

Period	Barristers	Attorneys	Vakils
1879–1883	11	23	42
1884–1888	16	8	77
1889–1893	14	14	123
1894–1898	18	6	129
1899–1903	21	2	146
1904–1908	23	2	201
Total	103	55	718

As a result, the vakils' overall numerical strength soon became much greater than the combined strength of barristers and attorneys, which allowed the vakils to dominate both the professional and public spheres by the turn of the century. The relatively small number of attorneys entering the profession resulted from the expensive 'double-agency' system. Combining the functions of a barrister and attorney, a vakil provided cheaper services than the rest. Moreover, the increasing number of vakils each year was another significant factor in a person's vigilant search for business. A novice tended to take whatever a client offered rather than rejecting a brief altogether. In contrast, ordinarily even a mediocre attorney did not reduce his fee. To do so meant lowering his professional reputation and standards and incurring debts.

The preponderance of vakils in the legal profession reflected the national trend among the college and university graduates. While many still preferred government employment—which promised better salary, job security and retirement benefits than other positions—graduates had begun to look elsewhere for similar opportunities. The legal profession promised the most at that time. In 1882, the Education Commission collected information on the activities of graduates and published its findings. Table 2, from the Commission's Report, provides a comparison between employment in government and the legal profession and employment in other professions, such as medicine and engineering.

The report made certain observations on the character of the legal profession, which ranked second only to government employment in its attraction of recruits. It observed:

TABLE 2
Indian Graduates and Their Career Choices[73]

	Madras	Bombay	Bengal	N.W.P. and Oudh	Punjab	C.P.
Number of graduates in 1871–82	808	625	1696	130	38	14
Having entered the public service, British or Native	296	324	534	61	21	8
Legal profession	126	49	471	33	5	—
Medical profession	18	76	131	—	—	—
Civil Engineering profession	—	28	19	6	—	—

At the Bar, a profession which in many ways is eminently suited to the best of the native mind, the ex-students of our colleges have made their way with honourable success. Even in the Presidency towns, though pitted against distinguished English lawyers, they carry off a large share of the practice, acquitting themselves with special credit in all civil cases. . . . Though pleading in a foreign tongue, they not seldom display an eloquence and power of debate which would command admiration before an English tribunal. . . . Government service and the Law . . . engage the attention of the majority of our graduates and undergraduates.[74]

Table 3 clearly shows the second most important characteristic of the legal profession in Madras: the overwhelming domination of brahmans.

Table 3 elicits a few additional remarks. First, despite their regional, linguistic and religious differences, brahmans' monopoly of the legal profession merely reflected their concentrations in public services. They held on to their position for many decades, even beyond the 1920s and 1930s when the non-brahman Justice Party in Madras introduced certain legislative measures to curb over-representation of any one group pursuing legal studies or

Table 3
Communal Representation of Graduates (in Arts and Law) in the Legal Profession[75]

Community	Total Number	Percentage
A. Brahmans		
1. Iyer (Saivas)	51	40.2
2. Iyengar (Sri Vaishnavas)	23	18.1
3. Maratha (Deshasthas)	17	13.4
4. Telugu	8	6.3
B. Non-Brahmans		
1. Chettiyar	4	3.1
2. Mudaliyar	3	2.4
3. Naidu	5	3.9
4. Pillai	4	3.1
5. Reddiyar	1	0.8
6. Menon and Nair	3	2.4
C. Christians	8	6.3
Total	127	100

practising the craft.[76] Because of this overwhelming majority of brahmans in the profession, a greater portion of briefs obviously fell into their hands. Second, the extended family system, with its hosts of individuals claiming kinship, also enhanced the network of clients and contacts among brahmans in the hinterland from whence most appeals arose. This did not mean that other communities had failed to exploit the system of family connections. But, in their case, this feature was less pronounced.[77] Third, among the non-brahmans, Indian Christians had a slightly greater proportional representation than any other community.[78] Four out of eight were Vellalars while the rest were (Catholic) Goan and Malabar Christians.[79] Finally, the list of graduates does not include any Muslim graduates, who practised law either as pleaders in the district courts or as High Court vakils. The reasons why Muslims failed to take advantage of the opportunities in the legal profession, especially considering that a century earlier they had served as *sadr amins* and *kazis*, have yet to be fully explored.[80]

Chapter 5

THE LIMITATIONS IN VAKILS' PRACTICE

> I am of opinion that whatever was the original intention at the time when the rule was framed, it is no longer advisable to maintain it in the general form. The effect of debarring pleaders from the present circumstances [seems] to be mischievous both professionally and politically.
>
> —Justice Abdur Rahim[1]

The Supreme Court had been established in Madras as the King's Court and Parliament had sole authority to enact laws defining its different jurisdictions. Naturally this brought certain exclusive rights to barristers and attorneys: they alone had the privilege to appear before it. Vakils had no such favours because their profession only aided suitors in the East India Company courts. Even when the High Court came into existence, representing the amalgamation of these two systems, the differences in practice between barristers and vakils persisted. Supported by law and conventions, the former enjoyed a clear monopoly over insolvency cases while the latter had none; their feeble but belated attempt at securing that privilege failed. In fact, that vakils constituted a separate group from advocates automatically precluded them from conducting cases on the insolvency jurisdiction of the High Court until 1928 when they too became advocates.

The absence of a professional body in India, similar to the Inns of Court responsible for regulating and controlling the activities of their members, also created much latitude in the development of a code of ethics among vakils. Despite their numerical growth by the turn of the century, the Vakils' Association had failed to attract even half of all the vakils settled in Madras. It was not successful in enforcing the rules of ethics or etiquette. The judges, in addition to their judicial functions, had other executive responsibilities, which created peculiar difficulties in watching over the activities of many vakils who practised in Madras High Court and many more who practised in the district courts. They had very little time or energy to nurture the profession or instil in others the high standards of conduct that they themselves had inherited from institutions at home. Since the High Court Charter empowered them to make periodic rules governing the legal profession, it became easier for the judges to frame guidelines and enforce them throughout the machinery of Presidency courts. Though they had misgivings about the constitutionality of their actions, judges were unwilling to modify the rules; they more or less knew that because of the prevailing tensions between the bureaucracy and the judiciary within the context of nineteenth century colonial authority no one was truly interested in challenging their decisions. Moreover, judges understood that rescinding a rule would not be easy because any regulatory rules that the High Court had passed generally tended to acquire almost a canonical status.

RESTRICTIONS IN INSOLVENCY COURT

In 1828, a parliamentary enactment established a special kind of court for 'the relief of insolvent debtors in the East Indies' in the three major cities of Bombay, Calcutta and Madras.[2] Subsequent legislation either modified this act or confirmed its continuation until 1848 when a new law totally replaced it. The 1848 act remained in force until 1909 when yet another statute, known as the Presidency Towns' Insolvency Act, became effective. These laws, between 1828 and 1909, admitted only advocates and attorneys to practise in insolvency courts of the three Presidencies. Even though the insolvency court was a separate judicial tribunal, the presiding officer, known as the Insolvency Commissioner, was a judge of the Supreme Court or later the High Court. As a distinct professional class, vakils, with a few exceptions, could not ordinarily become advocates or attorneys.

In 1888, however, vakils began to handle appeals that arose from orders of the Insolvency Commissioner but they remained shut out from acting or pleading in original insolvency cases.[3] During the insolvency proceedings of the notorious Arbuthnot Firm in 1907, V. Krishnaswami Iyer, a High Court vakil, appeared for certain creditors. When challenged by the opposite side as having no right to appear before the court in his capacity as a vakil, he 'doffed the gown he was wearing and . . . said he would argue as a party in person'.[4] When in 1909 the Presidency Towns' Insolvency

Act brought about the merger of the former Insolvency Court with the High Court, insolvency matters became 'one of several jurisdictions of the High Court'.[5] Among other features, Section 121 of the Act reaffirmed the existing privileges of lawyers, particularly in conducting insolvency cases:

> Nothing in this Act, or in any transfer of jurisdiction effected thereby, shall take away or affect any right of audience that any person might have had immediately before the commencement of this Act, or shall be deemed to confer such right in insolvency matters on any person who had not a right of audience before the Courts for the relief of insolvent debtors.[6]

Although vakils had zealously safeguarded their rights on the Original Side since 1876 and had defended that right as late as 1916, they were less concerned about handling original insolvency cases. Except for a short editorial which pointed out the unfairness of excluding them from the original insolvency cases, vakils had virtually remained silent.[7] That for almost 50 years they had done little or nothing to move the High Court to alter its rules brought criticism from the bench in 1923, when vakils unsuccessfully attempted to do so. Justice M. D. Devadoss summed up the judges' attitudes and the position of vakils when he said:

> For nearly a century, only advocates and attorneys were recognized as practitioners in the Court for the relief of insolvent debtors. For nearly half a century after the establishment of the High Court, no vakil claimed a right of audience in the Court for the relief of insolvent debtors. After the passing of the Act of 1909, there is nothing to show [that] . . . any vakil claimed the right of audience in the Insolvency Court. On the principle that vested rights should not be lightly interfered with and that the existing state of things should be maintained, Section 121 was enacted. *It denies vakils the right of audience when the High Court exercises original insolvency jurisdiction*.[8]

At a general meeting on 11 July 1923 vakils unanimously passed a resolution and sent it along with a letter to the judges.[9] The letter said that vakils had been entitled to 'appear and plead in all appeals from the decisions of the Insolvency Court and . . . to plead in all matters in Insolvency in the District Courts and in appeals therefrom to High Court'.[10] However, the Vakils' Association had earlier failed to pass a similar resolution objecting to the exclusion of vakils. How does one explain its reluctance to challenge the rules for such a long period? Knowing that the Government of India was about to repeal the 1848 Act and legislate a new law, why did the Association then neglect to make any prior representations requesting the removal of all restrictions? Answers to these questions can be sought by tracing the judges' attitudes on the subject and by explaining how their changing views influenced subsequent judgements.

The High Court Registrar replied on 23 October 1923, three months after the Association had sent its letter; he said that to amend the insolvency rules would be contrary to the Presidency Towns' Insolvency Act of 1909 and that it would be a matter for the legislature to decide.[11] Privately, the judges disagreed on whether the High Court had power to amend the rules. Notes prepared by the Deputy Registrar clearly say that 'the Judges have power to amend the rules . . . but . . . the right to practice has *always* been confined to advocates and attorneys'.[12] When the dossier was later circulated among the judges for comments, two-thirds of them held that statutory limitations prevented vakils from original insolvency cases.[13] Chief Justice Sir Walter Schwabe, a proponent of this view, according to one source, had a tendency to form conclusions early in the hearing of a case, which he seldom changed.[14] Those who disagreed with him held that Section 121 of the Presidency Towns' Insolvency Act of 1909 neither stood in the way of amending the rules nor overrode the general powers conferred on the High Court by Sections 9 and 10 of Letters Patent of 1865.[15] Justice M. Venkatasubba Rao observed: 'I am strongly of the opinion that the vakils must be given the right of audience . . . the matter is of sufficient importance to be discussed at a Judge's meeting.'[16]

Whether they ever met as a forum to discuss this question is not clear. That the judges approved the Deputy Registrar's letter to the Association without any further consideration seems to imply that, even if they had met previously, they had failed to agree to a change in the rules. Contrary to any wishful thinking by the majority of judges that they had permanently dealt with the question of vakils appearing in original insolvency cases, the Association remained unconvinced. The Council of the Association met again on 9 November 1923. Authorizing Alladi Krishnaswami Iyer, who later became the advocate general for three consecutive terms, to compose a reply to the Registrar, the Association instructed him to point out that 'the desired amendment of rules [was] not contrary to the intention of the Presidency Towns' Insolvency Act, 1919 [*sic*], as thought by the Hon'ble Judges'.[17] Krishnaswami Iyer sent his reply to the High Court on 8 January 1924.[18] However, new developments in the proceedings of the court further intensified disagreements between judges and vakils. No longer were deliberations confined to the closed walls of judges' chambers. Instead, passionate arguments took place in the open court, where contestants sought to apply their legal expertise and vested interests sought to protect special privileges.

G. Krishnaswami Iyer, a High Court vakil, filed a special application at the end of 1923 to review the orders of the Deputy Registrar on a vakalat issued to him by Chakrapani Achari, a creditor. The Deputy Registrar, after having examined the vakalat, had returned it 'on the ground that vakils had no right of audience in the Insolvency Court'.[19] Justice David G. Waller reviewed Krishnaswami's application and decided against the vakil on the grounds of precedent: vakils had never appeared in original insolvency cases since 1828.[20] Against Waller's ruling, Krishnaswami Iyer proferred an appeal in January 1924, and a Full Bench heard the arguments in public.[21]

In the meantime, this episode had acquired 'almost a sensational importance by reason of a long-standing and perhaps natural jealousy between two important and influential sections of the Bar in Madras'.[22] Two of the three judges—Justice Charles G. Spencer (the officiating Chief Justice) and Justice M. D. Devadoss—had already participated in previous discussions when the Vakils' Association's petition had first circulated among the judges. They sided with the views of the former Chief Justice Sir Walter Schwabe, who was loath to modify the existing insolvency rules, which were obviously lopsided in favour of advocates and attorneys. The third member, Justice V. V. Srinivasa Iyengar, had been a member of the Council of the Vakils' Association prior to his elevation. As such, he had already supported the vakils' petition to amend the rules on the Insolvency Side. But now that he had been elevated to the bench, albeit temporarily, Srinivasa Iyengar changed his position; he claimed that as a judge he had to steel himself 'against all . . . preconceived bias and approach the decision of the question merely as a *dry question of law*'.[23] Despite his high-sounding devotion to the rule of law, the adverse judgment he delivered along with his brother judges can be explained differently. Had he dissented from the majority opinion, he would have been overruled. Whether he sided with the rest in order to 'show' his impartiality or to earn the esteem of his colleagues, one does not know. One can only speculate about the motives behind his strange volte-face.

The Full Bench decisions of 1924 and 1928 must be compared to appreciate the reasons behind the different views of the judges.[24] In 1924, the judges maintained, for reasons already shown, that they should not modify the insolvency rules because in so doing they would encroach upon legislative powers. Although they had long been aware of their constitutional powers to modify or issue any rules pertaining to the legal profession, they remained adamant in their view that the Insolvency Act of 1909, especially Section 121, did not explicitly confer any new rights upon practitioners. In taking this view, they made the Indian legislature appear to be more or less responsible for special treatment accorded to one class of legal practitioners over another. By 1928, the professional climate had changed. The All-India Bar Council Act of 1926 abolished the powers vested in the High Court under the Letters Patent. Instead, a newly constituted Bar Council in each Presidency was empowered to exercise the privilege of formulating the rules of qualification and admission of lawyers. This Act also removed the dubious distinctions between advocates, attorneys and vakils, and unified the bar by designating all three groups in one category, as advocates. Every vakil who had formerly practised in that capacity was able to enrol himself as an advocate without having to meet further educational or time-in-service qualifications. This was truly a boon for many vakils, who took advantage of the new provisions. One such vakil-turned-advocate was V. V. Devanadhan, who tried to file a vakalat on behalf of a party in an insolvency case.[25] The presiding Insolvency Commissioner, Justice C. V. Kumaraswami Sastri, ordered that the papers should be returned because under the existing insolvency rules an advocate could only appear and plead but not act. He had formerly dissented from his colleagues and wanted to demonstrate that nothing in the previous laws of 1848 and 1909 curtailed the powers of the High Court established under the Letters Patent.

When the Full Bench, therefore, assembled in 1928 the judges showed unmistakably that the Insolvency Act of 1848 did empower the Supreme Court, and later the High Court, to make rules consistent with the Act regarding practitioners who might appear in insolvency cases. And, they held, in no way had the Presidency Towns' Insolvency Act of 1909 vitiated the powers of the High

Court, even though it did not confer any fresh rights on any person by transferring insolvency jurisdiction to the High Court. Chief Justice V. M. Coutts-Trotter, one of the members of the Full Bench, managed to obtain a copy of the judgement written by Justice Kumaraswami Sastri at whose request the Full Bench had been constituted. When Justice Kumaraswami Sastri read the judgement, the Chief Justice merely expressed a few general remarks supporting the judgement. The third member of the Bench, Justice P. Walsh, also nodding his agreement with his colleagues, had nothing to add. The judgement, therefore, essentially reflected the views of Justice Kumaraswami Sastri, who had been a High Court vakil. He observed that under the Letters Patent, the High Court had *always* possessed powers to make *any* rules it wished with respect to advocates, but the judges exercised their powers only too sparingly. In his view, the provisions of the Indian Bar Council Act entitled 'an Advocate of the Madras High Court to appear, act and plead in *all* the jurisdictions of the Madras High Court'.[26]

This marked a significant turning point in the annals of the legal profession in the Madras Presidency, as advocates, many of them former vakils, could now exercise all the three functions of their profession and could appear in any court that came under the High Court jurisdiction. This decision also silenced many of the vexatious arguments—put forth by the judges, advocates and attorneys—on the nature of the original Court for the Relief of the Insolvent Debtor, on the inherent powers vested in the High Court to frame rules dealing with judicial administration, and, finally, on the capacity of the Indian legislature to confer any new special privileges on any one group of practitioners. The insolvency rules that the High Court framed under the authority of the Act of 1848, remained the same between 1862 and 1909. That an Indian legislature could nullify a parliamentary statute by passing new legislation caused no change of heart among the judges. They continued to enforce the rules until 1924 when vakils challenged the legality of precluding them from accepting original insolvency cases.

RESTRICTIONS ON TRADE OR BUSINESS

The High Court had issued other orders against the interests of vakils and pleaders; these orders regulated the fees paid to vakils, controlled their extra-professional activities, and defined various pleader-client transactions. While certain rules had statutory backing, others were framed entirely at the discretion of the judges. One such rule sought to keep vakils' activities narrowly circumscribed by the confines of law and law courts. It appears that sometime prior to March 1899, a High Court vakil who had been practising in the mufassal allowed himself to get involved in entrepreneurial and commercial activities—maintaining a grocery or retail dry goods store.[27] When the judges discovered that a vakil, supposedly a member of the 'learned profession of law', had ventured into business operations outside of his calling, they were indignant. Such engagements were not befitting to a law practitioner and had to be curbed. On 13 March 1899 the judges circulated an order thoughout all subordinate courts: 'No vakil shall carry on any trade or business without the previous sanction of the High Court. Any vakil carrying on a trade or business without such previous sanction shall be liable to suspension or removal from practice.'[28] This rule also applied to pleaders in all sub-courts under Section 6 of the Legal Practitioners' Act of 1879 and remained in force until 1916, when communications between the government, High Court and the Vakils' Association led to subsequent modifications.

When the Co-operative Societies Act came into effect in 1912, for example, 'a very large number of co-operative societies, especially those in towns and in places where there are Civil and Criminal Courts, [had become] dependent on the goodwill and co-operation of Vakils and Pleaders'.[29] The government requested the judges to make a general rule permitting lawyers to participate in co-operative societies, especially in localities where they practised.[30] The judges acceded to this request and modified the rule by adding a provisional clause: 'Vakils may take part in the management of Societies . . . in the areas in which they practise; but no vakils so taking part shall receive any remuneration other than the ordinary profits without the special leave of the High Court.'[31]

Until this time, the judges had never defined what they meant by 'carrying on any trade or business' as stated in the original order of 1899. Nor did they now elaborate on the meaning of 'ordinary profits' in the modified order of 1916. These inherent ambiguities or loopholes tended to place the judges on the defensive, especially as prominent leaders of the vakil bar raised doubts over the legality of the rule as well as its intended meaning.³² Between 1916 and 1925, vakils and pleaders received permission on the basis of this modified rule even though doubts persisted regarding the extent of its application: whether the rule should permit or prohibit participation 'in the management of other institutions organized on the basis of joint-stock enterprise'.³³ A representation, presumably sent by the Vakils' Association, met with the judges requesting clarification on this point, and the judges, as one journal put it, 'clutched' at the opportunity and offered a narrower interpretation. The modified version of the rule of 1899 passed through yet another transmutation. The 1925 version declared:

> Application from practising vakils to be permitted to become salaried Directors of banks will ordinarily be refused. Exception will however be made where the company is (a) a co-operative society, (b) a company whose primary object is charitable, educational or philanthropic. In no circumstance will a practising vakil be permitted to be a Director of a Bank other than a co-operative Bank.³⁴

This departure from the previous practice of granting permission on the merits of a particular application or on the reputation of a particular joint-stock company provoked consternation. Editorials in law journals discussed the inconsistencies of the rule when applied to Indian practitioners. They compared parallel provisions of the English Bar Council Rules, which did not prohibit members of the bar from serving as directors of companies.³⁵ Judges justified their position by stating that a 'Director-Lawyer' could hardly resist the temptation to take control of 'the finances for purpose of the litigation in his hands or . . . [to] make use of his knowledge of the financial position of his constituents for his getting on [in] the profession'.³⁶ The *MWN* virulently denounced these excuses as farfetched. Such arguments, in the views of the journal, might just as well be applied to attorneys who were outside the pale of the rule.

The Vakils' Association submitted its own memorandum, outlining the usefulness of vakils participating in commercial banks as being comparable to their role in co-operative societies. It also pointed out that in the face of complex banking laws the future economic prosperity of these institutions would be guaranteed if vakils properly supervised them. Moreover, certain prominent members of the vakil bar had already been involved with such banks as the Indian Bank, the United India Life Assurance Company, and other kindred institutions. Finally, the memorandum remarked upon the inability of vakils to comprehend why they alone should be singled out for such discrimination.[37] The judges relented and, once again, altered the rule. In 1926, they announced that permission would ordinarily be granted for becoming a director of a bank as long as the applicant's motive and the institution's character proved unimpeachable. That the judges were willing to restore the original practice allayed, once and for all, the anxieties of many vakils and pleaders. Henceforth, they felt free to assume positions in commercial enterprises without the prior sanction of the High Court. These changes, however, applied only for involvement in institutions which styled themselves as banks, funds and *nidhis*. Many such institutions had recently been spawned throughout the Presidency, specifically in the southern districts.[38] Notwithstanding this relaxation of rules, individual vakils and pleaders still had to obtain permission before they could engage in profit-accruing activities outside of their profession.

It would be instructive to examine how unanimous the judges had been in making the rule which originally prohibited vakils from taking on extra professional duties. Did they differ with one another as they had done in the matter of allowing vakils to appear in original insolvency suits? Under what statutory provision did they make the rule? Even if they possessed some unspecified broad powers, whether implicit or explicit, to regulate the conduct of vakils and pleaders, by what procedures did the judges deal with individual applications? In other words, how did such factors as professional, social and economic standing influence a judge's decision either to grant or deny a request? Original documents containing the judges' views on the subject are yet to be discovered in the High Court archives. However the numerous files selected from the administrative records provide tentative answers.

Although Chief Justice Sir Arthur Collins had managed to approve the rule with support from his colleagues[39] in November 1899, a later document reveals that their decision was not altogether unanimous. The Chief Justice and Justices Benson and Boddam thought that a rule ought to be made, but Justices Davies, Shephard and Subramania Iyer opposed it because they saw 'no compelling reason' for its formulation.[40] Since the judges disagreed equally how did the rule ever get majority vote? It is possible that the Chief Justice may simply have imposed his own views on those who dissented. He might have even insisted that, in framing the rule, he was not so concerned with reaching a total agreement among the judges as with ensuring what he saw as the proper conduct for vakils and pleaders. Otherwise, it is difficult to explain how the positions of Justices Davies, Shephard and Subramania Iyer could have been overridden; they continued to express strong disapproval of the existence of a general rule.[41]

Eight months after the rule had come into operation, R. Sriramulu Sastri, a High Court vakil, petitioned the judges to extend the time limit imposed on him for winding up his dealings with the Portland Cement Factory. By then, Arnold White had inherited the mantle of the Chief Justice. Promoted from his previous position as Advocate General of Madras, his views altered the balance. Justices Benson, Boddam and Lewis Moore (a civilian appointed temporarily), advocated that permission should not be accorded to the petitioner because his former application had already been rejected. Supporting the application, however, the new Chief Justice along with Justices Davies, Shephard and Subramania Iyer, thought that encouragement ought to be given for such enterprises so long as a vakil's involvement was not 'derogatory to the profession'.[42]

Except for the Chief Justice Arnold White and Justice Moore, others were members of the old regime under Sir Arthur Collins. In March 1899, when the High Court approved the rule, Arnold White had been in Madras only for seven months as Advocate General. A newcomer to the local legal scene, he desisted from expressing any personal opinion on the efficacy of the rule even though as the head of the bar he could have done so discreetly. Perhaps, he was not then concerned about a rule dealing with vakils and pleaders. The petition from Sriramulu Sastri now presented Chief Justice White with a unique opportunity. In a rather long minute he wrote:

> My own view is that the petitioner should be allowed to continue the working of his factory. *I am not clear where our power comes from to pass a rule, in general terms, prohibiting vakils from carrying on a trade or business without our sanction.* Of course, if the trade or business is inconsistent with the vakil's duties as a vakil, or derogatory to the dignity of the profession, the High Court would have the inherent power to interfere. It is very desirable to have a rule like the one in force in reserve, but I see no objection, on principle, to a vakil's investing his capital in, and exercising a general supervision over an undertaking like the petitioner's. I don't know whether it is a fair analogy. *But no objection is raised for this sort of thing being done by barristers or solicitors, at home.* Of course . . . it would never do to

allow a vakil to carry on the business of a money lender, or a retail trader.[43]

Those who took the opposite view strongly contended that any active involvement in commercial purposes would keep a practitioner away from his duties. Whether the High Court had powers to frame a rule such as the one under consideration did not concern them. That a rule had been passed and sent to all subordinate courts in the districts and taluqs itself was sufficient to legitimize the assumed powers of the High Court. There were other minor considerations as well. As early as 1899, Justice Boddam wrote, 'I have had already more than one insolvent vakil before me and each added insolvency tends to degrade the whole profession. I think the rule is a good one and should be enforced.'[44] In 1916, Justice Coutts-Trotter adduced yet another reason for preserving the rule. He said,

> I am conscious that my views . . . must be coloured by ideas formed in England, where conditions are quite different. Personally, I have the strongest objection to any practising advocate engaging either directly or indirectly in any industrial or trading concern. It must tend, especially in a small district, to put him in possession of knowledge regarding his neighbour's business affairs and finances which he ought not to possess; and it gives opportunities for obtaining professional work, I will not say by illegitimate means, but certainly on illegitimate ground.[45]

Whereas Justice Coutts-Trotter's arguments for retaining the rule received criticism from the *MLJ* as being far-fetched, hypothetical, and even unfair to a particular segment of the legal profession, Justice Boddam's concerns seemed more reasonable.[46] The notoriety of one insolvent vakil, in his view, damaged the reputation of the entire profession. Moreover, once a particular rule had assumed status as a canon, it could not be easily nullified even though the judges admitted its controversial nature.[47] To do anything contrary might make the judges look whimsical and arbitrary. That the supreme judicial body in the Presidency vacillated between leniency and stringency in granting permission to vakils, especially during the 1920s, suggests that the judges were more preoccupied with the enforcement of the rule in as many cases as possible than debating its legality.

No wonder that the manner in which the High Court reviewed and granted permissions to hundreds of applications should vary. The judges usually looked for information in four broad categories:

the nature of a vakil's involvement, the time he was likely to devote to it, the monetary compensation he received for his duties, and the actual or potential conflict that might arise between his professional duties and commercial or economic interests.[48] When the rule came into operation, the judges were initially less stringent in approving petitions from vakils and pleaders. For example, G. F. Mackenzie, the District Judge of Coimbatore, made certain requests on behalf of some High Court vakils and local pleaders that they might be permitted to continue in their positions as Directors of the Coimbatore Varthaka Vridhi Dharmajana Sangam, the Jana Upaharam Vridhi, Ltd., and the Coimbatore Spinning and Weaving Company, Ltd. He assured the judges that the responsibilities of these individuals as directors in no way 'clashed with their professional duties'.[49] Therefore, the judges sanctioned the petition without further verification.

A large number of applications sent to the High Court dealt with directorship in several local commercial enterprises, whether co-operative societies or limited joint-stock companies.[50] A few practitioners submitted their petitions for trading in 'food stuffs',[51] operating printing presses,[52] conducting newspapers and law journals,[53] acquiring mica mines,[54] and some other temporary activities.[55] There were numerous reasons, whether altruistic or opportunistic, on the basis of which both vakils and pleaders tendered applications. Unfortunately, not every applicant obtained permission. In some cases, the judges automatically denied permission without explaining why. Even when the majority of them thought that an application merited consideration, their final verdict was a cold refusal because some of their members disagreed. The case of C. R. Parthasarathy Iyengar provides the best example. In 1922 he applied for permission to start a Telugu weekly newspaper. Eight out of ten judges favoured the request on the grounds of precedent and only two, Justices Oldfield and Coutts-Trotter, opposed. After discussing the matter in a meeting behind closed doors, their 'Lordships' for reasons unknown decided to refuse permission and informed the petitioner accordingly.[56]

Important as the services of vakils and pleaders might have been to the survival of many commercial or financial institutions, the judges were leery of the volume of applications they had to screen each year. That there had been a steady growth in several 'fraudulent Provident Societies' or 'bogus companies' in the Presidency at the turn of this century,[57] that some of these institutions had come under criminal investigation,[58] and that some vakils had filed insolvency petitions or abused the privileges conferred on them,[59] caused judges to deal quickly with offenders who had not obtained permission from the High Court.[60] Furthermore, the judges' anxiety over the number of petitions that flooded the High Court led them to opt for other less successful measures. That is why in 1925 they seemed to have departed from their usual lenient practice of permitting any bona fide petitioner, by redefining, in a narrower sense, who could become directors of co-operative or charitable institutions.[61]

If some practitioners had been guilty of abusing the special favours conferred on them by the High Court, the judges, too, were not always objective in according permission. Such factors as social and economic pre-eminence, professional standing and, not least, personal acquaintance seem to have influenced the judges' decisions whenever they passed orders on applications. The petition of P. Anandacharlu serves as the best illustration. In 1902 he sought permission from the High Court to assume control over the Vaijayanti Press into which he had 'sunk a large sum of money'. The judges were divided in their response. Justice Lewis Moore argued that since Anandacharlu had failed to inform them of the extent of his investments in a previous application which had been turned down, he should not now be permitted to take full possession of the press. Justice V. Bhashyam Iyengar, on the contrary, pointed out that the petitioner had operated his press long before the 'prohibitive order' ever came into force and therefore there were no legal or technical grounds for denying permission.

If Justice Bhashayam Iyengar supported the application primarily on the force of law, Justice Boddam took a different view altogether:

> I think this case is one in which we may give sanction to Mr Anandacharlu to carry on his Vijianti [sic] Press. *Mr Anandacharlu's position is exceptional.* He had acquired a character and status in his profession which would justify us in permitting him to carry on a business, which might [cause] a younger and less trust-worthy man to act unworthy of his profession and owing to the duties of his position as a member of the Viceroy's Council he has practically had to abandon the active pursuit of his profession. I think the conduct of a high class printing press is not derogatory of the profession of a vakil though I admit it is by no means easy to distinguish between a press which may and a press which should not be sanctioned. I think Mr Anandacharlu may be trusted to do nothing in carrying on the business of this press derogatory

to the dignity of his position as a vakil and a member of the Viceroy's Council and I think where we can sanction the carrying on of the business (which tends to the elevation and education of his fellows) we should. I would sanction the proposal.[62]

In the end, the chief justice and another judge nonchalantly appended their signatures and Justice Moore had to modify his previous views. This he did, of course, with mild protest.

Prominent vakils of stature—such as V. Krishnaswami Iyer, P. S. Sivaswami Iyer, C. P. Ramaswami Iyer, T. R. Ramachandra Iyer and A. Ramaswami Mudaliar—had no difficulty obtaining approval. Judges never doubted their integrity, but insisted on strict adherence to the rule whenever juniors were involved. Thus, the partiality shown by the judges enhanced the advancement of elite vakils and they moved quickly on to other spheres of activities which brought them even more social esteem and honour.[63] In contrast, both juniors and not-so-successful vakils received half-hearted treatment. The judges did not realize that in reality the underdogs probably needed their unstinting encouragement more because of an overcrowded bar and stiff competition within the profession. In passing a rule prohibiting vakils and pleaders from taking part in trade or business, the Madras High Court was not alone, however. Other High Courts in Allahabad, Bombay and Calcutta also framed similar rules.[64] The judges from Allahabad even went so far as to specify various activities a vakil could legally pursue outside of his profession.[65]

The judges ordinarily granted permission to vakils who had a flair for journalism, writing text-books and law commentaries, and for assuming leadership in social or literary movements. Insofar as vakils and pleaders were not personally engaged in alleged seditious activities or had not openly criticized the British administration of justice, they were left alone to regulate their affairs. Ironically, this relative freedom from the annoying interference of officialdom created an atmosphere for exchanging different political ideologies. It inadvertently promoted agitational strategies in many district bar associations where entry was limited to the privileged few. In this respect, whatever the High Court had hoped to achieve by framing a rule against vakils who were often interested in augmenting their income, the judges were powerless to stem the tide of vakils' influence in politics during the first few decades of this century.[66]

Part III

THE VAKILS' ASSOCIATION, 1889–1920

Chapter 6

THE ASSOCIATION'S LEADERS AND PRIVILEGES

> I must note that the Native bar, as it exists at present is without an organization and therefore, without much power for good. The time has come for the formation of a Vakils' Association which may in course of time, take up a position analogous to the Inns of Court . . . and thereby the whole body of legal practitioners in the country [may be brought] under wholesome professional control.
> —Sir T. Muthuswamy Iyer[1]

The Madras Bar Association enforced rules designed to maintain the professional norms and dignity of barristers. These rules prohibited their members from accepting briefs from vakils on the Original Side and from giving commissions to nonprofessionals; the rules also enjoined all barristers to adhere to the fee standards for services they provided. Although a few uncompliant newcomers or junior members occasionally challenged the rules and norms, the barristers by and large succeeded in enforcing rules that safeguarded their own professional aspirations, income and mobility. Though fewer than vakils, barristers exerted considerable influence upon the decisions of the local government, especially in securing appointments to higher law offices, and had the lion's share of legal practice. They also provided leadership and usually set the standards for the three groups of law practitioners.

Vakils owed much to barristers for inculcating the methods of advocacy and traditions, for setting an example in legal scholarship, and for developing a sense of responsibility in civic or social activities. As apprentices or juniors, they were associated with barristers, but, unlike their European mentors, vakils had failed to establish a professional organization in order to consolidate their own position and to press their claims for official patronage. In 1882, Sir T. Muthuswamy Iyer, the first Indian judge of the Madras High Court, observed in his convocation address to the law graduates that vakils should have a professional organization to strengthen their position and to exercise control over numerous vakils.² Sometime after 1882 vakils formed an association,³ but it did not attract many members and soon died. At the end of the 1880s, 'some friends' suggested to the High Court vakils that they should resuscitate the association. It is not clear who these friends were or why they made the suggestion. However, a circular invited vakils to attend a meeting to discuss possibilities for reviving the association.⁴ Twenty-two vakils responded and attended the meeting on 1 March 1889. They founded an organization known as 'The Madras High Court Vakils' Association', and named K. P. Sankara Menon its provisional secretary; they also set up a special committee to draft rules for the working of the organization.⁵

OFFICERS OF THE ASSOCIATION

When on 15 April 1889 the vakils reconvened to consider the draft rules formulated by the special committee, they unanimously accepted the rules and elected the executive officers.⁶ Tables 4–6 provide the names of elected officers of the Association.

TABLE 4
*Presidents of the Vakils' Association, 1889–1931*⁷

No.	Name	Term(s)
1.	Raja T. Rama Rao	1889–1891
2.	Sir S. Subramania Iyer	1891–1895
3.	Sir V. Bhashyam Iyengar	1895–1901
		1906–1908
4	Sir C. Sankaran Nair	1901–1906
5.	Sir P. S. Sivaswami Iyer	1908–1912
6.	R. Sadagopachariar	1912–1915
7.	J. L. Rozario	1915–1917
8.	S. Srinivasa Iyengar	1917–1920
9.	T. R. Ramachandra Iyer	1921–1931

A perusal of names found in these three tables permits a few observations. First, there was a preponderance of brahmans (both Saivas and Sri Vaishnavas) in positions of leadership. Of the eight different presidents between 1889 and 1920, only two vakils were non-brahmans.⁸ With the exception of Rama Rao and Sadagopachariar the rest of them later became either advocate generals or

Leaders and Privileges 121

TABLE 5
Secretaries and Joint-Secretaries, 1889–1921[9]

No.	Name	Term(s)
1.	K. P. Sankara Menon	Provisional Secretary
2.	V. Krishnaswami Iyer	1889–1901
3.	K. Krishnamachari (Offg. Sec.)	1890
4.	K. R. S. Sastri (Jt. Sec.)	1899–1902
5.	P. S. Sivaswami Iyer	1901–1906
6.	K. Ramachandra Iyer (Jt. Sec.)	1902–1903
7.	V. V. Srinivasa Iyengar	1902–1903 1916–1920
8.	P. R. Sundara Iyer	1906–1911
9.	C. P. Ramaswami Iyer (Jt. Sec.)	1906–1907
10.	C. Venkatasubbaramiah (Jt. Sec.)	1907–1908
11.	K. C. Desikachari (Jt. Sec.)	1908–1911
12.	S. Srinivasa Iyengar	1911–1912 1915–1916
13.	T. R. Ramachandra Iyer	1912–1916
14.	V. Masilamani Pillai (Jt. Sec.)	1912–1916
15.	K. Srinivasa Iyengar	1914–1915
16.	Vepa Ramesam (Jt. Sec.)	1916–1917
17.	T. V. Gopalaswami Mudaliar (Jt. Sec.)	1917–1921
18.	T. R. Venkatarama Sastri	1920–1921

TABLE 6
Some Members of the Managing Committee[10]

No.	Name	Term
1.	P. Anandacharlu	1889–1893
2.	C. Sankaran Nair	1889–1890
3.	K. P. Visvanatha Iyer	1889–1893
4.	P. R. Sundara Iyer	1889–1908
5.	M. Venkataramiah Chetty	1889–1894
6.	V. Bhashyam Iyengar	1889–1894
7.	C. V. Sundaram Sastri	1889–1893
8.	C. R. Pattabhirama Iyer	1894–1897
9.	C. Ramachandra Rao Sahib	1894
10.	M. R. Ramakrishna Iyer	1897
11.	T. Rangachari	1908
12.	T. Ethiraja Mudaliar	1901–1908
13.	P. R. Ganapathi Iyer	1908

judges of the High Court or both.¹¹ Among the secretaries or joint-secretaries or members of the managing committee, only seven were non-brahmans.¹² Second, in spite of the overwhelming majority of brahmans in positions of leadership, widespread communal hatred was scarcely evident during the early years of the organization even though one might, in retrospect, sense the inevitable outcome of such brahman monopoly. For many vakils, whether brahmans or not, withstanding the competition and rivalry from European barristers was the most common goal; the Vakils' Association provided members with an identity and a cause to fend off challengers. Third, a clear pattern that emerges from the extant records is that some ambitious individuals successively sought nomination to the managing committee, then became the secretary, and finally reached the position of president.¹³ Fourth, the Association was primarily the brain child of a small coterie of vakils who zealously watched over the growth, activities and reputation of the vakil bar.¹⁴ These few vakils religiously attended the meetings, formulated policies governing the Association's internal operations, made representations to the judges and local government, and strenuously strove to keep the Association afloat in the face of insufficient resources and inadequate facilities.¹⁵

DUTIES OF OFFICERS

The President

The rules adopted by the Association did not stipulate any specific responsibilities for the president. Primarily a ceremonial figure of the vakil bar, he had pre-eminence and represented the vakils in all formal proceedings in the High Court and in all social gatherings.¹⁶ Occasionally he addressed the court on issues that impinged upon the interests of vakils.

The Secretary

If the president had possessed merely formal or ceremonial powers, the secretary had real authority to liase between the Association and the outside world. Unlike the president who could opt to be absent from meetings, a prerogative he often exercised, the secretary was almost always present at the deliberations of the Association. He convened the general and special meetings, maintained a record of all discussions, kept accounts of all incomes and disbursements, corresponded with others, and prepared the annual reports. He voiced the opinion of the Association in the columns of journals and local newspapers. The rise and fall of the Association largely depended upon the imagination, commitment, skill and energy of the secretary. Such were the traits of V. Krishnaswami Iyer, the first elected secretary, who continued in that office for nearly twelve years. His sagacity and industry were unparalleled.[17]

The Managing Committee

According to the original rules, seven resident members were elected to the managing committee; these individuals along with the president and secretary formed the backbone of the Association and only they had powers to control and regulate its operations. Specifically, the managing committee was empowered to convene special meetings, control the flow of funds, and to make further rules 'not inconsistent with the [general] rules' of the Association.[18] During the first few years of its existence, the managing committee made decisions with respect to hiring employees, purchasing law books and other documents, and furnishing the premises of the Association.[19] The committee also recommended to the general body that vakils should forthwith appear in formal attire, wearing professional gowns like barristers.[20] It also laid down policies for collecting subscriptions towards establishing a library, for instituting legal proceedings against defaulters, and for opening its doors to vakils residing in outlying districts.[21]

ELECTION OF OFFICERS

Rule IV of the general body of rules adopted by the Association provided for election of officers.[22] Between 1889 and 1908 the convention seems to have been that the president, a major figure in the vakils bar, was always elected unanimously.[23] In the early years, the secretary and members of the managing committee were also re-elected to their respective offices.[24] At the turn of the century, however, competition for offices became more common, especially after V. Krishnaswami Iyer stepped down from his position as secretary. For example, in 1901 both Sankaran Nair and K. R. Subramania Sastri were elected unanimously to the offices of the president and joint-secretary respectively, but the secretaryship became an object of contention between P. S. Sivaswami Iyer and S. Kasturi Ranga Iyengar.

The rivalry of these two eminent figures throws some light on the changing nature of the vakils' profession. They attended the Presidency College together and both met all the requirements to become High Court vakils in 1885.[25] Whereas Sivaswami Iyer chose to remain in Madras and commence practice, Kasturi Ranga Iyengar opted for Coimbatore, a prosperous and emerging municipality where there was relatively less competition. In 1894, Kasturi Ranga Iyengar returned to Madras because he wanted to get involved in the city's public affairs.[26] The political landscape of Madras had by then changed considerably. Unlike the two previous decades, when a few subservient government officials alone had presided over public discussions, numerous energetic and young professionals, lawyers mainly, had now appeared on the stage. For example, vakils dominated the proceedings of the Madras Mahajana Sabha, an organization established in 1882 to represent the interests and grievances of local Indian communities.[27]

By the end of the century vakils had managed to revive and reorganize the already defunct Madras High Court Vakils' Association. The new organization for all practical purposes was in the hands of those vakils living in Mylapore, an important suburb reputed for its ancient temple and brahman orthodoxy; Mylapore became commonly, but perhaps derogatorily, known as the 'legal sanctuary', in contrast to the enclave occupied by those in Egmore, another suburb of Madras. Success in career and leadership in the newly established bodies bred rivalry and jealousy between individuals from Mylapore and Egmore.[28] This new vakil rivalry obscured the former antagonisms between barristers and vakils on the one hand, and between veteran bureaucrats and professional upstarts on the other. Although Kasturi Ranga Iyengar lived in Mylapore, after his return from Coimbatore his professional affiliation and sympathy were with his colleagues from Egmore. While the latter readily welcomed him, the Mylaporeans resented the intrusions of a mufassal vakil, in spite of his 'connections' in the city and the High Court. However, he managed to obtain a membership in the managing committee in 1897, from which position he desired to climb the professional ladder.[29]

In this context of Madras urban and professional politics the otherwise insignificant election to the Vakils' Association secretaryship must be placed. In the election Kasturi Ranga Iyengar lost to his rival Sivaswami Iyer, 16 to 23.[30] In 1902, members elected nearly unanimously both president and secretary but the competition to get into the managing committee proved intense.[31] The Association minutes, unfortunately, do not contain any information on the total number of members who actually contested the election, the number of votes the other contestants got or how many votes each member was permitted. Only 39 members were present at this meeting, and as many as 36 members voted for P. S. Sivaswami Iyer; this was a remarkable testimony to his popularity and leadership qualities.[32] Again, in 1906, while the election of the president was unanimous, the offices of the secretary and joint-secretary, and membership in the managing committee became arenas of scramble.[33]

During the early years only a few vakils willingly shouldered the responsibilities of the Association; but as it grew in strength, popularity and recognition, many aspired to control and influence its policies, despite the honorary nature of the positions. Competition for the offices reflected the professional rivalry between Iyer and Iyengar vakils and between those in Mylapore and Egmore. Consequently, the elections, far from being dull and mechanical, became more heated and political.

RESOLUTIONS OF THE ASSOCIATION

Membership

The rule regarding admission of vakils to the Association stated that any High Court vakil was eligible to become a member after approval of the managing committee.[34] Apparently, the committee rejected no applications. This is understandable because the Association hoped to open its doors to as many vakils as possible: it encouraged not only the city vakils but those in the districts and taluqs as well. It even offered a reduced membership fee to vakils living outside Madras because it thought that they would not make frequent use of the facilities easily available to city members.[35] In spite of such concessions, the Association was not very successful in attracting a large number of High Court vakils, either from Madras or from outside.[36] Nor was it able to persuade the several district bar associations to affiliate themselves with the city body.[37] When the Association was first formed in 1889 there were about 100 vakils in Madras, of whom only 59 became members.[38] In 1939 the aggregate membership represented approximately one-sixth of the total number of law practitioners in the entire Presidency.

A corollary to the initial difficulties the Association faced in attracting a large membership was the onerous and often unpleasant task of collecting dues, whether for the monthly subscription or the library fund. The managing committee recommended a rule to undertake the collection of funds for the proposed library. It stated 'that every member shall on admission subscribe to the library fund a sum of at least Rs 50 payable in a lump sum or in monthly instalments not exceeding 10.'[39] The general body decided to start the actual collection on November 1889.[40] Sixty-four vakils were members at this time and they pledged Rs 3200 towards the library fund, out of which Rs 2000 was outstanding or in arrears by March 1890. The committee asked the secretary to 'write an earnest appeal to the members . . . to pay up the arrears as early as possible'.[41]

The first annual report for the period ending on 30 April 1890 indicated that a sum of Rs 382 had been collected as 'ordinary monthly subscription' from 64 members. Of these, 54 came from Madras and the remaining ten from the mufassal. The amount of arrears as of 1 May 1890 was Rs 113. Likewise, of the total of Rs 3085 payable in instalments towards the library fund, only Rs 1905.6.0 had been collected.[42] Twelve years later the situation was no better: Rs 2189 and Rs 345 were in arrears in the library fund and monthly subscription, respectively. The committee observed with regret that 'unless more stringent measures [were] adopted it will not be possible to collect the heavy arrears, and while it would not be able to meet even its current expenditure the library cannot be improved by the addition of useful books that come out from time to time'.[43]

The managing committee adopted certain tactics to check this intractable delinquency. By ordering many volumes on credit in anticipation of collecting the arrears,[44] the committee apparently presumed that it could persuade members to pay their dues, but this approach proved futile.[45] It then framed a rule for the dismissal of defaulters.[46] On 10 September 1891, the committee resolved to remove seven vakils if they did not reduce their arrears within a week.[47] While some defaulters responded to the committee's resolute measures, others simply ignored the warning. At last, the Association authorized the committee to take recourse to law by instituting legal proceedings against members who had not paid any of their subscriptions.[48] By the turn of the century, it dismissed a few members each year for failure to contribute their share of support.[49] In 1939, in the midst of jubilant festivities, the Association admitted that the question of arrears had been a problem from its inception and that there could be no solution unless all members voluntarily co-operated by reducing the arrears. For all that, the Association had about Rs 20,000 in bank deposits at this time.[50]

Position of the Profession

One of the primary objectives of the organization was to protect and promote the interests of vakils.[51] There were many vakils of stature throughout the colonial period. V. Bhashyam Iyengar, S. Subramania Iyer, Raja T. Rama Rao and R. Balaji Rao, to name only a few from the nineteenth century, were no less competent than barristers either in legal knowledge or in subtle reasoning and advocacy. But as a rule vakils had no public status.[52]

1. *Attire*. Whereas High Court barristers paraded themselves as members of the 'fraternity of the long robe' whenever they appeared before any judicial tribunal, vakils could not even dream of adorning themselves in such impressive costume. Indeed, the appearance of an average vakil made it difficult to identify him when he stood in the midst of a motley crowd in court. Occasionally, a court-keeper would mistakenly try to remove certain vakils whose apparel made them indistinguishable from their clients.[53] Naturally, vakils felt that such indiscriminate and disrespectful treatment was an insult to their profession and that some remedy was called for. As Sivaswami Iyer put it, 'Whether in the matter of general education and attainments, or in the matter of legal qualifications, we felt we were not a whit inferior to the other section of the Bar, which considered itself to be solely and pre-eminently entitled to be called "the Bar".'[54] Therefore, the vakils decided to appeal to the High Court.

In July 1889, the managing committee recommended to the general body that vakils should wear gowns, and made representation to the judges as well.[55] On 4 December 1889 the committee passed two further resolutions: that vakils should wear black coats and white turbans 'with or without lace' from 1 January 1890 onwards, and that 'it [should] be optional to wear boots and trousers'.[56] The judges in support promulgated a new rule requiring vakils to appear before the High Court in black gown.[57] The local

Indian newspapers congratulated the judges for their favourable response to the vakils' request, and the vakils for the well-merited distinction that they had earned.[58]

Although later generations of practitioners took the dress rule for granted, to vakils of that day the new rule was tantamount to the judges' public acknowledgment of their talent and merit. At long last the vakil profession in Madras had come of age. In Calcutta, vakils waited until 1907 before they could obtain the privileges of wearing professional gowns.[59] Madras vakils, in contrast, wore their gowns not only in the High Court but also in the civil and sessions courts of the districts. Thus, 'the black gown' became a symbol of status distinguishing the vakils of the High Court from those of the lower courts, namely the first and second grade pleaders.[60] In 1905, the High Court issued an order extending the same privilege to those High Court vakils who had previously been appointed as district munsifs or sub-judges.[61]

2. *Apprentices-at-Law.* The High Court judges required that vakil candidates should serve a year of apprenticeship, after completing the B.L. degree, under a practitioner who appeared on both sides of the court. By 1891, they realized that the rule existed only on paper and had never really been enforced. As Justice Horatio H. Shephard put it:

> It is important to make the study in Chambers a reality instead of allowing the requirement to degenerate into a form. There is reason to believe that reading in Vakil's chambers does not *in fact* represent any study or work on the part of the apprentice and anyhow there is no assurance to the contrary.[62]

Justice T. Muthuswamy Iyer concurred with his colleague's views, adding that it should be 'incumbent on the apprentice to keep a diary showing the work *actually* done by him from day to day and get it initialled' by the vakil under whom an apprentice entered a contract.[63]

In 1903, the Association authorized the secretary to address the judges on the desirability of holding two examinations a year for apprentices, instead of only one as had been the case previously.[64] Why the Association even suggested the change is unclear, but a few members thought that if some candidates could not take the examination, they should not have to wait for another year before having another opportunity. The professional disadvantages to young vakil aspirants of having to wait for another year were obvious. The members of the Association, therefore, wished to let the judges know their strong views on the subject and recommended that efforts should be made to remedy the situation.

3. *Vakil-Advocates*. Originally the advocates of the Madras High Court included those 'fresh' barristers from England and Ireland, advocates from Scotland, and those from Calcutta, Bombay and Allahabad High Courts. Advocate candidates had to produce certificates of professional training and testimonials of character before they could be admitted to the Madras High Court. Not many Indians went to England to study at the Inns of Court during the nineteenth century because the expenses were too high. Even if one could manage the expenses and wished to undertake travel across the sea, the fear of pollution, excommunication from caste, and other religious sanctions stood in the way. An easier solution, therefore, was to sit for the much harder Master of Law examinations at the local university, then undergo a period of apprenticeship for 18 months with an advocate of the High Court, and, finally, get oneself admitted.[65] An Indian advocate usually had a higher status than a vakil, and enjoyed the customary courtesy in being heard first during any proceedings of the court, while a senior vakil waited his turn. As advocate, he appeared in insolvency courts but a vakil never had that privilege.

In 1895, the judges considered the possibility of elevating a number of vakils as advocates because they thought that the admission rules discouraged vakils from becoming advocates. They even referred the proposal to the Vakils' Association but it resolved to defer the matter.[66] It is not clear whether the Association ever discussed the subject formally and the records are silent. One passing reference from P. S. Sivaswami Iyer sheds some light. He wrote that vakils rejected the proposal 'on the ground that it would relegate the large majority of Vakils to a distinctly lower category and would militate against our attempts to win a position of equality with the Advocates' branch of the profession for the whole body of Vakils'.[67]

In a later general meeting, the Association discussed the rule regarding admission of advocates. In the light of the stringent rules of the High Court, vakils thought they suffered a double hardship. If a vakil desired to become an advocate, the rule requiring a second term of apprenticeship could only be seen as redundant and obnoxious. Therefore, the Association commissioned both

P. S. Sivaswami Iyer and V. Viswanatha Sastri to draft a memorandum to the judges expressing vakils' interests in becoming advocates without having to serve an additional period of 18 months.[68] When the Association submitted this memorial or how the judges responded to it are questions that cannot be answered with certainty. That the judges were not persuaded by the vakils' arguments is clear, since the rule remained unaltered for many more years.[69]

PRIVILEGES OF MEMBERS

The fundamental reason for having a professional association arose out of the common interests and needs of High Court vakils. Prior to the reorganization of this body, barristers and members of the commercial community in Madras city had already established their own loosely structured associations.[70] In 1893 attorneys followed the example of others.[71] Several other cultural or quasi-religious and political organizations, which did not represent any one particular professional interest, had also emerged during the second half of the nineteenth century.[72] Common to all these institutions was the mutual need for some forum that could unite those of like interest. Within each organization, colleagues usually gathered, discussed topics of the day, and enjoyed whatever recreation facilities were available.

Some years after the American Revolution, large cities in the U.S. had their bar associations where lawyers met for social, professional or disciplinary purposes.[73] This description of American bar associations quite neatly applies to the Vakils' Association which came into existence almost a century later. When it formulated the general rules in 1889, it outlined its basic objectives as follows:

    a. To maintain a high standard of professional conduct,
    b. To protect and promote the interests of vakils,
    c. To make representations from time to time to the authorities on matters affecting suitors or the profession, and
    d. To form and maintain a library.[74]

It would be extremely difficult to evaluate objectively how well vakils succeeded in achieving these goals, especially the ideal of maintaining a high standard of conduct. For many, such ideals were important, while others thought them impractical in the face of stiff competition and limited opportunity. In his pamphlet, *The Madras Bar and How to Improve It*, Anandacharlu had admitted the coexistence of these two types of lawyers. However, the Association provided a library and meeting place for members, while it lobbied for chambers and higher appointments. For the first time, under the aegis of the Association all vakils in Madras assembled for social interaction, setting aside their status or differences.

Library and Meeting Place

Apart from personal libraries of a few well-to-do vakils, the only libraries to which vakils had any access were those belonging to the Association, High Court, law college, and university.[75] The Association collected library fund dues from members in order to acquire volumes of imperial and local statutes, law reports and textbooks.[76] The managing committee slowly built up the library in spite of some members' chronic delinquency in remitting dues. Occasionally, the library received donations of books from individuals as well.[77] When the Association celebrated its fiftieth year, well over 30,000 volumes had been acquired for the library.[78]

The library served multiple purposes. Not only did it house books and law reports but it also created an atmosphere for business interaction. As vakils waited for their cases to be called, the library provided a convenient gathering place. Here they also met with their clients. Time spent at the library provided opportunities for vakils to keep up with the gossip of the day, to build friendships with fellow vakils, and to hear senior vakils expatiate on their feats in court. The Association made special representation to the judges and obtained two rooms for its use in the old High Court buildings situated in front of the harbour.[79]

Chambers for Vakils

During the first 30 years of the High Court, vakils did not have any chambers within the court premises. They commonly rented offices in the streets near the High Court.[80] The Association sought to remedy the inconveniences felt by vakils and applied to the government for constructing a number of separate chambers within the new court complex.[81] After a lengthy correspondence between the Association, judges and government, the latter finally acceded to the petition.[82] This was a boon. The occupants enjoyed the proximity of the court without having to hurry back and forth from their previous offices; renting a chamber within the High Court buildings also marked a practitioner's mobility and success. If a vakil had his own chamber, a client from the districts had little difficulty in locating him; there was every certainty that the vakil would show up in court where the client could meet with him.

Even though the judges had originally recommended 100 rooms, it is unclear how many chambers were constructed.[83] Forty vakils, most of whom belonged to the Association, occupied 44 chambers.[84] Although it is difficult to discover the actual number of vakils practising at this time in the city, that these 40 vakils fared better than most others is obvious. To those who had neither a reasonable income nor good standing in the profession, the Association rendered a singular service. If a vakil could not afford a chamber or the necessary law books and reports, it provided such facilities, giving members access to tools essential for their profession.[85]

Professional Appointments

The revival of the Vakils' Association in 1889 enabled vakils to acquire a sense of solidarity and capacity to run their organization smoothly; it also provided them with both a platform for protest and a vehicle for expressing grievances and promoting fulfilment of their aspirations. As vakils competed with barristers and attorneys for a fair share of legal business, the Association earned a reputation as a nursery of indigenous professional talent. For example, in 1888 the government appointed S. Subramania Iyer, one of the leading vakils, as the Government Pleader. After 1889, whenever a vacancy arose both the government and the judges had to consider eligible vakils, many of whom belonged to the Association. During the 1890s, they obtained appointments which had been denied earlier: High Court judgeship, advocate generalship, district judgeship, and an assistant professorship at the law college.[86] Many other subordinate judicial offices also came within their reach.[87] The only non-European professional body in Madras with a clear sense of purpose and direction and with a large membership and talent, the Association thought that it alone had the entitlement in enjoying such rewards. Whenever the government elevated a vakil, the Association rejoiced and celebrated his accomplishments, while diplomatically excluding other non-member vakils from such festivities.[88]

Little wonder then, that vakils, pleaders or even munsifs who had settled down in the districts became aggravated. The partiality shown by the authorities in selecting High Court vakils from the city caused deep resentment. Their encroachments upon the privileges of others 'who [could] hold their own against any vakil practising at the High Court bar' brought further agitation.[89] Welcoming the action of the government in 1914 in the appointment of W. L. Venkataramayya, who had been a public prosecutor, as an acting district and sessions judge of Behrampur, the *West Coast* commented:

> The highest place in the Judicial service a mufassal pleader can now aspire to is that of a munsiff, or at the utmost that of a Sub-Judge, the High Court bar enjoying a monopoly of higher appointments. Who will say that, for instance, Mr T. M. Appu Nedungadi of Calicut, Mr Narayana Kurup of Tellicherry or Mr Lobo of Mangalore, all senior pleaders, are not fit to discharge the duties of District Judges as some *well connected and much advertised* Ramaswami carrying on his trade in the High Court?[90]

Annual Gatherings

During the earlier years of the Association, relations between the bench and the bar were less cordial: at the slightest neglect of duties, whether wilful or otherwise, judges tended to react harshly with all practitioners, vakils in particular. In 1889 two long editorials in *The Hindu* dealt with the need for mutual respect and recognition between judges and lawyers; it urged that the bench and senior members of the bar should take the initiative in bridging the professional and social gulf which existed between themselves and a large body of nameless and faceless lawyers. There is no evidence to show that the bar had actually carried out this exhortation. Absence of long-standing indigenous traditions in law practice or partnership among vakils had exacerbated the lack of common identity and collegiality. Other social or religious taboos stemming from orthodox life-styles vitiated what little chance there might have been for personal and professional intercourse.

In 1904, however, for the first time members of the Association assembled to 'rub shoulders' with each other. V. Krishnaswami Iyer, then a member of the managing committee, proposed the idea of an annual gathering and hosted the first event. He hoped that the event would enable vakils to meet informally and freely exchange views on the condition of their profession.[91] In the next 24 years, 20 such annual gatherings took place;[92] sponsored by senior vakils, whose traditional hospitality indirectly alluded to their professional success. These events attracted several hundred city vakils.[93] Primarily intended as a social event, the gatherings later acquired a serious dimension. Amidst fun and frivolities members organized a plenary session and openly discussed topics related to internal governance as well as opportunities for vakils. On occasion the hosts arranged for a quasi-academic forum in which a leading member read a paper on a topic of law and judicial administration or reviewed the state of the profession.[94]

Two important issues seem to have received more than lip service in these presentations: the quality of professional ties between senior and junior practitioners and the establishment of a fund for less fortunate members of the profession. Whether these 'less fortunate' ones came from the entire class of vakils or only from Association members is less clear. That members grappled with such serious issues instead of spending the time socializing seems to reveal the crisis within the vakil bar at this time. To outsiders vakils appeared successful and enterprising in their competition with advocates and attorneys. Yet a close scrutiny revealed murmurs of professional disaffection among them. The reasons for discontent were neither hidden nor groundless: discontent arose because the underdogs in the profession, the juniors, felt that seniors virtually monopolized the practice. This exclusion not only deprived juniors of proving their mettle by competing with seniors but also denied them the much needed and very valuable courtroom experience without which any hopes of securing business were unfounded. Juniors became jealous and suspicious of seniors, who, in turn, thought that juniors were obstreperous, arrogant and impatient.[95] Against this atmosphere of monopoly and complaint, the Association appointed a committee in 1919 to study the existing conditions and future prospects for juniors.

In December the committee submitted its recommendations to be discussed during the next annual gathering. The six resolutions passed subsequently resembled the resolutions that barristers had passed about 50 years earlier in the controversy between seniors and juniors.[96] The full text of the resolutions is provided here because it brings out clearly the underlying grievances of juniors. The resolutions read:

> It is expected that no vakil of over 10 years standing will ordinarily accept an engagement in any matter on the Appellate or Original Side

of the High Court over Rs 5000 in value without another vakil of less than ten years standing appearing in the case.

Whenever [two] vakils appear in a case, the junior shall be entitled to not less than one-third [of] the senior's fee when the senior's fee does not exceed the regulation fee.

The High Court should be moved to make a rule allowing [two] vakils' fee as costs in cases of the value of Rs 5000 and above.

When a brief is transferred from one practitioner to another, the latter shall be entitled to a reasonable proportion of the former's fee.

No vakil shall suggest to the client the engagement of another practitioner as junior in the case when the client himself suggests a junior or a junior has already been engaged.

No vakil shall accept an engagement from a client who has already engaged a vakil in the case unless the consent of the latter in writing is obtained.[97]

While it is not certain that these resolutions brought forth the intended results or improved their lot, the Association knew it could no longer remain apathetic to struggling juniors.

The plight of 'less fortunate' vakils also generated some discussion in the annual gatherings. Although what constituted the state of being less fortunate or what criteria the members used in determining the positions of practitioners are not easily known, the question of how to ameliorate the conditions of such vakils had been under discussion for many years. T. V. Seshagiri Iyer, the first to take notice of this situation, observed during the annual gathering in 1913 that 'Many a man is stranded in life for reasons which bring him discredit. Many a young life is snatched away early. It is the duty of those who are in the profession to make provision for the family of these unfortunate brethren of ours.'[98] He proposed that a Benefit Fund be created, following the rules accepted in England for similar purposes. In the next few years, K. Srinivasa Iyengar, V. Ramadas and K. Bhashyam dwelt on the issue. Bhashyam devoted an entire paper to this growing concern,[99] and according to reports his paper was well received. Despite their expressions of professional *dharma* in caring for the needy, vakils did not adopt any concrete action.[100] Due to apathy and inertia on the one hand, and preoccupation with local and national politics on the other, the Association failed to achieve its aspirations. In 1943, only after the initiatives of Sir C. P. Ramaswami Iyer, the Association established a fund to help the needy vakils.[101]

The last annual gathering of vakils took place in 1927, when the institution that had lasted for 24 years came to an abrupt end. It began primarily as a social event which lasted but for a few hours and it later became an all-day affair, attracting more practitioners than any other regular meetings. Apart from providing mirth, music and recreation, the gatherings assumed an atmosphere of open forum generally absent in the Association's ordinary business meetings. While members freely discussed the plight of vakils struggling to eke out a living, they did not achieve the solidarity they had hoped for between seniors and juniors. Their diverse social background, economic standing and status did not fully contribute to the development of brotherhood among them. That at the end of the second decade some disgruntled vakils in Madras organized the Non-Brahman Lawyers' Association lends credence to this view. However, an unanticipated result was that these annual gatherings caught the imagination of High Court advocates and members of the district bar associations, who followed the lead of Madras vakils and organized their own annual meetings.[102]

Chapter 7

COMPETING VOICES IN THE ASSOCIATION

Beyond providing facilities or creating opportunities for members, the Association played the role of a watch-dog, ensuring that vakils maintained a high standard of professional ethics.[1] Periodically, it made special representations to the governments in Madras, Calcutta (later Delhi), and in England, and to the High Court protecting vakils' interests against demands from barristers and civilians for patronage. The Association also offered its opinions on various bills introduced in the provincial and central legislatures.[2] Since its inception, the leadership rested almost always in the hands of a few brahman vakils. The ascendancy of brahmans through higher education and government service during British rule naturally created widespread resentment and opposition from the non-brahmans. Contrary to the claims that leaders of the Vakils' Association had made, certain non-brahman lawyers thought that it did not truly represent the interests of all vakils regardless of their political, professional, sectarian and social differences. Therefore they decided to break away from the Association and found a separate organization, while others sought to unify the profession, which included both High Court vakils and First and Second Grade Pleaders in the Presidency. This chapter explores the alleged unity and dissent within the Indian legal profession.

FUNCTIONS OF THE ASSOCIATION

Supervision of Members

Among the three groups of lawyers in Madras, the vakil branch was the youngest and therefore had little historic reputation to protect or ancient traditions to regulate its conduct.[3] Despite their claims, even some barristers and attorneys wandered away because of high competition and limited professional opportunities. Occasionally, the High Court censured them for their unprofessional practices.[4] A number of vakils equally abused their special privileges as officers of court and received criticisms from the bench as well.⁵ Although provisions in the amended Letters Patent of 1865 and the Legal Practitioners' Act of 1879 empowered the judges to deal with instances of professional misconduct,⁶ they exercised their prerogatives rather sparingly towards barristers and attorneys because their own societies in England had jurisdiction over such matters.⁷ Only with vakils did judges strive to uphold the dignity of that profession and in so doing, they were unsparing and zealous crusaders. Both the press and legal journals politely pointed out that they must be impartial when dealing with allegations of professional misconduct and only in situations where all evidence was unquestionably clear could the judges institute legal proceedings.⁸

In 1893 V. Bhashyam Iyengar, addressing the graduates of Madras University proposed the formation of a law institute vested with powers to supervise the conduct of local barristers, attorneys and vakils. 'The duty of the proposed association,' he said, 'will be to bring to the notice of the [High] court cases of professional misconduct and also to report to the court on cases, which, as a rule, should in the first instance be referred to it for investigation.'⁹ Bhashyam Iyengar apparently thought that should such an institution ever come into operation it would play an intermediary role between the High Court and the legal profession, by conducting initial enquiries against alleged cases of professional misconduct. Only on the recommendations of the institute could judges pronounce their judgement on a guilty lawyer. Thus, the institute would not only put a check on the judicial impulse to undertake proceedings, as had been before, but also save the members of the profession from unwarranted publicity and humiliation which usually accompanied such inquiries in open court.

The proposal was received favourably by certain members on the bench and most of the bar supported it. Moreover, the editorial in the *Madras Law Journal* particularly encouraged vakils to take the initiative in forming the institute by themselves, should barristers and attorneys not wish to co-operate.¹⁰ The journal's homily bore no fruit and the institute never became a reality. Not until the 1926 passage of the Indian Bar Councils' Act was there a local bar council somewhat resembling Bhashyam Iyengar's original proposal. During the mid-1890s the judges took a different attitude in handling complaints of professional misconduct. Even though the High Court accepted complaints against vakils as before, the judges began to invite vakils' opinions.¹¹ At times, the Association also received complaints against vakils from individuals who did not wish to resort to the actions of the High Court; they requested the leaders to take whatever action was necessary. For example, Reddy Branson, an attorney, sent certain newspaper clippings to the Association 'bearing upon the conduct of H. Raghavendra Row', and it concluded that it was 'not justified in taking any action on the matter'.[12] Substantial information on allegations of professional misconduct, however, comes from the records of the local government, the High Court, and the law reports. A select example will suffice to show the important position that the Association occupied in determining the fate of innumerable vakils, even if they were not its own members.

In 1908, a series of correspondence took place between the Court of Wards, the Madras government, the High Court and the Vakils' Association; since the Ward had lost an important appeal in the High Court, it urged the local government to move the High Court to alter one of the rules of practice.[13] Briefly put, the Court of Wards sought the advice of 'two eminent vakils of long standing and wide practice in Madras',[14] on a suit connected with the minor zamindar of Palayapatti. When the sub-court in Madura decided the case against the zamindar, the Court of Wards, which administered the estate of the minor decided to appeal. The Ward sought the assistance of the two vakils. They declined to conduct the appeal on the grounds that they had already been engaged by the opposite party. Eventually, the Ward engaged some other vakils but lost the appeal. Defeated twice in litigation and denied services of the two vakils who had previously handled all its matters, the Ward began to raise 'considerable doubt whether [the] conduct of the vakils could not amount to a breach of professional etiquette'.[15]

The Court of Wards then wrote to the Vakils' Association explaining the conduct of the vakils and eliciting opinion from that body. V. C. Desikachary, the joint-secretary, confirmed the 'doubt'. He said that there were rules of practice applicable to practitioners on the Original Side of the High Court as well as those in the mufassal courts; he added that 'the principle of these rules [was] regarded by Vakils as also binding on them where a vakil has acted for a client without a vakalat'.[16] Yet the Association thought that it was not possible to frame rules similar to those of the English Bar Council. In England where the system of double-agency prevailed, an advocate did not directly come into contact with his client but only through a solicitor. In India, however, the vakils did 'the whole work of acting, appearing and pleading' for their clients; therefore, they 'would not feel bound by any rules framed by Vakils, but would be absolutely unhampered in the conduct of their litigation'.[17]

Subsequent correspondence between the Ward, the High Court and the Judicial Department shows that they all agreed that the two vakils had acted unprofessionally; however, the government had decided not to take further action in the matter since not all the vakils concerned were still alive.[18] This episode clearly describes the prominent role that the Association played by giving its opinions on questions of misconduct and by delegating members to attend the proceedings against vakils.[19] Acknowledging the High Court for the courtesy extended to the Vakils' Association, the *Madras Law Journal* observed:

> ... we hope this practice will be invariably followed to the advantage both of the Profession and the Judges themselves. On the one hand, the voice of the Association will be effective as the practitioner concerned will have the condemnation of his own brethren if he happens to deserve it and there will be less room for false sympathy; on the other hand, the Judges will have the strength of the support of a reasonable body like the Vakils' Association in its condemnation of professional [mis]conduct.[20]

Representation to Authorities

Even before there had been any formal association, under the leadership of V. Sadagopachari and R. Balaji Rao, vakils petitioned the judges in Madras and the Indian government in Calcutta for permission to practise on the Original Side or to retain that privilege as a special concession. Zealously guarding every advance they had made, vakils looked for other frontiers to explore. Unlike in the 1860s when their numerical strength was low, their professional status inferior to barristers, and their organization nonexistent, they now had a permanent association headed by leaders of experience, imagination and talent. Their knowledge of law or skill in court was in no way deficient compared to that of local European barristers.[21] Their newly-founded association enabled them to push forward their claims to positions of power, status and income. Professional equality and solidarity which they never before possessed was now theirs.

Through personal and collective representations, vakils obtained several privileges following the rebirth of the Association. Their rights to wear professional gowns, have their own rooms within the High Court, and occupy private chambers were only some of the more obvious gains within just a few years. Additional encouragement also came at the end of 1891 when one of their own members, S. Subramania Iyer, was appointed to a temporary vacancy at the High Court.[22] The first vakil ever to become the Government Pleader in 1888, Subramania Iyer's later appointment to the bench considerably increased the prestige of the vakil bar.[23] An editorial in *The Hindu* explained:

> There is not another Hindu gentleman in this Presidency in whom the community has greater confidence or who has more endeared himself to them not merely by his attainments and highly engaging manner but by the valuable service he has rendered to the public.[24]

The elevation of Subramania Iyer so excited his fellow vakils that they arranged for a special celebration in his honour.[25]

Actively pursuing higher positions of power became one noteworthy feature of vakils' activity in the 1890s. Hitherto, by bureaucratic conventions, all higher appointments had gone to barristers. Vakils had accepted whatever positions were thrown open to them, especially such lower judicial positions as district munsifs. With the appointment of a fellow-vakil to the High Court bench, vakils were encouraged to enlarge their sphere of professional opportunities. Using a conventional but effective method of exerting pressure on the rulers by persistently and determinedly submitting memorials and petitions, the Association made its grievances and demands known: more and younger members of the profession should be given encouragement. Both the Indian-owned press and legal journals frequently gave publicity to the vakils' cause, just as the English-owned newspapers and journals had done previously for the cause of barristers. One editorial in *The Hindu* remarked that 'all the ministerial appointments are held by the Barristers. . . . Why should they in preference to the sons of the soil who have passed through an University ordeal more difficult and comprehensive, be elevated to position of trust and honour?'[26]

Supporting the employment of younger vakils within the existing judicial machinery, the Association submitted petitions in 1895 and 1896. It requested the local government to consider the appointment of a junior law reporter and it sought one of the positions of deputy registrarship from the High Court.[27] Although its efforts failed, the Association was relentless. Recommencing the memorial campaign, it directly petitioned the Secretary of State for India in England. In February 1897, deteriorating health obliged J. H. Spring Branson, the Advocate General, to return home. News of his impending departure caused 'a considerable flutter of rumours that a local vakil might be appointed to act during his absence.[28] The new Acting Advocate General, as announced by the government, turned out to be none other than V. Bhashyam Iyengar.[29] No sooner had the news of his appointment been released than both barristers and vakils showered petitions upon the Secretary of State. Barristers in Madras demonstrated against the appointment, requesting that one of their own members should have that position. The Vakils' Association, in contrast, implored him to confirm Bhashyam Iyengar permanently in his new office.[30] Unmoved and unwilling to accede to either request, the Secretary of State appointed a London barrister, C. Arnold White, to the post.[31] This may have been due to pressure from local barristers who had political contacts.

In 1900, the Association sent yet another petition to London, railing against the actions of the local government in 'purposely' misinterpreting a rule regarding temporary appointments to the High Court. As early as 1895, a lengthy correspondence between London, Calcutta and Madras dealt with the appointment of a possible fifth permanent judge in the High Court.[32] The Association desired that a second member from their ranks should be appointed but their wish was unfulfilled.[33] On 9 February 1900, an editorial in *The Madras Mail* on 'The Acting High Court Judgeship' referred to a secret communication from the Secretary of State to the local government, disapproving 'the appointment of practising barristers or lawyers generally to acting judgeships of the High Court'.[34]

Aroused by the editorial, the Vakils' Association wasted no time in asking for a copy of the Dispatch from the government.[35] But the latter refused to comply by simply informing the former that it might be 'inexpedient' to furnish a copy.[36] Thwarted in its attempts, the Association finally decided to send yet another memorial to the Secretary of State; the Madras government forwarded this petition to the Government of India explaining its own position:

> The Secretary of State's orders related, it is true, to the appointment of barristers, but it appeared to the Governor that the reasons which

render objectionable the appointment of practising barristers to short acting appointment upon the High Court Bench apply with equal force in the case of practising vakils. Accordingly, in the absence of suitable native candidates, *outside the ranks of practising vakils*, His Excellency the Governor in Council selected for the appointment Mr Lewis Moore, of the Indian Civil Service, a District Judge of long standing, who had previously acted with credit as a Judge of the High Court.[37]

Nothing came of the memorial sent to the Secretary of State except subsequent public criticisms of his policy and the erroneous, if somewhat biased, interpretations of his correspondence by the local government.[38]

By 1900, the authorities realized that, in order to avoid any further open criticism, future selection for these two most important offices—the advocate generalship and the High Court judgeship—should be based on the aspirations and talents of vakils rather than on claims to any particular professional, ethnic or even religious affiliation. Although many lawyers sought special treatment from the government, it could not satisfy their desire and they naturally became disappointed; but in each battle for official 'loaves and fishes', the Association generally managed to stage a colourful show of professional strength which could not easily be matched by others.[39]

Advisory Role

By supervising the conduct of members and by making periodic representations to authorities, the Vakils' Association only endeavoured to protect its reputation and further the advancement of its members. Other professional or occupational bodies would have done much the same. What marked the legal profession as the most unique among the modern professions—medicine, clergy and army—was that only lawyers assumed the mediating role: between government and people, court and people, government and court, and finally, between litigants. Versed as they were in the language of the legislative process, in the obtuse enactments,[40] and in the intricate technicalities, procedures and traditions of courts, the roles that lawyers filled became indispensable. Involved in the source and art of conflict resolution, their primary task was to apply the law through the machinery of courts in order to satisfy the interests of clients.

Though the concept of representation, that is, mediation of one party for another, was not alien to traditional or pre-modern

India, the modern legal profession certainly was not indigenous. This is a rather controversial point. Opinions of scholars have been divided on whether or not there ever was a legal 'profession' in ancient India.[41] However, the Indian vakil should be seen as a synthesis of both Indian and Western cultures. With the advent of the Company rule, his knowledge was not simply restricted to the substantive religio-legal texts, but he became familiar with a body of enactments contained in various regulations, codes, statutes and procedures. Thus, the modern legal profession did not fully evolve out of the indigenous social or cultural developments but the British transplanted it as a logical consequence of their rule in India.[42]

Since the legal profession was largely a transplant on Indian soil, it became subject to a greater measure of bureaucratic control, whether legislative or judicial. From the beginning, various statutory regulations guided the profession and therefore, little room was left for any natural development of traditions or etiquette. Many factors contributed to the development of a distinct identity of the vakil profession: spread of English education, advent of modern universities in major cities, a new judicial system, and the gradual political awakening. These factors tended also to differentiate the leadership that vakils provided from that of the commercial and administrative elites.[43] As the vakil profession grew steadily in numbers and talent, and as the Association became more stable, unlike other shortlived political associations of the time, government agencies solicited its opinions. But there were also instances when it did not shy away from making known its unsolicited criticisms on nonprofessional matters.[44] A single but important example of how the Association took a momentous step in dealing with a crisis situation would, perhaps, suffice.

In January 1907, the split in the Indian National Congress led to the emergence of two radically opposing groups: the Moderates and the Extremists. Widespread anti-government activities, such as publishing scathing criticisms in the English and vernacular press and hurling open attacks on the rulers through organized political meetings became more frequent. One of the ringleaders of this anti-British campaign was Lala Lajpat Rai, the well known lawyer-turned-politician of Punjab.[45] He said that he would like to have the 'same influence' over imperial troops as he had over the masses. Alarmed by the implications of such utterances and their subsequent threat to the rubric of political stability, the rulers in Calcutta swiftly introduced a bill to prevent any possible mutiny in the armed forces. The bill had two parts: Part One dealt with various regulations against political meetings, while Part Two laid down rules for the 'prevention of the circulation among troops of documents likely to seduce them from their duty'.[46] The Government of India forwarded a copy to all local governments, eliciting their opinions. In no uncertain terms did the Government of India express its readiness to quell any outburst of sedition. The cover letter from the Officiating Secretary said:

> He [the Governor General] recognizes to the full the evils of executive interference with the liberty of the subject untrammelled by judicial control, but he regards as paramount the imperative duty that lies upon him to preserve the country from the horrors of bloodshed and anarchy which would be the inevitable consequences of a serious armed rising.[47]

Ironically, the Madras government did not sense the urgency of the tone of the letter and offered no criticisms; it merely assented to the intended measures of the bill. In contrast, both the press and other public bodies throughout India protested vehemently. A flood of telegrams from these institutions, including the Vakils' Association, reached the Government of India. At a meeting convened on 23 October 1907 the Association cabled its unanimous resolution to the Viceroy. The resolution read:

> Association respectfully but emphatically protests Seditious Meetings Bill. Hurried legislation Simla most objectionable. Time wholly insufficient Public discussion. Legislation unnecessary. Existing law amply sufficient. Bill sure to alienate even most moderate loyal subjects and create impression Government determined to crush freedom. If passing determined Association suggests necessity restricting legislation itself to disturbed areas limiting to one year.[48]

In spite of mounting protests, the bill was rushed through the Imperial legislature and became law in 1908.[49] Viewed from the top the Association's action was nothing but a dim voice in the midst of thunder which echoed in different parts of the land. Yet in the city of Madras, the resolution represented the distinct response of an elite professional body and as such it received publicity in the local press.[50] In the wake of the Montagu-Chelmsford Reforms of 1919, the Jallianwala Bagh massacre, and Gandhi's Non-Cooperation Movement, the Association had numerous opportunities to express its 'political' opinions.[51] By then, it functioned as one of the more influential bodies in Madras, whose interests and activities exceeded the limits of law courts. Frequently drawn into the arena of local and national politics, many of its members found themselves caught in a dilemma. Fulfilment of personal ambition and acquisition of political power clashed with ideals of personal sacrifice and public service for the cause of the country.

DISSENT AND UNITY

From the beginning, leaders of the Vakils' Association mainly came from the two major brahman communities: Iyer and Iyengar. Between 1889 and 1920, only two non-brahman vakils held the office of president.[52] Brahman vakils wielded so much influence in shaping the Association's character, that their predominance in the legal profession must be seen as a natural consequence of an ongoing social and historical process. A large number of brahmans (some from such far-away places as Malabar and Tinnevelly) had steadily migrated to the city in pursuit of education and employment.[53] The newcomers usually joined the most successful individuals and participated in local politics. In time, rivalry broke out between those whose families had 'originally' settled in Madras and the newcomers or 'aliens'. Such rivalry was especially fierce among vakils and other professionals, mainly government servants.[54]

The three important suburbs of Madras—Egmore, Mylapore and Triplicane—eventually came to be compared to Grey's Inn, Lincoln's Inn and Middle Temple because during the 1880s and 1890s some of the most prominent vakils lived in these suburbs. While C. Sankaran Nair was one such vakil in Egmore, V. Bhashyam Iyengar and S. Subramania Iyer were leaders in Mylapore; T. Rama Rao and M. O. Parthasarathi Iyengar resided in Triplicane.[55] From the beginning, those in Mylapore attempted to create a spirit of co-operation and inquiry among themselves. A band of about a dozen vakils regularly gathered in the home of Subramania Iyer to discuss important questions of law. P. S. Sivaswami Iyer described these meetings:

> I may pass on to mention another institution. I am applying too great a name when I call it an institution. It was quite an informal affair that we used to have in those early days, but it was certainly a most valuable gathering, and contributed not a little to the advancement of large

knowledge of those who joined. . . . What we did was, we discussed the important decision[s] in the 'Indian Law Reports'. The four series were distributed among four of the juniors. We had to read the cases, propose for discussion such decisions as were questionable. We did not trouble ourselves with any unimportant questions, or with decisions the soundness of which was not open to question. But any important questions, as to which there was a doubt as to the correctness of the decision, were brought up for discussion. The discussion, was, generally, most edifying and helped to clarify ideas, and very often many of the results of those discussions appeared in the Law Journal in one form or other. It was an institution of great value.[56]

This tendency of close interaction and mutual assistance among lawyers, especially brahmans, continued beyond the nineteenth century. Govind Swaminathan, a leading advocate in Madras, observed that during the 1920s and '30s, a coterie of brahman lawyers dominated both the Original and Appellate Sides. As inimitable 'schemers', these legal pundits used to discuss in anticipation the different aspects of a case in order to put on an able performance in court. Some leaders even received informal assistance from the clerical staff of the High Court, as most of the clerks had a common brahman background and thus willingly provided 'hints' on cases admitted in the court. A vakil of little substance or stature had small chance of breaking the monopoly of brahmans on the Original Side.[57]

Similarly, Swaminathan continued, 'in the Appellate Side they were all "fed" from the districts' where barristers and vakils had usually cultivated contacts. During the long vacation many lawyers visited their friends and relatives in the districts they originally came from. For example, vakils from Madura went to Madura, those from Trichy to Trichy and the Tanjoreans to Tanjore. Even criminal lawyers toured in the Ceded Districts where they met with members of the local bar and established friendship with them. Such personal contacts forged with local vakils, as Swaminathan put it, were based on a 'pattern of community and caste'. That is, a local Naidu vakil would support a fellow Naidu vakil in the High Court and a Gounder would only help a Gounder.[58]

Political Rivalry

At the turn of the century, the increased sharing of responsibility between Europeans and Indians in making government decisions created new tensions among rival groups. As the arena of encounters between different groups frequently shifted, conflicts occurred within the corporation, the university senate, the High Court, and the secretariat; these became centres of power, influence and 'wire-pulling'. Through intricate webs of patronage, appointments obviously went to those who commanded the strongest political connections and resources. Professional and political rivalries between those in Egmore and Mylapore affected their styles and ideologies in playing politics both in the city and outside, since no one conducted his business on altruism alone. While Mylaporeans gradually managed to gain greater representation and therefore greater influence in several bodies of the city, the influence of the Egmore stalwarts waned. A maxim of the time was: 'What Mylapore thinks about today, the Fort St. George puts into action tomorrow.'[59]

A few common threads bound these two groups together: they all had university degrees, came from higher communities, commanded wealth and popular support, and had membership in the Indian National Congress at one time or another. Between 1885 and 1907, the Congress essentially remained a movement of Western-educated, urban-based professionals who wished to steer the country towards greater political participation through constitutional processes rather than through agitations. Both groups provided leadership in the Congress and recognized each other's merit and talents in local politics.[60] Nonetheless, the advent of the Home Rule Movement in 1916—spearheaded by Annie Besant, who had many Mylapore brahman followers—and the certainty of reforms in the air, led the rival groups to redefine their ambitions of gaining more political power for themselves.[61] Interestingly, no longer were arguments based on competition between the 'traditional' versus 'new' elites or between original settlers and migrants. Instead, the new-fangled ideology which separated one group from the other was based on 'communalism'. Like a virus, this new approach to politics profoundly affected and altered the vocabulary, goals and strategies of politics in Madras for the next 20 years. The pontiffs of this new doctrine accused the brahmans, a small minority of the population, of conspiracy against other communities and of monopoly of positions in the government, especially in the revenue, education and judicial departments.[62] The leaders of communal politics, under the banner of the Justice Party, wanted a larger representation of jobs for their community members, both in the legislative council and in government services. The Justicites argued that they had been denied their rightful opportunities for a long time.

A Rival Association

The development of communal politics also affected the legal profession and, as a result, tensions among the High Court vakils, especially in the Association, flared up. Individuals like T. Ethiraja Mudaliar,[63] A. Ramaswami Mudaliar,[64] R. K. Shanmugam Chetty[65] and O. Thanikachalam Chetty[66] found that the heat generated by the communal controversy was advantageous to the professional aspirations of non-brahman vakils. They decided to form a separate Non-Brahman Lawyers' Association,[67] whose purpose would be to seek the appointment of their members to the High Court and recruitment 'in the higher grades of the Judicial Service'.[68] The chief function of this rival association was to pass resolutions and forward them to the government for implementation. The officials' normal response was to note, 'No action seems called for [and] the papers . . . [may] be recorded.'[69] The officers of the Non-Brahman Lawyers' Association soon realized the futility of their strategies and began to look elsewhere for opportunities. They used their clear majority in the local Legislative Council to exert pressure on the government to accept their subsequent resolutions.[70]

How did the Vakils' Association respond to the challenges posed by the Non-Brahman Lawyers' Association? What were the accomplishments of the rival association and why did it not survive? The emergence of the Non-Brahman Lawyers' Association, as one individual put it, was the result of the 'new urge' that began to sweep across the Presidency in 1916. Under the leadership of Dr T. M. Nair, the Justice movement strove for adequate representation for non-brahmans in politics, government services and professional organizations. Since the Vakils' Association had mainly been started, nurtured and controlled by brahmans, non-brahman vakils had had little or no opportunity to voice their aspirations. Such individuals thought that there was a legitimate need to address openly the interests of non-brahmans in the context of a well defined forum. The Non-Brahman Lawyers' Association served that purpose. Additional support, though indirect, also came from Sir C. Sankaran Nair, a judge of the High Court between 1908 and 1915.[71]

Attempted Compromise

From the outset, the Vakils' Association opposed the formation of a separate professional organization exclusively representing the interests of any community. At that time in 1920, S. Srinivasa Iyengar was both President of the Vakils' Association and Advocate General. In the latter capacity, he led the entire legal profession. From this platform, he decried all attempts at creating a separate association. He argued that any division of a professional association along caste lines would weaken the solidarity of the present Vakils' Association, which had *always* stood for the advancement of *all* vakils. As in the Tamil proverb, 'Guard the milk while being friendly to the cat,' he had a dual role to play. As President of the Vakils' Association he needed to represent that body in the midst of competing demands from other sections of the bar, but as Advocate General he could not support any one segment or community within the bar. Srinivasa Iyengar had to find a way to extricate himself from this awkward situation.

The solution was organization. For the first time in India, he planned an ambitious conference representing all advocates, attorneys, vakils, and all first and second grade pleaders in the Presidency. The proposal received enthusiastic support from the legal periodicals of Madras.[72] A 'Manifesto', published widely, and signed by 70 practitioners from the city as well as from outside, claimed:

> At a time when every interest, social, political or professional organizes itself for its own protection and advancement, continued indifference on the part of the Bar to its own interest is bound to tell seriously on its position and influence. A permanent unifying agency representative of the Mofussil as of the Madras Bar . . . has become indispensable.[73]

When the delegates met on 24 and 25 January 1920, more than 600 practitioners participated in the proceedings. This gathering clearly demonstrated Srinivasa Iyengar's skills in organization and leadership, and mobilized support for his ideas, however impractical or absurd they might originally have appeared. Leading Madras vakils read papers on special topics.[74] As President of the Conference, Srinivasa Iyengar delivered the keynote address in which he sought to justify this great gathering of all legal brethren. He remarked:

> [I]n the matter of legal reform, professional ethics and etiquette, the rules of practice of the courts, the position of juniors, training of

apprentices, legal education, law reporting, prevention and reduction of unnecessary litigation, protection of interests of the litigant public, provision of legal assistance to the poor, effacement of any sectarian feeling in the profession and the reorganization and unification of the bar, an association such as this would be of greatest help.[75]

The conference subsequently passed several resolutions both on general concerns of the profession and on particular gains to be made on behalf of the profession, especially with respect to direct recruitment to the bench from the bar.

While almost all barristers in Madras voluntarily kept themselves aloof from the conference, it is unclear whether anyone belonging to the Non-Brahman Lawyers' Association participated in the proceedings. Moreover, the topics that were dealt with in the presidential address and in special presentations were not new; many had already been under discussion in one form or another by various agencies interested in and connected with the judicial administration. What, then, was the real achievement of such an august gathering? It seems clear that Srinivasa Iyengar was concerned about preserving vakils' solidarity in the face of open rivalry from certain non-brahman city lawyers, most of whom belonged to the vakils' class. He used his position as Advocate General to demonstrate the collective strength of vakils and pleaders, both brahmans and non-brahmans.

The extant records show that the original resolution No. VII, which the conference passed on the recruitment policy, contained six separate clauses but a copy of the same resolution sent to the government had only five. The omitted clause read, 'that recruitment should take place without reference to communities and with sole regard to the higher interests of the administration of justice'.[76] An editorial in the *Madras Weekly Notes* commented that 'the Bar must set its own house in order before coveting fresh fields for the adventure, and we wish some of the local members directed their passionate zeal to find a practical solution to some of these problems rather than to provoke heated controversies on communal differences'.[77] It is obvious that the Lawyers' Conference opposed the emergence of a non-brahman professional faction because this grouping advocated that recruitments to judicial service be based on communal ratios. This explains why P. R. Ganapathi Iyer, the Secretary of the Lawyers' Conference, sent a copy of the original resolutions to the government, omitting sections that dealt with communal issues.

But, by so doing, he tried to down play the importance of communal feelings among the participants.

In spite of its 'big flourish of trumpets', the Madras Lawyers' Conference ultimately proved a dismal failure.[78] Within a year after the conference had met and elected its officers, the institution had virtually ceased to function. That it did not survive very long, despite its claims, suggests that either the conference idea was impractical or that its officers were least prepared to translate its resolutions into action. By merely forwarding the resolutions of the conference to the government, the leaders accomplished nothing. The authorities again noted 'no action seems necessary'.[79]

Several startling parallels between the two rival camps demand attention. First, both institutions were short-lived. Leaders as well as members of these bodies had more than one sustaining interest; therefore they were not able to devote enough time to keep the institutions alive. Second, the leaders' inability to fulfil what they promised also contributed to the ephemeral nature of these bodies. They could not influence the government's recruitment policy even for a short period because the authorities simply shelved their petitions. Third, the two bodies were mainly interested in securing appointments for their own members. In the case of the Non-Brahman Lawyers' Association, the officers thought that because of the preponderance of brahmans in the judicial service only lawyers belonging to the non-brahman communities should be selected.[80] However, the Madras Lawyers' Conference hoped that one-half of the district judges and one-third of the subordinate judges should be recruited directly from the ranks of the practising lawyers, including a number of non-brahmans. It preferred that the bar should have a greater proportion of appointments to district judgeships than the provincial service.[81] Thus, while the non-brahman vakils compared themselves to brahman vakils, the brahman vakils, who represented the Vakils' Association, competed with those ICS 'mandarins' in the judicial service. Ironically, with such formidable competition, both took refuge under the recommendations of the Public Service Commission Report.[82]

Yet there was one major difference that separated these two groups. As noted earlier, many non-brahman vakils managed to enter the legislative council, where members of their party had a clear majority over any other political or professional group. They managed to pass resolutions beneficial to themselves and their supporters. Gains they had been unable to earn for themselves through professional competition they now obtained through manipulation of political machinery. Leaders of the Vakils' Association, in contrast, continued to wait for patronage from the imperial rulers, in the time-honoured fashion of the past century. They wielded no political power to achieve their ambitions. The Vakils' Association, however, remained one of the most powerful and influential professional organizations. It had (and still has) the largest following and continued to play a significant role in bringing about reforms in the profession in the years that followed.

Part IV

PROTEST AND REFORM, 1921–1928

Chapter 8

WINDS OF CHANGE

> The very magnitude of our [vakils'] achievements and even our versatility have provoked jealousy and organised opposition. Should we surmount these obstacles, there yet remains the tremendous obligation that is ours of shaping the legislative and the political future of our land, at a time when each experiment is a trial of strength.
> —C. P. Ramaswami Iyer[1]

The Madras Lawyers' Conference, which S. Srinivasa Iyengar organized in January 1920, provided inspiration for other regional and provincial associations. Both High Court vakils and subordinate court pleaders realized how they, as special interest groups, could come together to discuss various professional concerns and to pass resolutions demanding privileges that had been denied them. They organized many conferences throughout India after 1920, especially in such important legal centres as Allahabad and Calcutta.[2] In the same year, European and Indian attorneys and barristers met in Nagpur to create national solidarity among their members.[3] Many leading practitioners who participated in these conferences were also members of the newly expanded Legislative Assembly which had been constituted under the Montagu-Chelmsford Reforms in 1919.

The political and administrative changes of the 1920s brought an additional blessing for the professional status of vakils. In the Indian Legislative Assembly, vakils far exceeded any other group.[4] From this vantage point, they introduced various resolutions passed during the professional conferences demanding certain definite and urgent reforms. The newly appointed Viceroy, Lord Reading, who had been himself the Chief Justice of England, sympathetically heard the grievances of Indian practitioners. When a deputation of vakils from different parts of India waited on him, he openly acknowledged that he had heard 'with admiration the work done in India by lawyers' and that the welcome address given by vakils 'was intended as a tribute from lawyers to a lawyer'.[5] Moreover, the Law Member in the Viceroy's Council was Tej Bahadur Sapru, one of the prominent vakils from the Allahabad High Court. Whereas S. Srinivasa Iyengar conceived the idea of a conference of both vakils and pleaders on a regional level, Sapru suggested the possibility of a gathering on a national scale. That he had been a guiding force behind this movement was an open secret, admitted by the president of the Allahabad Vakils' Association as well as by C. P. Ramaswami Iyer, who presided over the conference.[6]

Assured of support from fellow-vakils and of a favourable, if not enthusiastic, hearing by those in power, vakils in the Assembly set themselves to the task of demanding equal status with barristers. Their demand was twofold: the creation of an Indian bar, which alone should be responsible for formulating policies on legal education and a code of ethics, and the elimination of all distinctions between barristers and vakils. No doubt that vakils would have gradually achieved these objectives given the political climate of the country, but the procedure they adopted at this point in time, namely, seeking legislative intervention, incurred stiff opposition and 'stonewalling' from the barristers. If the vakil element had a broad support group in the Assembly—including some key European and Indian officials, professionals and fellow-vakils— the barrister element was formidable, even though it ultimately lost the battle. Prolonged Assembly debates and lengthy consultations between the Government of India, provincial governments and various professional bodies characterized 'the war of words' between these two equally powerful and influential groups, vakils and barristers.

REMOVAL OF SEX DISCRIMINATION

Until the end of the First World War, the profession of law throughout the world had been a male preserve. In the United States, for example, women had not been admitted into prestigious law schools. As Jerold S. Auerbach has pointed out, 'For women, that unique minority group that actually constitutes a majority of the population, sex discrimination was still rampant. For decades elite law schools had excluded them altogether.'[7] In England, the Inns of Court also kept them out until the passing of the Sex Disqualification (Removal) Act in 1919.[8] Nevertheless, certain women candidates, both in England and in India, publicly demanded the opening up of the legal profession.

The Pioneer Role of Cornelia Sorabji

Cornelia Sorabji, a member of the Parsi community, completed the requirements for the degree of Bachelor in Civil Law (B.C.L.) at Oxford in 1892, but did not receive her degree until 1922; she advocated that women should be allowed to study and pursue a career in law.[9] On her return to Bombay in 1894, she had many opportunities to establish a personal rapport with the *zenana* women of two Princely States—Indore and Kathiawar. Her many first-hand experiences with women, who ordinarily avoided any encounter with outsiders, convinced Sorabji of the potential for women equipped with legal training. Secluded, illiterate, and ignorant of their legal rights, *purdahnashins* (lit. 'sisters behind the curtain') had often been deprived of personal rights to property due to the malversations of their male agents and kinsmen. Both in Indore and in Kathiawar, Sorabji had occasion to deal with such complex questions under the Hindu Law as inheritance, succession, maintenance allowances and *stridhan* that affected the lives of these 'veiled women'.[10]

In 1902, Sorabji published a plea in *The London Times* under the title 'Purdahnashins in India', informing readers of the disabilities under which zenana women and widows suffered. They had not only lost valuable properties but had also been drawn into unnecessary litigation due to poor advice from 'fifth rate mukhtars or vakils'. She concluded:

> Oxford and Cambridge and sister Universities are producing women who do good, cool-headed [and] non-hysterical work. Let the best of such be secured for a position which would need tact and sympathy as well as legal knowledge and business capacity. I leave the question to the brains and hearts of a country which has responded nobly to a similar want in regard to medical aid for Purdahnashins.[11]

It is difficult to ascertain how readers in England responded to Sorabji's article. In India, however, the response was mixed. Some thought that her reasons for advocating more women legal advisors were either insufficient or impractical because implementation of her proposal would only serve a negligible percentage of the total litigant population. Resources, both in legal personnel and in monetary rewards, were too limited.[12] Yet others saw some redeeming value in the scheme and offered qualified support.

The editor of *The Law Digest and Recorder* of Madras, for example, dealt with this subject. Under the caption, 'Need for

Women Lawyers in India', his article was very progressive in terms of its objective treatment of the issue and its recommendations. Not only did he criticize the denial of women's entry into the legal profession because of their gender, but he also pointed out avenues in which they could provide valuable services. He showed that the institution of *purdah* was more scrupulously observed among women in the North. Women in the South, though equally illiterate and ignorant of their legal privileges, had more freedom to move about within their respective communities and localities. Also, they had a 'deep and abiding concern' in 50 per cent of all the suits brought to court, but their scheming relatives or greedy touts usually handled the legal matters. The appointment of qualified women legal practitioners could alleviate many of the anxieties that these women felt entrusting their cases to men. Indeed, much of the money wasted in litigation might be saved. 'We feel,' the editor concluded, 'that it is an injustice to deprive women of this privilege both on *a priori* grounds and on consideration of expediency.'[13]

In 1904, Sorabji became a Legal Advisor to the Court of Wards, for handling all cases related to purdahnashins in Bengal, Bihar, Orissa and Assam.[14] No other woman had ever been employed in that position in any part of the country. However, if executive attitudes and actions in appointing a woman appeared more consistent with changing times, the judges in Bengal were still conservative and resisted the change. A Full Bench decision of the High Court, delivered on 29 August 1916, refused the enrolment of Regina Guha as a pleader.[15] On 23 November 1921, when S. B. Hazra applied to the Patna High Court, her application also met with similar rejection. The Patna judges took the view that the reference to 'person' in Section 6 of the Legal Practitioners' Act of 1879 did not include 'a female'.[16] One of the judges even thought that the Indian legislature, by passing the Legal Practitioners' Act, 'was of opinion that it would be repugnant to ideas of decorum to permit women to join in what I may call the rough and tumble of the forensic arena'.[17]

A breakthrough occurred when the Allahabad High Court ignored the verdict of the Calcutta High Court and admitted Sorabji as a vakil on 24 August 1921.[18] The judges' decision in permitting women to practise law can be explained in the light of what had already taken place in England, where, as a result of the Sex Disqualification (Removal) Act in 1919, women candidates were now being admitted and were later called to the bar. The ripples of that legislation reached Indian shores and caused gradual changes in judicial attitudes.

The Legal Practitioners' (Women) Act of 1923

The Legislative Assembly in India, constituted under the Reforms of 1919, followed enactments resulting from the suffragist movement in England. In the course of debate on a suffragist resolution, the Assembly addressed the subsidiary question of enabling women to become legal practitioners. On 1 February 1922, Hari S. Gour introduced the historic amendment on this issue. A barrister and a champion of the cause of women,[19] he moved that the government should remove the sex bar which disqualified women from enrolment as law practitioners in Indian courts. Assured by Sir William Vincent, the Home Member, that the Government of India would elicit opinions from local governments, High Courts and professional bodies, Gour withdrew the amendment.

The Government of India sent a copy of the Assembly debates to the Madras government, soliciting the views of various local bodies and individuals.[20] The Advocate General, Vakils' Association, Women's Indian Association, and Women's Graduate Union each unanimously supported the enrolment of women as lawyers. The Bar Association, however, failed to express any view because it was not concerned with the issue. At that the Assistant Secretary remarked, 'It is doubtful if that body is now a living association.'[21] The High Court judges, however, were divided. Those who had long argued for the admission of women into the profession of law accepted the principle embodied in the Indian government's proposal; they thought that 'the time [had] come when these antiquated sex disabilities should be removed.' Justice C. Krishnan, for example, wrote: 'Surely we may follow the lead of the Inns of Court in this matter.'[22] The dissenting voices echoed the earlier cries that the proposal was still 'uncalled for and premature'.[23] Justice Coutts-Trotter, standing alone, thought that 'the proposal will affect so few women for so long a time to come, that it does not matter one way or another'.[24] Before forwarding these views to the central authorities, the local government also appended its own 'guarded' opinion:

> [While the Governor shares the] opinion of some of the Honourable Judges that for a long time to come there is not much chance of women

lawyers coming in in large numbers and while [he] does not think that the presidency has suffered for want of lady legal practitioners, . . . [the Governor] sees no harm in giving duly qualified women the right to be enrolled . . . and accordingly recommend [sic] the adoption of Dr Gour's suggestion.[25]

The opinions from other parts of the country also fell into the three categories of attitudes taken by the Madras High Court judges. The Home Member informed the legislators that a majority of those who had been consulted favoured the 'principle' and that on the whole there was no objection. Yet the Government of India remained unconvinced; nor did it wish to take a definite stand because, the Home Member said, the authorities had not had sufficient time to scrutinize the bill so as to amend the Legal Practitioners' Act of 1879. 'Our acceptance or our omission to oppose this first motion,' he said, 'is not to be treated afterwards as in any measure having committed us to any attitude towards this Bill at a subsequent stage, and we are at perfect liberty to take any attitude that we might think necessary later.'[26] That occasion never arose. The bill was passed on 21 March 1923 and became law on 2 April 1923.[27]

The Case of B. Ananda Bai

The enthusiasm that the legislators showed towards enabling women to practise law seems to have been largely superficial. The token appearance of women practitioners evoked both sentimentality and curiosity in the bar rooms.[28] The prospects for women in securing a decent position in the profession, which for decades had been competitive and male-dominated, were grim. The case of B. Ananda Bai in Madras serves to illustrate the kind of experiences that women could expect if they had hoped to pursue law as a career. As the first woman law graduate of the Madras University, Ananda Bai had the privilege of meeting with the governor, when she explained to him the 'peculiar position' in which she had found herself. She later sent him a letter, requesting a position in government service. As she put it, 'to set up practice in this city as a lawyer is hardly possible for a young woman taking into consideration the present . . . condition of social and professional life'.[29] She also claimed that the first women law graduates in other provinces had been offered 'responsible positions' in High Courts and similar arrangements might also be made in her case.

No sooner did Ananda Bai's petition reach the government than the latter undertook a nationwide investigation to ascertain how many women law graduates had been employed by provincial governments or High Courts. Replies from Bombay, Bengal, Burma, Bihar and Orissa, and the United Provinces showed that no woman law graduate had been provided with employment under any government. The letter from the Chief Secretary of Burma indicated that his government had appointed one woman in the provincial judicial service as an assistant registrar of the High Court. 'It is not proposed,' the letter added, 'to employ her as a Judge.'[30] The Madras government then contacted its own High Court, inviting remarks on her application. The Registrar, A. C. Happel, promptly communicated the judges' views, indicating that any 'responsible post' in the High Court would be normally filled by such individuals as had experience either in office administration or at the bar. Ananda Bai had neither. She would therefore have to wait until she had acquired that experience. 'If she finds it difficult,' the judges admonished, 'for various reasons . . . to acquire that experience, she should have considered that before she joined the legal profession.'[31] Accordingly, Ananda Bai was informed on 23 May 1928 of the inability of the government to comply with her request. By then, however, she had already become an apprentice to V. V. Srinivasa Iyengar and showed every intention of settling down to practise law in Madras.

Why did the judges take such a 'cold' attitude towards Ananda Bai's application? First, their letter shows the crucial connection between experience in government service and promotion, and between experience at the bar and judicial appointment. Not only were they loath to appoint a fresh law graduate, and a woman at that, to any non-clerical position in the High Court, but they also anticipated that such an appointment would arouse murmur from advocates, vakils and members of the subordinate judiciary. Second, the difficulties of apprentices and juniors in securing briefs kept mounting, despite the concerns that senior lawyers expressed to remedy the inequality. The judges' admonition that Ananda Bai should have considered the odds before joining the legal profession was no empty warning; it only reinforced the practical wisdom essential in choosing any career, particularly the profession of law. Finally, unemployment among educated young people was rampant during the 1920s. The Madras government, in 1927, appointed a special committee, under G. F. Paddison, to study this ever-increasing problem in the Presidency. A few years later, in 1935, the special committee headed by Sir Tej Bahadur Sapru found growing unemployment in the legal profession.[32] It was extremely unlikely, therefore, that a woman law candidate fresh from training could have succeeded against such obstacles.

The same year that Ananda Bai became an apprentice-at-law, Seeta Devadoss enrolled as an advocate in the Madras High Court. Having completed her legal education in England, she had been called to the bar at the Inner Temple.[33] Despite the common experience between Ananda Bai and Seeta Devadoss on account of their gender, the latter had better chances for success and a relatively easier start in the profession, because of her superior educational qualifications and contacts with those in power. Justice M. D. Devadoss was her father, whose personal or professional connections established prior to his elevation to the High Court were well-suited to the building of Seeta's career. However, no clear information about her career is obtainable.

Today about 425 female advocates practise in the Tamil Nadu Bar. They constitute just about four per cent of all practising lawyers. Recent research shows that this pattern is not very different in the rest of the country and that the profession is still a male-dominated one.[34]

DEBATES ON THE INDIAN BAR COUNCILS

Although the amendment to the Legal Practitioners' Act of 1879 was a progressive measure, the new law did not automatically remove every form of discrimination against women, nor did it dramatically alter the composition of the profession. Men with English or Indian training monopolized the courts and judicial appointments, while some of their leaders contributed significantly to the growth of law and judicial administration. Yet certain 'historical accidents' continued to institutionalize these two groups ('English' and 'Indian') as separate entities. Retention of separate identities resulted in professional rivalry and antagonism between these groups. Those who had been educated and had subsequently been called to the bar in England considered that they alone represented the best traditions of the profession. In contrast, their Indian counterparts could neither reflect the glory of any historic past nor feel unduly proud of their training (and 'old school' ties); they had to rely on their own sense of worth and actual accomplishments.

Vakils generally conceded that a few European barristers, who had formerly practised at the four major High Courts in the late nineteenth century, were superior. The Indian vakil profession was at that time in its infancy, but now vakils denounced any claims to intrinsic superiority of their own countrymen who had been trained and certified in England to practise law in India. It is important to bear this distinction in mind. Otherwise, it is possible to conclude erroneously that the heat generated in subsequent controversies was another manifestation of the traditional rivalry between barristers and vakils and that such antagonism was somehow inevitable. Indian vakils resented the special privileges accorded to Indian barristers, but now that vakils held a majority in the Assembly, they galvanized their numerical strength under one banner to seek redress for their grievances.

Protest in the Assembly

1. *Munshi Iswar Saran's Resolution.* Vakils constituted a clear majority in the Legislative Assembly, which met in New Delhi for the first time in 1921. With skill and speed, they introduced various resolutions aimed at the establishment of an Indian bar and the removal of all distinctions, whether of status or of appointment. The distinctions against which vakils crusaded had developed over many years on account of powers conferred upon the High Courts under the charter. As autonomous institutions, each possessed enormous powers over the provincial judicial machinery. Occasionally, one court might consult with others on matters of mutual interest, but no court was ever bound by any rules of practice, precedent or etiquette followed by the rest.

When, in February 1921, Saran introduced his resolution in the Assembly, privileges accorded to vakils throughout the country by High Courts were anything but uniform. In some instances, the freedom of vakils had been curtailed by the rules of some High Courts.[35] The report of the All-India Bar Committee summed up vakils' grievances when it said that they 'could count amongst their number many very eminent lawyers and judges' but 'resented what they regarded as inferior status of vakils'.[36] It spelled out seven different handicaps under which vakils struggled. First, the Calcutta

High Court totally excluded vakils from the Original Side. Second, in Bombay vakils had to pass an additional examination to qualify for enrolment as advocates on the Original Side. Third, in Madras vakils did not have the privilege of acting or pleading in the insolvency court. Fourth, invidious distinctions between advocates and vakils tended to undermine the quality, ability and performance of vakils in all High Courts. Fifth, the arrogance of even the most inexperienced advocate against the most able vakil brought insult to the profession.[37] Sixth, every High Court required vakils to file vakalatnamahs for appeals, while exempting advocates from such requirements. Finally, Calcutta High Court maintained distinctions in professional robes between barristers and vakils. Such restrictions or disabilities 'offended the self-respect of the Vakils'[38] even though some of their own members had risen to positions of power and had been instrumental in the political transformation of the country.

Public statements from legal experts in England and India also added weight to vakils' arguments.[39] Indeed, it is possible that Viscount Haldane might have suggested the creation of an autonomous Indian bar because of political concerns rather than professional interest in Indian lawyers; many who had flocked to the Inns of Court from India had subsequently engaged in anti-British activities. Support for vakils also came from an altogether unexpected quarter. Veteran barrister Eardley Norton, whose law practice in Madras and Calcutta spanned over 40 years, openly favoured removing the disabilities under which vakils carried out their duties. Norton seemed to have undergone a real change of attitude: from being a crusader in Madras for upholding the status quo of barristers, to that of a sympathetic legislator at Delhi, who publicly acknowledged the ability of vakils.[40]

Saran's resolution, however, did not go unopposed. Nand Lal, who represented the interests of barristers, criticized it as impractical and likely to create further 'disunion, conflict and differences' between the two branches of lawyers.[41] J. B. Bryant, another member in the Assembly, also rebutted the resolution, suggesting that it should be thrown out insofar as it anticipated the transfer of jurisdiction over legal practitioners from the High Courts to a council comprised of legal practitioners.[42]

Tej Bahadur Sapru, the Law Member, intervened. Though a vakil who had risen to his present position, he took a neutral attitude because of his new role. He acknowledged that long before the vakil profession had attained sophistication and recognition, members of the English bar had contributed significantly to the growth of constitutionalism in India and that British lawyers had fought for India's freedom. Sapru complimented members of the English bar for introducing their traditions into India, for their sense of duty to their clients, for their independence, and for their maintenance of high professional standards. Yet Sapru acknowledged that vakils throughout India had long been obliged to practise under severe disadvantages. The absence of an organization solely responsible for formulating and enforcing rules of professional etiquette had deprived vakils of the means for developing their own traditions. Sapru conceded that the anxieties felt by Saran and his supporters were justified.[43] He cautioned, however, that any changes in the existing conditions of the profession would involve a thorough overhauling of the legal machinery and that the Assembly should not be hasty in bringing about such changes without first consulting a 'smaller body of experts'. On behalf of the Indian government, he promised to 'be guided by the expression of definite constructive public opinion'[44] from local governments, High Courts and numerous professional bodies. On this assurance, Saran withdrew his resolution.

In May 1921, the Indian government sought recommendations from the provinces for the creation of an Indian bar.[45] After protracted consultations, the information so gathered eventually found its way to New Delhi. But vakils were impatient; they realized that the wheels of the administration moved rather slowly and exerted more pressure by prodding the select committee to hasten deliberations on the recommendations received from the provinces. Some vakils even engaged in continual and sustained debates in the Assembly by successfully manoeuvring the political machinery to introduce two more bills. While K. C. Neogy's bill dealt with the question of removing all distinctions between barristers and vakils in appointments to the High Court bench, T. Rangachariar's bill anticipated the creation of provincial bar councils.

2. *K. C. Neogy's Bill*. This bill, introduced in the Assembly in September 1922, sought to amend the Legal Practitioners' Act of 1879, under which the High Courts had formulated various rules of admission and privileges of barristers and vakils. Its aims were to admit vakils on the Original Side of Bombay and Calcutta High

Courts and to abolish barristers' precedence over vakils. Although the High Courts had powers to alter or even annul any rules that had been in force, Neogy argued, they were reluctant to do so. No body other than the central legislature had powers to effect a uniform practice in India. Gour opposed Neogy's efforts on the grounds that the bill was a piece-meal legislation and that the question of removing *all* distinctions was interconnected with the broader question of the creation of an All-India bar. Although the Law Member silenced Gour's arguments by permitting the bill for further discussion, the subsequent tactical procedures of the Indian government for gathering information delayed any immediate action on Neogy's bill.

3. *T. Rangachariar's Bill*. Two years after Saran had introduced his resolution, the authorities hesitated to take any action although a 'large mass of opinion' had been collected. Therefore, Rangachariar submitted his own bill on the question of an 'Indian Bar for India'. An energetic campaigner for reform, his bill embodied three propositions. First, the legislature should expedite the founding of an Indian bar without allowing the provincial High Courts to frame rules for its operation because the creation of that body was essentially a national question. Second, in view of the country's complex administrative system and the impending devolution of more autonomy to the provinces, the creation of separate provincial bar councils was more practical than a pan-Indian body. Third, these councils should have jurisdiction over all matters of qualification and admission, while the High Courts retained authority on questions of professional discipline.[46] Rangachariar's speech reflected his determination: 'I want an Indian Bar, an autonomous Bar, an independent Bar, and we ought not to depend upon other countries for recruiting to the Bar of this country.'[47]

The government saw that it must act at once because Rangachariar's bill had received wide support of barristers and vakils in the Assembly. By attending to the proposed legislation, it could avoid criticisms from politicians, but circumstances stood in the way. As adjournment was imminent, neither the Assembly nor the authorities had time for gathering further opinions from the provinces. Instead, the Home Member, Sir Malcolm Hailey, proposed a different course of action:

> [T]he whole question is one which has been engaging the anxious consideration of the Governor General . . . for some time. The opinions

on this difficult subject vary widely in different parts of India; the interests engaged are diverse; and any change which would involve an infringement of the long standing rights and jurisdiction of the High Courts, would be momentous and could only be taken with the greatest hesitation. . . . We believe that the *only solution* is to appoint an authoritative committee. . . . I say at once that it is our desire to get the whole of the legislation put on one side until we have received the Report of the Committee to which I refer, which will, we hope, deal in a comprehensive manner with the whole question, and if legislation is to be undertaken at all, will enable it to be framed in a more satisfactory form and spirit than now appears possible.[48]

The government subsequently appointed a special committee, commonly known as Chamier's Committee, dismissing the two previous bodies constituted to study the proposals of both Saran and Neogy.[49]

Chamier's Committee Report

On 24 November 1923 this Committee met in Bombay. It consisted of four barristers, three vakils (and pleaders), two civilians, and one attorney.[50] The members investigated the feasibility of creating an Indian bar, on either a national or a provincial basis, with particular reference to its constitution, statutory recognition, function and authority, and its position *vis-à-vis* High Courts.[51] They also studied the implications of removing the distinctions between barristers and vakils enforced by statute or practice.[52] An informed correspondent wrote in *The Times*: 'A solution that is generally acceptable will be hard to find. But it may be anticipated with every confidence that an existing anomaly in the practice of the Courts will not survive the results of the investigation.'[53]

After visiting several places, ascertaining the views of judges, lawyers and law officers of governments, Chamier's Committee submitted its findings and recommendations on 1 February 1924.[54] Its report consisted of three major sections: a description of the organization of the bar in India, a breakdown of different categories of lawyers, and the proposals for the establishment of provincial bar councils. Chamier's Committee suggested a total reorganization of the profession by enrolling all groups under one nomenclature, namely 'advocate', who would be entitled to practise in the High Court and in any subordinate court of the province. Moreover, all distinctions between barristers and vakils should be eliminated so that they as advocates might have the same privileges.

In Bombay and Calcutta High Courts, however, where 'special conditions' had been maintained on the Original Side, the distinction between advocates entitled to practise on the Original Side and those who did not should be retained.[55]

The committee also advised the establishment of provincial bar councils, instead of a national body, under the supervision of their respective High Courts in matters of discipline:

> The constitution of the Bar Councils of any kind is an experiment the value of which can only be tested by experience, and it is in our opinion unthinkable that the first flight should carry the Bar in India to a position which the English Bar with centuries of traditions and experience in self-management, has never yet aspired to.[56]

Finally, as far as the Madras High Court was concerned, equal opportunities should be given to barristers (or advocates) and vakils on the Original Side. Should an advocate prefer to assume the position of a vakil who alone could perform all three functions—acting, appearing and pleading—he should be so entitled. If a vakil wished to assume the position of an advocate, with privileges of appearing and pleading only, he should be permitted likewise. Also, the anomaly of vakils appearing on the Original Side in all matters except in insolvency should be abolished. The 'curious inequality' of awarding fees for services rendered by attorneys and vakils on the Original Side should also be removed.[57]

For the most part, the committee members were unanimous in their evaluation of the profession and in their recommendations for the inauguration of provincial bodies. On the question of either retaining or setting aside the system of double-agency, they disagreed. Separate memoranda appended to the report by Justice Coutts-Trotter and Rangachariar brought out their differences, although they both came from Madras. Justice Coutts-Trotter favoured the double-agency but his arguments for its retention seemed to lose force because of the coexistence of two separate systems in Madras High Court. Even though the double-agency had been in vogue for many years, it had never been totally adhered to, and the clients always had the choice of employing either an advocate, instructed by an attorney, or a vakil unaided. This arrangement satisfied the judges who frequently acknowledged that vakils had executed their duties competently on the Original Side. Without the double-agency, the judges knew that the court conducted its business and that practitioners fulfilled their obligations to clients and to court.[58] For a judge to allow the coexistence of both the dual system and the 'vakil system' in his own court but recommend the double-agency for others appeared hypocritical.[59]

Indian Bar Councils' Act of 1926

The Indian government sent copies of the report to all provincial governments, requesting their views.[60] Sir Alexander Muddiman, the Home Member, observed that the replies 'took a very long time in coming in'.[61] The government then prepared a bill based on suggestions of the bar committee and on opinions garnered from different professional bodies throughout the country. A select committee reviewed the bill in order to place it before the Assembly.[62] When on 26 August 1926 the bill formally reached the floor a heated debate ensued between vakils and barristers, each supported by non-officials or other professionals. Throughout the debate, members of the two groups made personal jibes at each other. Barristers demanded the recirculation of the bill by complaining that it was 'materially different' from the original draft which had been introduced in the Assembly in 1925. They also argued that the practice of recognizing seniority should be continued even after the bill had become law and all the practitioners were enrolled as advocates. The privilege of seniority, as Gour described it, was 'the most valued of all privileges'. Seniority carried with it 'a certain professional and social status' and gave an advocate 'the right of preaudience in a court of law'.[63] Regardless of one's experience or age, an individual who had been called to the bar in England led a senior and most experienced vakil in court because of the established custom in India that a barrister must precede a vakil. While many flaunted their 'superior' education and the historic traditions of the Inns which they had attended, some actually claimed that they had also imbibed the bar traditions while in England. It proved difficult to contradict such assertions.

Ironically, no barrister in the Assembly cared to enumerate what these traditions were, how carefully they were followed 'in India' or how many Indian barristers abided by them. 'After all, the tradition of the English Bar,' retorted S. K. Datta recalling his own experiences in England, 'was not enshrined in merely attending lectures, passing examinations and eating a stipulated number of dinners.' Datta further observed, 'Where was this tradition specifically cultivated? The tradition was in Chamber practice under an English barrister. . . . It was easy for Australian or Canadian students to obtain this privilege, but very difficult for Indian students though members of an English Inn to obtain this specific experience.'[64]

Another strategy that barristers employed was to insist that the High Courts alone should have the responsibility for framing rules of admission and the bar councils should merely serve as advisory bodies. The barrister-lobby maintained that it would be 'disastrous if the High Court were to surrender its jurisdiction as regards this matter'. Not only on matters of admission but also on questions of discipline, no encroachment should be made on the powers of the High Courts. In spite of their strategies, barristers soon realized that they were fighting a losing battle. Vakils far outnumbered barristers in the Assembly. One barrister, K. Ahmad, in his exasperation could hardly resist the temptation to caricature the Assembly as the 'Vakil Raj'.[65]

By demanding its recirculation if barristers sought to thwart the objectives of the bill, vakils fought just as vehemently to accomplish their opposite goals; and they received support from government authorities. Indeed, the Indian government was set on pushing the bill through the legislative machinery as quickly as possible. Vakils castigated barristers for perpetuating inequalities which they described as a professional 'caste system'. Barristers, they charged, expected special treatment even at this critical juncture when the entire profession was at the threshhold of reorganization and unification. Except for the High Courts of Bombay and Calcutta, where stringent rules had long been enforced against the incursion of vakils on the Original Side, no other court in the country so zealously protected the interests of barristers. Vakils objected to all such obnoxious rules. One vakil, Rangachariar, labelled the Calcutta High Court as 'a stronghold of prejudice in favour of barristers' who were conniving to kill the bill.[66]

Sir Alexander Muddiman informed barristers that the government was intent upon passing the legislation, despite their eleventh-hour clamour for recirculation. Since the country was gearing itself for the third Assembly election, the rulers had other pressing issues on the agenda. Yet he assured barristers of his willingness to eliminate certain parts of the bill dealing with the question of seniority and preaudience; these issues would be later introduced in the Assembly as separate amendments. Sir Alexander reminded the Assembly members that the bill was but a step in the right direction towards the creation of a united Indian bar.[67]

Despite its commitment to pass the bill, or its sympathy with vakils' grievances, the Indian government carefully preserved the existing structures of power, hierarchy and authority. Members of the Viceroy's Executive Council understood the soundness of maintaining equilibrium in the judicial administration.[68] They did not wish to engender a constitutional crisis between themselves and the judges, even though this legislation was consistent with the changing political trends and had received support from the majority in the Assembly; they could not invest the bar councils with any jurisdiction in matters of admission or discipline. Furthermore, under the Letters Patent and the Legal Practitioners' Act, the High Courts had exclusive powers over all lawyers and to transfer those powers to the bar councils would undermine the judicial prerogatives that had been established for well over sixty years.[69] The government merely empowered the bar council to undertake enquiries that the High Court had directed to it. Final authority, however, remained unchanged.[70]

The High Courts of Bombay and Calcutta, last of all, retained whatever rules they had enforced on the Original Side, particularly on double-agency. This system, non-existent in Madras, did perpetuate the interests and status of advocates and attorneys.[71] Provincial bar councils in these cities could only play an advisory role. It follows, therefore, that the vakils got less than they demanded. On 9 September 1926 the Viceroy approved the Indian Bar Councils' Act containing four major sections: constitution of bar councils, admission and enrolment of advocates, professional misconduct, and miscellaneous provisions.

Results of the Act

Apart from these major considerations that influenced the actions of the rulers, vakils did gain certain concessions. First, differences in the nomenclature among practitioners, either advocates or vakils, came to an end. Vakils automatically became advocates by paying a nominal fee of Rs 10 and a change in designation also removed their alleged inferior status.[72] Second, the Act modified the rules of seniority to the satisfaction of vakils.[73] Henceforth, seniority would be determined either from the date of a person's call to the bar in

England or from the date of a person's admission to the High Court. Third, every advocate, whether he had been an advocate or vakil, had to file a vakalatnamah whenever he acted for his client on the Appellate Side. Fourth, a special Bench of the Madras High Court decided the eligibility of all advocates to act and plead in the original insolvency court.[74] Finally, the Madras High Court cancelled the two different methods of awarding costs. One method benefited attorneys by awarding cost based on the total number of items included in the Attorney's Bill of Costs, while a second method determined the cost solely on the basis of the value of a suit. The Chief Justice, V. M. Coutts-Trotter, who had so dutifully defended the double-agency, realized that the two entirely different methods of dealing with litigation costs on the Original Side were unnecessary:

> With regard to *ad valorem* fee I can see no possible object in retaining it. On the Original Side of the Madras High Court it is in nine cases out of ten *a mere sham*; in the tenth it may operate to put money into the practitioner's pocket which he has not earned by the work done on the case. In all cases it inflicts in practice a gross injustice on one or other of the litigant[s].[75]

This 'antiquated rule', as Justice H. O. C. Beasley described it, had been in force for well over 120 years in Madras.[76] Every practitioner who had successfully contested in a suit could now bring in his own Bill of Costs to be taxed by an officer of the court.

THE FIRST MADRAS BAR COUNCIL

Although V. Bhashyam Iyengar had proposed the founding of a law institute as early as 1893, it failed to gain any ground during the next 35 years. During this time, the Vakils' Association acted as a professional watch-dog but this function neither had a constitutional backing nor a wide recognition. Still barristers and attorneys stood outside of its influence and non-member vakils refused to accept its rules. The Indian Bar Councils' Act, however, unified all who had been enrolled in the High Court.

Attitudes Towards Its Formation

1. *The High Court Judges*. The reasons why the Indian government was chary of interfering with the High Court's jurisdiction over the legal profession have already become clear. The judges strongly

disapproved of the transfer of disciplinary power that they had enjoyed for so long. The Madras government understood their position but remained adamant about investing the bar council with plenary powers to deal with the misconduct of its members. This clash between provincial executive and judiciary branches remained unresolved. On three different occasions the Madras government, at the behest of the Government of India, solicited opinion from the High Court on various resolutions introduced in the Assembly.[77] Each time, the judges disapproved the formation of an autonomous institution and strongly protested against transferring their powers to it.[78] For example, even after the publication of Chamier's Committee report, the judges took a negative attitude towards the efficacy of provincial bar councils. F. G. Butler, the High Court Registrar, conveyed their general view to the local government:

> The proposal to form Bar Councils does not commend itself to the . . . Judges as a body. The fitness of such councils to exercise disciplinary action over the members of the Bar is doubted by some of the Judges and it would therefore seem advisable to defer their formation for the present.[79]

Some of the judges who supported the recommendation of the Indian bar committee had themselves been vakils; they sided with their former colleagues in the profession rather than with their colleagues on the bench.[80]

In 1926, the High Court again received for review the Indian Bar Councils' Bill. While it guaranteed the judges their retention of disciplinary jurisdiction, it also enjoined them to refer cases of professional misconduct to the bar councils. The judges could and did accept this provision. Most of them considered the bill 'entirely satisfactory', but some alluded to the political climate which might 'choke' its implementation. Justices Devadoss and Odgers both thought that there was no need for the proposed bill. They said, 'Bar Councils for India are apt to be swayed by political, social and other influences which have little weight in the Inns of Court in England.'[81] In reality, the judges were generally reluctant to share their power with a body of practitioners who for well over 65 years never had a voice in shaping the course of their own profession.

2. *Barristers and Vakils*. During the 1920s the Bar Association was significantly smaller than the Vakils' Association and was never able to generate or rally any widespread protest against the

reforms that vakils had been seeking. In fact, it failed even to make its opinions known when the government approached it for information. On two different occasions, in 1921 and 1924, the Association failed to forward any views on resolutions dealing with the creation of an Indian bar and the admission of women to the legal profession. The opinions that it did submit, either on the report of the bar committee or on the bill to constitute provincial bar councils, merely dealt with special provisions to be sanctioned on behalf of its representatives, most of whom were barristers.[82]

In contrast, the Vakils' Association was by far the largest single professional organization, pursuing its interests more actively than either the Bar Association or the Attorneys' Association. Through numerous resolutions, petitions and memoranda, vakils continually strove to publicize their own grievances and agitation. Former members P. S. Sivaswami Iyer, T. V. Seshagiri Iyer and T. Rangachariar, all of whom had found a seat in the Assembly, supported the demands of their colleagues. Moreover, Rangachariar, who engineered the original bar councils' bill, boldly disagreed with Justice Coutts-Trotter against retaining the double-agency and went on record with a dissenting minute to the report of the bar committee. His 1923 speech in the Assembly signalled his determination to create an autonomous, independent Indian body that would deal with all professional matters. It is hardly surprising that, when the first election to the Madras Bar Council took place in 1928, former vakils alone had a clear majority in that body.

3. *The Madras Government*. Unlike the High Court, the government consisted of heterogeneous elements with particular expertise and skills essential for its innumerable daily functions. The judicial administration, in this sense, formed only part of the total role of the rulers; yet they commanded resources that enabled them to employ the best individuals, who as heads of departments would advise the governor; he often accepted their opinions unquestioningly.[83] Both the advocate general and the government pleader, for instance, regularly advised the government on almost every question of law and represented it in court. Moreover, the law member of the Governor's Council possessed even greater powers to ensure that sound laws were passed and enforced in the Presidency.

Between 1921 and 1930, the government generally appointed vakils as law officers and the only exception was C. Madhavan

Nair, who had been called to the bar in England.[84] As law officers, these former vakils supported the reforms that their fellow members were demanding and in many ways helped to mould the government's attitude. Since the governor commonly accepted the recommendations of the law member or the advocate general, these individuals' views ultimately became those of the government. For example, the government's opinion on Saran's resolution reflected the positions of Sir K. Srinivasa Iyengar and C. P. Ramaswami Iyer, Law Member and Advocate General, respectively.[85] Not only did the governor unequivocally recommend the formation of an Indian bar but he also wanted the power to exercise disciplinary control to be bestowed on that body. This recommendation frustrated the judges, who thought that the Indian bar councils should only be vested with certain limited powers or, better still, no changes should be made in the existing arrangements for the indefinite future.

C. P. Ramaswami Iyer, as the Law Member in 1924, articulated government views on publication of the Chamier's Committee report. Although the judges offered adverse comments on the constitution of provincial bar councils, he wrote 'I am not in agreement with the High Court as a body when it deprecates the formation of Bar Councils and I concur with the views of Sir K. Srinivasa Iyengar in this matter and the previous position of this government.'[86] Thus, the government's responses, whether under the governorship of Willingdon or Goshen, to questions of reform within the legal profession reflected the views of law members, who as former vakils gave weight to the arguments and aspirations of fellow-vakils.

Creation of the Madras Bar Council

The Indian government, by passing the Bar Councils' Act, hoped to achieve a compromise between those who opposed the formation of such bodies and those who demanded them. While the Act reserved for the judges the powers relating to matters of discipline, and while it even made the High Courts responsible for formulating initial guidelines for the constitution of bar councils, the provincial bar councils, under the Act, also received authority to decide matters of professional qualification, admission and etiquette. The Act became a statute on 9 September 1926, but its implementation took more than 21 months. Judges did not know how to formulate rules for a body whose right to exist they generally doubted. No other similar agency existed in India, they claimed, to which they could even refer. The Madras High Court finally consulted other High Courts to ascertain what rules, if any, they had framed. Replies from Allahabad, Bombay, Calcutta, Lahore and Patna were disappointing; they too, after all, faced the same dilemma. Pressure from the central government to create the local bar council at the earliest date possible and judges' anxiety over inordinate delays eventually forced them to seek help from outside India.

The judges obtained a copy of the regulations and by-laws from the General Council of the Bar in England, which provided a framework for making rules applicable to the Madras Bar Council. The rules passed on 4 August 1928 dealt with several aspects: constitution of the council; its powers; qualifications of contestants; and procedures for conducting elections, election of officers, and disbursement of funds in meeting election expenses.[87] Chief Justice V. M. Coutts-Trotter later admitted that these rules had been framed 'more or less in the dark', and expressed willingness to reconsider them should difficulties arise.[88]

No sooner had the High Court announced the introduction of the Indian Bar Councils' Act in Madras, effective from 16 July 1928, than many vakils and attorneys began to enrol as advocates. Initially there was confusion among vakils in lower courts. They thought that should they fail to become advocates under the new rules they might lose that privilege. They feared that the Act, instead of achieving a unification of the bar, might divide lawyers into two camps: those who became 'advocates of the High Court' and those who remained 'vakils of the High Court'. Thus, the latter might lose their privileges and status because the Bar Councils' Act offered no statutory guarantee for retaining their former designation.

A long correspondence took place in the local dailies. Vakils from the mufassal eventually received assurance from the judges that there would be no penalty if an individual chose to remain a vakil. Even though a vakil would not be able to practise before the High Court he would not suffer a loss. But the sooner a vakil enrolled himself as an advocate, the more assured would be his seniority among the new crop of advocates.[89] Approximately 1850 former vakils became advocates, of whom about 850 came from the districts while the rest came from the city.[90]

First Election to the Bar Council

The enrolment of vakils as advocates was less eventful than holding the first election to the Madras Bar Council. As accredited members of the bar, 15 individuals constituted that body: ten to be elected, four to be appointed by judges, and one to be the advocate general functioning as ex-officio chairman.[91] The Bar Councils' Act originally authorized the judges to send two of their own representatives, but they relinquished this privilege to maintain a balance among different groups represented within the profession.[92] Therefore, they nominated four advocates; but for elected positions there was a great scramble.

Editorials in the *Madras Weekly Notes* show that the contestants viewed the election as a ticket to political office. Some advocates even toured the districts, making themselves known to the local bar members, while others canvassed votes through door-to-door visits in the city or through imaginative advertisement campaigns. Still others viewed the election through particular professional or communal spectacles. The real contest of strength, however, was between urban advocates and those from the districts. The latter even staged a conference in Tanjore to select their own candidates who would represent their interests in the bar council. Country advocates had long resented their city cousins who enjoyed many official rewards. In the words of one speaker:

> The need for a separate organization would not at all have been felt if the Madras members were taking any interest towards the Mofussil Bar. The experience of the past had shown that the Madras Bar had that . . . human element which had the merit of having the best merit suppressed.[93]

The city advocates had their own supporters as well; they argued that because a large number of advocates lived in Madras and practised before the High Court, the Bar Council 'in the main should consist of members from the City'. They believed that their own traditions resulting from long association with English barristers and their proven experience in the High Court would enable them to uphold the independence, rights and privileges of the bar and to enforce a high sense of duty among the members.[94] Moreover, they held, unification of the profession would be possible only when voters willingly buried their territorial, linguistic and communal differences.

180   *The Legal Profession in Colonial South India*

The election took place on 22 September 1928. Fifty-four people—12 from the districts and 42 from the city—contested for the ten seats. Table 7 clearly demonstrates, however, the strong influence and reputation of the urban advocates in spite of loud protests from their competitors in the districts.[95]

TABLE 7
Members of the First Madras Bar Council

No.	Name	No. of Votes
1.	S. Srinivasa Iyengar	1021
2.	T. R. Ramachandra Iyer	897
3.	T. R. Venkatarama Sastri	883
4.	Alladi Krishnaswami Iyer	736
5.	T. Rangachariar	736
6.	K. Bhashyam Iyengar	705
7.	K. P. M. Menon	653
8.	P. Venkataramana Rao	573
9.	K. S. Krishnaswami Iyengar	557
10.	S. Duraiswami Iyer	516

By virtue of his position, Advocate General C. V. Ananthakrishna Iyer became the Chairman, and the judges nominated Nugent Grant, Muhammad Ibrahim Sahib, C. Venkatachalam Pantulu and T. A. Ramalingam Chettiar. Together, these 15 advocates constituted the members of the first bar council. But it had no brief and functioned primarily as an advisory body. Yet the table above is revealing. Brahmans constituted two-thirds of the entire council, despite the efforts of some non-brahman lawyers in 1920 to organize a rival association based on communal interests. The brahmans remained the leaders of the bar, while some non-brahman vakils, along with their political allies, controlled the city corporation and the legislative council. Moreover, all elected members had previously been closely connected with the Vakils' Association: two had been presidents, three secretaries, two honorary librarians, and the rest managing committee members.[96] All ten elected members came from Madras and no one from the districts was elected. This suggests that city advocates were by far the most influential, powerful and successful practitioners in the Presidency. Their numerical strength, forum of practice, personal and professional skills, participation in local and national issues, and most of all, their long affiliation with the Vakils' Association, which they could harness to their electoral aspirations, were factors which criss-crossed in enhancing personal prestige and capacity for leadership.

On 9 October 1928 members of the Bar Council assembled for the first time as a forum. Chief Justice V. M. Coutts-Trotter addressed the gathering and promised every co-operation from the bench 'to help the Bar Council in its duties' during its initial years. 'The most responsible and arduous parts,' he admonished, 'will be those connected with disciplinary jurisdiction over the profession, and which are really devolved upon you from the Judges,'[97] but the judges still retained ultimate authority in deciding whether a lawyer found guilty should be removed from the rolls, suspended, censured, or simply acquitted. They thought that a professional body which consisted of advocates only 'could not be expected to command the confidence of the lay public' when questions of morality and ethics were involved.[98]

CONCLUSION

This study began with the observations of Charles Lockyer and Sir Thomas Strange describing conditions in the Madras bar. In the eighteenth century, Lockyer compared the few Englishmen who practised law to 'broken linen drapers' who sought their fortunes by their wits; they had no formal training, except familiarity with the kind of legal jargon used in England. When the East India Company established its rule throughout South India in 1801, rulers introduced a hierarchy of courts and institutionalized the legal profession, but the profession developed rather slowly. The 'regulations . . . provided no definite qualifications for [pleaders], no precise mode of proceedings, [and] no rules of evidence.'[1] Pleaders simply drew up pleadings and answered questions that a judge raised. Every pleading, motion or petition that they submitted had been reduced to written statements; oral argument was virtually absent except in courts below the district court.[2] Such conditions justified the observations of Sir Thomas in 1830 when he stated that the 'Native courts had no learned bar'.[3] In contrast, C. P. Ramaswami Iyer's assertions in 1920 reflected the existence of a different kind of Indian bar: vakils' achievements during the 120 years since the 1800s were rather impressive. With increase in political stability and opportunities under the British administration, vakils assumed prominent positions in local society.[4]

The history of the legal profession between 1802 and 1928 fell into four major periods. The East India Company's introduction of the practice of law as a distinct profession and the years between 1802 and 1846 marked its beginnings within the context of judicial administration. Next, the face-to-face argument of English barristers and Indian pleaders in the sadr courts and the systematic training of pleaders took place between 1846 and 1860. The following decades between 1860 and 1920 brought further refinements in the practice and status of vakils. Finally, the vakils' long struggle to obtain equality in the profession culminated in their complete success between 1921 and 1928.

Regulations X of 1802 and XIV of 1816, set the standards for law practice and prescribed pleaders' duties. As officers of the

Conclusion 183

court, holding positions similar to those held by English solicitors, pleaders had no power to influence the court policies or to protect their own interests. They mainly came from Hindu and Muslim communities and displayed their ignorance of the Anglo-Saxon procedures or provisions for conducting suits. By adopting various dilatory tactics to prolong suits rather than aiding judges, pleaders incorporated more details in their written pleadings and, as a result, they often received criticism, if not censure, from judges.

When authorities in England raised doubts about the very notion of retaining pleaders in judicial proceedings, Sir Thomas Munro intervened on their behalf.[5] His correspondence clearly shows that, while the decision-makers recognized the existence of 'an evil so generally acknowledged', they did not wish to do away with the institution of vakils, who had been an integral part of judicial administration for such a long time. The Court of Directors suggested to the Madras government that some sort of remedy should be devised in retaining pleaders, instead of abolishing their profession altogether.[6] In response, the government admitted a number of men to law classes conducted at the Fort St. George College from 1816 until 1836. Communications between the College Board and the government show that most students obtained certificates in spite of their superficial understanding of law and related matters, because of the demand for qualified pleaders in the courts. Later, many individuals, who had been trained at government expense, had no suitable positions. The government, therefore, decided to discontinue the law classes. After 1836, George Norton personally taught a small group of interested boys the rudiments of law, but he too soon dropped his lectures on account of lack of enthusiasm.

Between 1846 and 1860, barristers and pleaders argued side by side in the Sadr Adalat, in consequence of the enactment of Act I of 1846. Hitherto, barristers had practised only in the Supreme Court, where English law and procedure prevailed. The new legislation brought a mixed blessing. Pleaders gradually learned from barristers the art of cross-examination and developed the ability to sift masses of evidence, construct cases logically, and argue eloquently in the English language, but they also acquired a rather conservative approach to legal problems as well as 'a tendency to judge everything by the standard of English law'.[7] The founding of the 'High School of the Madras University' in the 1840s marked the dawn of modern higher education.⁸ The High School became 'a veritable nursery of talent'.⁹ Many graduates from this institution subsequently emerged as renowned administrators, judicial officers, lawyers and teachers.

At the beginning of the 1850s, judges of the Sadr Adalat became acutely aware of deficiencies in the formal training of pleaders; their concerns coincided with discussions pertaining to the renewal of the Company's Charter in 1853. Several individuals in England also urged that the entire judicial machinery should be reorganized and not just the institution of pleaders alone. Critics of the system attributed the backlog of arrears in the courts to the incompetence of judges and pleaders since neither had any adequate legal training. As a remedial measure, the Madras government introduced law lectures at the Presidency College in 1855. John B. Norton became the first professor, whose lectures served as the foundation for the evolution of legal education in South India. Criticism against the administration of justice in the Presidency resulted in a furious 'pamphlet controversy' between Norton and William Holloway,¹⁰ drawing much attention from the press in India and England. The open debate that ensued from a series of publications confirmed the view that the judicial system had become outmoded and needed a thorough overhauling. Before the end of the 1850s, the Mutiny took place, and the Crown assumed total control of the Indian Empire. Charles E. Trevelyan, Governor of Madras, appointed a select committee to study the ways in which both the Supreme Court and the Company's courts could be amalgamated into a unified structure.¹¹

The third period, between 1860 and 1920, forms the nucleus of this study. Both the original and amended Letters Patent of 1862 and 1865 empowered the High Court to enrol advocates, attorneys and vakils, and to formulate rules for their qualification and admission. On 18 August 1862, the High Court met for the first time and the judges permitted advocates to conduct all kinds of suits—original, appellate and insolvency—but vakils received only limited privileges. They could conduct appeals and could occasionally handle extraordinary original civil litigation, involving intricate questions of Hindu law. This distinction in privileges came from the notion that the Original and Appellate Sides of the High Court represented the former functions of the Supreme Court and the Sadr Adalat. Since vakils had never enjoyed audience in the former, the judges initially thought any innovation would be detrimental to the interests of barristers; they acquiesced to the demands of barristers by framing rules that would guarantee them an upper hand in law practice.

The cost of legal services for cases over Rs 500 in value, however, moved the judges to reconsider their rules of 1862, because litigants experienced considerable expenses on account of the employment of the double-agency. Some believed that a cheaper medium would alleviate the difficulties of suitors. Vakils provided that medium since their life-styles and professional attainments, on the whole, were not as elaborate as those of Europeans. The judges knew that a reduction in fee would not engender any real hardship in engaging qualified men because vakils possessed sufficient training both in the liberal arts and in law. The judges, therefore, permitted vakils on the Original Side, but this concession ultimately brought the demise of the barrister-attorney coalition, a result which the judges had never anticipated. Had they known that vakils would eventually eliminate from competition barristers if only to compete among themselves, and had they imagined that vakils would gradually rise to such heights in national and provincial politics, the judges might not have considered vakils as a 'cheaper medium'. But cheaper medium was what vakils had been ever since 1863 when they first commenced practice on the Original Side. Although this measure brought relief to many litigants, it also unleashed forces of professional animosity and competition between vakils and attorneys, which lasted for many years. Even after the Full Bench decision in 1876, upholding the right of vakils on the Original Side, tensions between vakils and attorneys never diminished. Fifteen years later, barristers in Madras continued to give vent to their anger over the decision. The editor of the *Indian Jurist* wrote:

> The unfair elevation of the vakils . . . has completely and irretrievably ruined the pure portion of the mixed bar of Madras, and there is no longer a career worth having to tempt promising young barristers and attorneys in Europe to seek their fortunes in the benighted Presidency. . . . And it will be indeed an evil day for the Madras legal world when the supply of new blood from Europe shall have ceased forever.[12]

Judges clearly sympathized with attorneys for the losses they subsequently sustained and showed that they were not totally oblivious to the grievances of attorneys, by imposing limitations on vakils. They introduced two different systems of awarding fees.

Whereas the Taxation Officer mechanically approved whatever an attorney included in the Bill of Costs, a vakil could charge what became known as an *ad valorem* fee, computed as a percentage of the total value of a suit—the Taxation Officer refused any other claims that a vakil made, regardless of their merit.

Although vakils had obtained special privileges on the Original Side, they enjoyed no such privileges in insolvency court; their exclusion rested on a narrower interpretation by the High Court that the 1828 original insolvency law allowed only 'advocates' to appear in such cases. Yet another rule, passed in 1899, enjoined vakils to obtain permission from the judges before they engaged in any trade or business outside their profession. This rule sought to ensure certain ethical quality and dignity among vakils. Some merely considered their profession as a profitable job and in that light also got involved in retail business. While the judges were more lenient in granting the requests of vakils who were leaders in the bar or who had acquired prominence in local or national politics, it was not always easy for juniors to get permission; not only did the process consume considerable time, but there were also considerable uncertainties whether the High Court would grant or refuse a request. A number of young vakils, therefore, embarked upon clandestine commercial ventures that brought about their undoing. This rule applied neither to barristers nor attorneys, and vakils saw it as being unfair and resented it.

In 1910 the High Court stipulated that vakil candidates should attend a series of lectures on professional conduct before they could apply for admission to the bar. Considering that their profession did not have a long-standing history or tradition and that a large number of candidates sought enrolment each year, the judges thought that this requirement might provide an occasion for them to acquire and maintain a sense of ethics. Yet this also proved irritating for those who had been prevented from making an earlier enrolment on account of failure to attend the requisite number of lectures.

The influence of English barristers on vakils was considerable, despite their rivalry; such names as Branson, Grant, Mayne, Norton and O'Sullivan lingered long in the memories of vakils. Barristers led the way, whether in establishing a professional organization, obtaining judicial positions, providing leadership for the bar, or developing legal journalism. As early as 1865, they assembled under the aegis of the Madras Bar to advance their interests. Vakils formed their own association in the beginning of the 1880s, but not until the end of that decade did it become effective. In energy, vision and dedication, vakils subsequently surpassed the achievements of either barristers or attorneys.

The associations of barristers, vakils and attorneys held several common threads, in spite of their differences in size and reputation. Their memberships were small when compared to the total number of lawyers in the Presidency and each group had a significant internal stratification. Hierarchy, mutual rivalry for business, and official patronage of the rich and mighty were common. Leaders generally came from among those with high reputation and income; they alone formulated and enforced the rules and they alone defined group goals. Their rules promoted the aspirations of the powerful and failed to protect the weak. Such behaviour resulted in various unethical or unprofessional dealings by beginners or by mediocre lawyers. The financial moorings of the associations were so weak that barristers and vakils especially found it difficult to remain solvent.

The Vakils' Association differed in certain respects from the organizations of barristers and attorneys. It had the largest membership because many vakils joined that body in order to benefit from the facilities it offered. The organization took extraordinary pains to build up a good library to serve the needs of many who could not themselves afford to buy the tools essential for their profession. In its general constituency and leadership, the Association was, however, predominantly brahman. This naturally led to the formation of cliques seeking their own interests. Some vakil families contracted strategic alliances with a view to keeping business within the family. This propensity to protect one's own interests in the profession, as well as to inbreed within one's own community (or subcaste), led to a situation comparable to that described by Gary B. Nash relating to the Philadelphia bar during several decades of the nineteenth century: manifestation of a high degree of self-interest and preservation throughout the legal profession.[13]

That a large number of law graduates enrolled as vakils each year and that district bar associations looked up to the Vakils' Association for guidance in all professional matters earned that body a *de facto* legitimacy, allowing it a major leadership role. It periodically made representations to judges and the government on behalf of vakils' interests; its officers were present in court to witness proceedings instituted against vakils, even when those vakils were non-members. The Association's preoccupation with various political and social issues became indistinguishable from its desire to earn more concessions for vakils. Many leaders became members of the corporation, the university senate and the legislative council.[14]

Although brahmans generally held the clearest majority within the Association, changes in Madras politics during the 1910s promoted the aspirations of non-brahmans, contributing to the formation of the Non-Brahman Lawyers' Association; but this was short-lived. It neither gained a broad support base nor commanded exceptional talent to compete with the Vakils' Association. The rival association was mainly interested in securing special appointments for its own members. Although an assessment of the Vakils' Association's reactions to the formation of a separatist, communal organization is difficult, that the former (now the Advocates' Association) is still functioning and that it still is one of the most influential organizations in Madras testifies to its ability to survive and to endure opposition.

The preponderance of brahmans both in government service and in professions, especially the legal profession, as a political and social issue merits discussion. A common assumption is that brahmans had an indisputable lead in higher education and in government employment during the last century,[15] that their ascendency in the administrative, professional and political spheres eventually spawned considerable antagonism and jealousy in other communities, especially in a 'monolithic' non-brahman organization,[16] and that a decline in brahman influence coincided with the emergence of a 'Dravidian' or non-brahman movement. In spite of their oversimplification, the general validity of these notions is not an issue here. Such notions, however, often ignore the complex structures and practices within the brahman communities. Not only did philosophical and religious (or doctrinal) identities—such as Smarthas, Sri Vaishnavas and Madhwas—divide brahmans themselves from one another, but distinctions along the lines of language and culture also served to widen the gap. Even within each language or cultural group—be it Tamil, Telugu, Malayalam, Kannada, Marathi or Gujarati—there were other major divisions among brahman communities. Each major region, then, had clusters of brahman castes and subcastes. Even though members of one particular subcaste might ordinarily interact and interdine with members of other subcastes or with a larger segment, they would never enter into marriage contracts with anyone who did not belong to their own group.[17]

In the wake of introduction of English education throughout the Presidency, not all brahman communities responded with the same vigour and determination. Even though some communities generally spent a good deal of their inheritance in the pursuit of English education, there were others who shied away from it,[18] while still others spent their entire lives in the editing and publishing of ancient classical Tamil texts.[19] To assume, then, that all brahmans took to English education is to overlook many historical, social and economic factors that forced them to move away from their ancestral villages and occupations, in search of new forms of employment or in pursuit of new paths to higher education.

Among the many brahman communities that took to English education and government service, certain internal differences separated them from each other. At what point a community began to move from one tradition to another and to what extent it sacrificed its traditional values in order to become more 'secular' are questions yet to be fully explored. During the heyday of the East India Company, the Deshastha or Maharashtrian brahmans dominated in the administration.[20] Then came Tamil brahmans, followed by the Telugus, Kannadas and Konkanis. The Malayali or Nambhudhiri brahmans in the nineteenth century showed little interest either in Western education or in careers in government and law.

While some brahmans realized that the 'caste politics' of the later years was the result of their own blindness, vanity and conceit, most of them did nothing to assuage the mounting tensions in the city.[21] Why this was so needs further investigation. As early as 1904, one writer included vakils as a group among those 'Western educated' Indians, who were notorious for their snobbery. He wrote:

> The native snob is a product of our modern University system. Having divested himself of the calm demeanour and oriental courtesy of his forebears, the native snob is flighty and inquisitive. . . . In this class of snobs may be included the Zemindar snob, the Vakil snob, and the

well-read snob who has Mill and Adam Smith at his fingers' ends and spouts Wordsworth and Browning and thinks he is a Mathew Arnold or a Carlyle come to judgement.[22]

Very little is known, therefore, about how brahmans in the Madras Presidency united as a community under a common ideology or how they mustered their strength to ward off the acrimonious discussions in the press or in the legislative council.[23] In the wake of militant anti-brahman activities in recent years, brahmans in Tamil Nadu have finally resolved to organize themselves in order to counter such attacks. As a result, the Tamil Nadu Brahmins' Association has set up about 3000 branches and has a considerable following.[24]

The controversy over the question of equality between barristers and vakils culminated in heated debates; vakils sought redress in the Legislative Assembly against the arrogance of barristers. Their goal was to create an All-India Bar Council, vested with powers for framing policies on all professional matters and enforcing them in India. Removing every kind of discrimination against vakils and pulling down every distinction of privileges would also come under its jurisdiction. Between 1921 and 1926, Indian legislators introduced three distinct changes within the profession. In 1923, they admitted women to law practice but very few actually benefited from such measure; not only did they find that the bar was highly competitive and overcrowded, but obtaining judicial appointments was equally impossible. In 1924, the Indian government approved the formation of provincial bar councils. After frequent correspondence between various government agencies and professional bodies, and after a well-staged confrontation in the Assembly, vakils found support in the Indian Bar Committee report. The Indian Bar Councils' Act became law in 1926 and took effect in 1928 at Madras. In many respects a compromise, the new law safeguarded the powers of High Courts, ensuring that the judges retained their power in dealing with issues related to professional ethics; it also protected the interests of barristers in Calcutta and Bombay, where double-agency continued. Yet it laid the foundations for equality of vakils: they immediately became advocates and their members dominated the newly established bar council, which advised judges on all points of concern. When in 1928 elections to the Madras Bar Council took place, the results showed that the council was in the hands of the same brahman oligarchy which controlled the Vakils' Association.

Conclusion

The All-India Bar Committee recommended to the Indian government that the High Courts be requested to make uniform rules for admission and practice, removing as far as possible every distinction between vakils and barristers. The statutory constraints which had previously preserved the office of the chief justiceship for barristers were also removed by an act of Parliament: members from either group of lawyers became eligible to hold that office. The Madras High Court voluntarily decided to do away with existing disparities in fees awarded to vakils and attorneys. Moreover, vakils also enjoyed the privilege of handling original insolvency petitions, having become advocates. Their long struggle over the alleged superior education, prestige and skill of barristers had ended. Vakils stood on a par with barristers.

Appendix I

REVISED RULES OF THE MADRAS BAR, 1882

A. *General Rule*

   I. The members of the Bar agree that under no circumstances and in no manner will they give commission or other payment directly or indirectly to law agents or other persons bringing business.

B. *Rules Relating to Cases Arising within the Presidency Town*

   II. In cases arising on the Original Side of the High Court, in Appeals therefrom, and in Session Cases, no member of the Bar shall be at liberty to accept a brief from, or to hold a brief with a Vakil.

   III. No member of the Bar shall be at liberty to accept any brief unless it is accompanied by the fee marked thereon, save under very exceptional circumstances.

   IV. No member of the Bar shall be at liberty to hold an interview with the client elsewhere than in Court except in the presence of the Attorney or his Clerk. This rule does not apply in Sessions Cases where Counsel is assigned by the Judge to defend a prisoner.

   V. The members of the bar are at liberty to appear in the presidency Small Cause Courts and Police Courts instructed either by Attorneys or by Vakils or by the parties in person.

   VI. No member of the bar accepting a fee shall accept less than the minimum fee.

   VII. Wherever two Counsels are retained in final disposal of Original Suits, Sessions Cases, Police Court Cases, Commissions to examine witnesses and examinations *de bene esse*, the minimum fee for Senior Counsel is 25 Pagodas and for Junior Counsel 15 Pagodas.

   VIII. Where two cases come on for hearing together, a refresher or the minimum fee shall be required in one case only.

   IX. Where a case begins after tiffin no refresher shall be required for the second day.

   X. The general and special retainer fees are respectively Pagodas 50, and Pagodas 15.

   XI. In all Small Cause Court Cases the minimum fee should be that fixed for Counsel by the Court Scale upon the sum sued for.

   XII. Scale of minimum fees:

A. High Court, Original Side

	Pagodas
Final disposal (where the value of the suit does not exceed Rs 2500)	15
Commission to examine witnesses in such suits	10
Examinations *de bene esse*	10
Confirmation of certificate in such suits	10
Final disposal and commissions to examine witnesses and examination *de bene esse* where the value of the suit exceeds Rs 2500	25
Final disposal and commissions to examine witnesses and examinations *de bene esse* where two Counsel are retained:	
For Senior Counsel	25
For Junior Counsel	15
Consultation or conference	10
Confirmation of Certificate, Senior or Single Counsel	15
Confirmation of Certificate, Junior Counsel	10
Brief to hear judgement, Single Counsel	10
Brief to hear judgement, where two Counsel are retained:	
Senior Counsel	10
Junior Counsel	5
References	10
Brief in Insolvent case	10
Court motions (except by consent)	10
Chamber motions	5
Motions of course and briefs to consent to motions	5
Settlement of Issues	5

B. Sessions and Police Courts

	Pagodas
Where two Counsel are retained, Senior	25
Where two Counsel are retained, Junior	15
Where one Counsel is retained	15
To hear judgement for single or Senior Counsel	10
To hear judgement for single or Junior Counsel	10
Consultation to examine witnesses and examinations *de bene esse*:	
where two Counsel are retained, Senior	25
where two Counsel are retained, Junior	15
where one Counsel is retained	15

Appendix I 195

C. *Presidency Small Cause Courts*

	Rs A P
Suits up to Rs 500 in value	25 0 0
Suits up to Rs 1000 "	35 0 0
Suits up to Rs 2000 "	52 8 0
Motions (except for new trial)	17 8 0
Motions for New Trial in:	
(a) Suits up to Rs 1000 in value	25 0 0
(b) Suits up to Rs 2000 "	35 0 0
Refreshers in suits up to Rs 500 in value	17 8 0
Refreshers in suits up to Rs 1000 "	25 0 0
Refreshers in suits up to Rs 2000 "	35 0 0

Commissions for examination of witnesses and examination *de bene esse* the same fees as for hearing.

Appendix II

RULES AND REGULATIONS OF THE ATTORNEYS ASSOCIATION, MADRAS*

THE RULES OF THE ASSOCIATION

Name

1. The name of the Association is the 'Attorneys Association, Madras'.

Objects

2. The objects of the Association are:
   (a) To ensure, as far as possible, the proper conduct by Attorneys of the High Court at Madras of professional business.
   (b) To advance the best interest of Attorneys and their Clients, as well as the convenience and due remuneration of the former.
   (c) To fix a scale of minimum charges for professional work and to make other regulations with regard to the professional remuneration of the Members of the Association.

Members

3. Every Attorney on the Rolls of the High Court, Madras may become a Member of the Association on his paying an Entrance Fee of Rupees 15, and the whole or a proportionate part of the Annual Subscription provided for by the next rule.
4. Every Member of the Association shall pay in advance, on the 1st day of May in every year, an Annual Subscription of Rupees 12. Provided, that upon the subscription of any Member becoming in arrear for six months he shall cease to be a Member.

Officers

5. The Officers of the Association shall consist of a Committee of seven Members of the Association and of an Honorary Secretary, also a Member of the Association, who shall ex-officio also be a Member of the Committee.
6. The Committee and Honorary Secretary shall be elected at the first Meeting of the Association in each year and shall retire annually, but may be re-elected.

*The Indian Jurist 17:1 (January 1893): 32–5.

7. Should a temporary vacancy occur in either the Committee or the post of Honorary Secretary, it may be filled up by the Committee.

The Committee

8. The Committee shall manage the affairs of the Association, subject only to the control of the Members of the Association as expressed by Resolution in Meeting Assembled; and they shall elect their own Chairman and may make Rules for their own guidance and determine the quorum necessary for the transaction of business.
9. The Committee shall, on the professional misconduct of any Attorney of the High Court coming to their knowledge, refer the same to the Association who may take such proceedings with reference thereto as they may think proper, or be advised; and the costs and expenses of, and incidental to, any such proceedings, shall be defrayed out of the Funds of the Association.
10. The Committee may, in any matter in which they consider the interests of the Members of the Association are affected, appear and represent or instruct Counsel or Solicitors to appear and represent the Association before the High Court, or any other Judicial or Administrative Authority; and take such proceedings therein as they may think fit, and the costs and expenses of, and incidental to, any such proceedings shall be defrayed out of the Funds of the Association.

The Honorary Secretary

11. The Honorary Secretary shall attend the Meeting of the Association and of the Committee, and shall keep minutes of the proceedings thereat, and shall conduct such correspondence as the Committee shall direct.
12. The Honorary Secretary shall receive and keep an Account of the Funds of the Association. Such Funds shall be deposited in the Bank of Madras; and such part thereof as shall not be required for current expenses shall be invested in Government Securities in the names of two Members of the Committee, provided that a direction, by the Chairman of any Meeting of the Committee and of any two other Members of the Committee to the Honorary Secretary, to expend any sum of Money, or to the Members in whose names any Government Securities of the Association are standing to sell or transfer the same and expend the proceeds, shall be a sufficient authority to him or them to do so.

Members, their Obligations and Rights

13. Every Member of the Association, by joining the Association, undertakes that, so long as he shall continue to be a Member, he will

observe the Rules and Regulations of the Association for the time being in force.

14. Should any Member of the Association be struck off the Rolls of the High Court, or be temporarily suspended, he shall thereupon cease to be a Member of the Association.
15. Any Member of the Association may submit to the Committee for their opinion any question upon a point of practice, or in relation to the professional conduct of any legal practitioner or as to the interpretation or application of any of the Rules or Regulations of the Association, and the Committee may either express their opinion thereon or may refer the matter to the Association.
16. In case of alleged professional misconduct of any Member of the Association, or breach by any Member of the Association of any Rule or Regulation of the Association, shall be brought to the notice of the Honorary Secretary, he shall bring the matter to the notice of the Committee.
17. The Association may, by a resolution passed in Meeting, express their opinion as to the professional conduct of any legal practitioner or the breach of any Rule or Regulation of the Association by any Member of the Association, and may also direct the Committee to make any application to the Court with reference thereto respectively and may by a special Resolution expel any Member of the Association from the same.

Meetings

18. The Association shall meet on the second Saturday in the months of January, April, July, and October, every year, at such hour and at such place as the Committee shall appoint.
19. The Committee may from time to time call such other Meetings of the Association as they shall think fit.
20. Any five Members of the Association may, by a requisition in writing addressed to the Honorary Secretary, stating the object of the desired Meeting, require a Meeting of the Association to be called, and on receipt of such requisition, the Committee shall fix a day and hour (not exceeding ten days from the date of the receipt by the Honorary Secretary of such requisition) and place for such Meeting.
21. The Chairman, for the time being, of the Committee shall preside at and be the Chairman of every Meeting of the Association at which he shall be present; and in case of his declaration as to the decision of the Meeting shall be conclusive, unless a poll shall be demanded before the Meeting separates.
22. A poll may be demanded at any Meeting of the Association by any five or more Members present at such Meeting.

23. Any Meeting may be adjourned, from time to time, until the business before it is disposed of.
24. At least four days' notice of every Meeting and of the object of such Meeting shall be given to all the Members of the Association in Madras at the time, provided that no Resolution passed at any Meeting shall be invalid by reason of the want of or irregularity in any such notice.
25. Except for the purpose of passing a special resolution, a majority of votes of the Members present and voting at any Meeting of the Association shall decide any question before the Meeting.
26. A Resolution shall be deemed a special resolution of the Association fifteen days after the same has been passed by three-fourths of the Members of the Association present, and voting at any Meeting of which notice specifying the intention to propose such resolution has been given at least two days before such Meeting, and at which Meeting not less than nine Members of the Association shall be present.
27. No business shall be transacted at any Meeting unless five Members be personally present at the commencement of such business.
28. If within one half-hour from the time appointed for the Meeting, the required number of Members be not present, the Meeting, if convened upon the requisition of Members, shall be dissolved; in any other case it shall stand adjourned for one week at the same time and place. At every such adjourned Meeting, Members, whatever their number, shall have power to transact all the business which could properly have been transacted by the Original Meeting had the necessary quorum been present thereat, provided, however, that no special resolution shall be passed at any such adjourned Meeting unless six Members at least shall be present and vote in favour thereof.

Rules and Regulations

29. The following are the Regulations for the time being of the Association.
    (1) No Member of the Association shall attest any deed, document or other paper writing (which by law or by the rules or practice of any Court in Madras requires his attestation) which has not been prepared or approved either in his own office or in the office of another Attorney.
        This Regulation does not apply to wills or to documents prepared out of Madras or to Notarial attestations or to documents or forms used in Public or Government Offices.
    (2) The premium to be paid by an articled clerk to a Member of the Association, shall in no case be less than Rupees 2500.
    (3) No Member of the Association shall agree to undertake the prosecution or defence of any suit or proceeding in the High

Court or Insolvent Court or to deliver a brief to counsel in consideration of a lump sum in lieu of the costs according to scale.

(4) No Member of the Association shall in conducting any Suit, Criminal Proceedings or other business, charge or accept lower fees than those allowed by the Rules of the High Court, Insolvent Court or Small Cause Court, or by the scale of charges of the Association for the time being in force.

(5) Every Member of the Association shall keep books of account which shall contain true and proper entries of all receipts and disbursements in connection with his professional business.

30. The Rules and Regulations of the Association may from time to time be altered, added to or cancelled by a special Resolution.

Appendix III

RULES OF THE VAKILS' ASSOCIATION, PASSED ON 15 APRIL 1889

Rule I   The Association shall be called the High Court Vakils' Association.

Rule II   Any Vakil of the High Court may become a member of the Association on his sending a written application to the Secretary.

Rule III   Every member practising at Madras shall pay a subscription of one Rupee a month and every other member a subscription of eight annas a month.

Rule IV   There shall be a President, a Secretary and a Managing Committee consisting of the President, the Secretary and Seven Members all of whom shall be elected once a year.
(a) Five members shall form a quorum of the Committee.

Rule V   All Resident Members of the Association shall be eligible to be members of the Managing Committee.

Rule VI   The Managing Committee shall meet on the First Monday of each month, except when the High Court is closed on that day.

Rule VII   A General meeting of the Association shall be held at least once in three months. Twelve members shall be a quorum. The Secretary shall convene a meeting of the Association on a requisition signed by Five members. Some special meetings shall be convened not later than Five days of the receipt of such intimation.

Rule VIII   The Managing Committee shall have power to convene meetings as often as they think fit on giving one day notice of such meetings.

Rule IX   The Managing Committee shall have power to deal with the funds of the Association.

Rule X   The following shall be among the objects of the Association.
(a) To maintain a high standard of profession conduct.
(b) To protect and promote the interests of Vakils.
(c) To make representations from time to time to the authorities on matters affecting suitors or the profession.
(d) And to form and maintain a library.

Rule XI The Managing Committee shall have power to make rules not inconsistent with the rules herein before mentioned or with the object of the Association, but such rules shall be liable to be modified or cancelled by a General Meeting.

GLOSSARY

adalàt: court of justice.
agraharam: brahman village or street.
amin: civil judge or judicial officer above a munsif.
anna: 1/16 of a rupee.
arzi: petition.
chela: disciple.
choultry: resting place.
dakshina: offering or fee to a guru or a teacher.
dharma: virtue, legal or moral duty.
dikshitar: brahman temple priest at Chidambaram.
dubashi: a bilingual person; hence, an intermediary or broker.
durbar: court, audience or levee.
gomastah: agent, clerk, confidential representative or steward.
guru: teacher.
kazi: Muslim law expounder.
Mimamsa: a Hindu philosophical system.
mufassal: the country as opposed to the principal town or city.
mufti: principal law expounder.
munsif: Indian civil judge of the lowest rank.
namam: Vaishnava sectarian mark.
pagoda: gold coin worth about 3.5 rupees.
pandit: (also pundit) scholar.
Pongal: festival of South India, observed in early January.
Prabandhum: Vaishnava poetic literature.
prasadam: divine leavings; leftovers of food offered to an idol.
purdah: curtain; practice of screening women from strangers by means of a curtain.
purdahnashin: woman observing *purdah*.
raja: a king, prince.
Sadr Diwani Adalat: high court of civil jurisdiction.
Saivas: worshippers of Siva.
sanad: grant or charter; licence.
sowcar: (also saucar) an Indian banker.
stridhan: term in Hindu law referring to property belonging to a woman.

taluq: administrative division within a district.
Thengalai: a Vaishnava sect belonging to the Southern school.
Vadagalai: a Vaishnava sect belonging to the Northern school.
Vaishnavas: worshippers of Vishnu.
vakalat: (also vakalatnamah) power of attorney or authorization.
vakil: agent, ambassador, representative or an authorized practitioner in a court of justice.
Varicu: legal heir.
zamindar: landholder.
zenana: female quarters; the women of a family.
zillah: administrative unit or division.

NOTES

INTRODUCTION

1. Marc Galanter, 'Study of Indian Legal Profession', *Law and Society Review* 3:2–3 (November 1968–February 1969): 214.
2. M. C. Setalvad, *The Common Law in India* (Bombay: N. M. Tripathy, 1970), p. 225.
3. John Paul, 'Stages and Actors in the Drama of Indian Law: The Dismissal Proceedings of Munsif Vedanayagam Pillai (1826–1889)', Paper read at the Twelfth Annual Conference on South Asia held at the University of Wisconsin-Madison, 4–6 November 1983.
4. Richard L. Abel, 'The Underdevelopment of Legal Profession: A Review Article on Third World Lawyers', *American Bar Foundation Research Journal* (1982): 871–93 and C. J. Dias, R. Luckham, D. O. Lynch and J. C. N. Paul, eds., *Lawyers in the Third World: Comparative and Developmental Perspectives* (Uppsala: Scandinavian Institute of African Studies, 1981). The bibliographic information available from these sources is rich, varied, and comprehensive on lawyers both in western societies and in the Third World. The following publications especially provide references to lawyers in India. Marc Galanter, Comp., 'An Incomplete Bibliography of the Indian Legal Profession', *Law and Society Review* 3:2–3 (November 1968–February 1969): 445–62 and John Paul and Lata Krishnamurty, 'A Tentative Bibliography on Indian Legal Profession (with Special Reference to Tamil Nadu)', in *The Legal Profession: A Preliminary Study of the Tamil Nadu Bar*, edited by N. R. Madhava Menon (New Delhi: Bar Council of India Trust, 1984), pp. 244–62.
5. Such as law, medicine, engineering, journalism and teaching. See, John C. Hume, 'Medicine in the Punjab, 1849–1911', Ph.D. Dissertation, Duke University, 1977 (unpublished); Roger Jeffery, *The Politics of Health in India* (Berkeley: University of California Press, 1988); John J. Paul, 'Indigenization of the Western Medical Profession during the nineteenth century, with special reference to South India', Paper read at the Sixtieth Annual Meeting of the American Association for the History of Medicine, Philadelphia, 30 April–3 May 1987, and J. D. Shukla, *Indianisation of All-India Services and Its Impact on Administration* (New Delhi: Allied Publishers, 1982).
6. Nirmalendu Dutt-Majumdar, *Conduct of Advocates & Legal Profession: Short History* (Calcutta: Eastern Law House, 1974), pp. 1–25.
7. Ibid., p. 202.
8. M. K. Gandhi, *The Law and The Lawyers*, edited by S. B. Kher (Ahmedabad: Navajivan Publishing House, 1962), pp. 131–4. In Madras, only 36 lawyers seemed to have suspended their practice in support of non-cooperation but they eventually returned to their profession. David Arnold, *The Congress in Tamilnad: Nationalist Politics in South India 1919–1937* (London: Curzon

Press, 1977), p. 83. Criticisms of Gandhi's 'call' to boycott courts and legislative councils came from C. Sankaran Nair, a prominent vakil and one-time judge of the Madras High Court. *Gandhi and Anarchy*, 2nd ed., (Madras: Tagore, 1922), pp. 2–3.

9. J. S. Gandhi, *Lawyers and Touts: A Study in the Sociology of Legal Profession* (Delhi: Hindustan Publishing Corporation, 1982); Robert L. Kidder, 'Formal Litigation and Professional Insecurity: Legal Entrepreneurship in South India', *Law and Society Review* 9:1 (1974): 11–37; Charles Morrison, 'Social Organization at the District Courts: Colleague Relationship among Indian Lawyers', *Law and Society Review* 3:2–3 (November 1968–February 1969): 251–267; Sam W. McKinstry, *The Brokerage Role of Rajasthani Lawyers in Three Districts of Rajasthan, India As Evidenced through Lawyer-Client Relations: Fact or Fiction?* (Washington: University of America Press, 1980); Peter Rowe, 'Indian Lawyers and Political Modernization: Observations in Four District Towns', *Law and Society Review* 3:2–3 (November 1968–February 1969): 219–50.
10. Samuel Schmitthener, 'A Sketch of the Development of the Legal Profession in India', *Law and Society Review* 3:2–3 (November 1968–February 1969): 337–82.
11. G. F. M. Buckee, 'An Examination of the Development and Structure of the Legal Profession at Allahabad, 1866–1935', Ph.D. dissertation, School of Oriental and African Studies, London, 1971 (unpublished).
12. V. N. Srinivasa Rao, 'The Origin and Growth of Legal Profession in Tamil Nadu: A Historical Study, 1640–1947', in *The Legal Profession: A Preliminary Study*, pp. 47–121.
13. Schmitthener, 'A Sketch. . .,' p. 337.
14. Buckee, 'An Examination. . .,' p. 15.
15. Bankey Bihari Misra, *The Indian Middle Classes: Their Growth in Modern Times* (London: Oxford University Press, 1961), p. 164.
16. Interview with M. Raja, Secretary, Tamil Nadu Legal Aid Board, on 2 April 1982.
17. See R. E. Frykenberg and Pauline Kolenda, eds., *Studies of South India: An Anthology of Recent Research and Scholarship* (Madras: New Era Publications, 1985).
18. Ibid., p. 187.
19. R. Suntharalingam, *Politics and National Awakening in South India, 1852–1891* (Tucson: University of Arizona Press, 1974), pp. 104–92.
20. Srinivasa Rao, 'The Origin and Growth', p. 59.
21. Ibid., 60 and Charles Lockyer, *Account of the Trade in India* (London: 1711), cited by John William Kaye, *The Administration of the East India Company*, reprint edition (Allahabad: Kitab Mahal, 1966), p. 321.
22. Evidence of Sir Thomas Strange, formerly the Chief Justice of the Supreme Court at Madras, before the Select Committee of the House of the Lords on 11 May, 1830; House of Commons, Vol. VI of 1830, Paper No. 646, p. 261.
23. C. H. Phillips, ed., *Handbook of Oriental History* (London: Royal Historical Society, 1951), p. 78. I am also grateful to Professor N. R. Farooqi (formerly at University of Allahabad) for bringing this to my attention.
24. Srinivasa Rao, 'The Origin and Growth', p. 69.
25. *The Madras Mail*, 22 and 25 March 1882.
26. High Court Administrative Records (hereafter HCAR), No. 1108, 14 June 1916.

Notes 207

Chapter 1: BEGINNINGS OF A PROFESSION

1. See, Introduction, footnote 21.
2. Extract from the letter from Sir Thomas Strange to the Rt. Hon'ble Lord Winford, dated 19 January 1830, which was later read before a Select Committee of the House of Lords on 14 May 1830; House of Commons, Vol. VI of 1830, Paper No. 646, p. 272.
3. Pande Nawal Kishor Sahay, *A Short History of the Indian Bar* (Patna: Bhaktiniketan, 1931), p. 20; see also, V. N. Srinivasa Rao, 'The Growth of the Madras Bar', *Lawyer* 7:1 (November 1967): 9.
4. *The Regulation Passed in the year 1802 by the Governor in Council of Fort Saint George* (Madras: The Government Press, 1803), p. 155.
5. Regulation X of 1802, Sections II–IV.
6. Ibid., Sections VI–VII.
7. Ibid., Sections VIII–IX.
8. Ibid., Section X.
9. Ibid., Section XIII.
10. Ibid., Section XIV.
11. Ibid., Sections XV–XVII, XXI and XXX.
12. Ibid., Sections XIX–XX.
13. Ibid., Section XXV.
14. Ibid., Section I.
15. *The Indian Middle Classes*, p. 164.
16. Ramesh Chandra Srivatsava, *Development of Judicial System in India Under the East India Company, 1833–1858* (Lucknow: Lucknow Publishing House, 1971), p. 176.
17. Ibid.
18. Richard Clarke, Comp., *The Regulations of the Government of Fort. St. George in force at the end of 1847* (London: J. & H. Cox, 1848), p. 340.
19. Ibid., Section VIII, p. 341.
20. Ibid., Section XVII, p. 343.
21. Ibid.
22. Ibid., Section XVIII.
23. Ibid., Sections XIX–XX, p. 344.
24. Ibid., Section XXI, p. 345.
25. The British judges held the same kind of opinion about people in other areas of the empire, particularly the people in Sri Lanka. John D. Rogers, *Crime, Justice and Society in Colonial Sri Lanka* (London: Curzon Press, 1987), p. 40.
26. House of Commons, Vol. IX of 1831-2, Paper No. 735, Appendix I.
27. A. D. Campbell, *Code of Regulations for the Internal Government of the Madras Territories, From A. D. 1802 to A. D. 1834*, 3 vols. (Madras: Fort St. George Press, n.d.), 3:44.
28. Evidence of Richard Clarke before the Select Committee of the House of Commons on 28 February 1832; House of Commons, Vol. XII of 1832, Paper No. 735, p. 5.
29. Ibid.
30. Henry Davidson Love, *Vestiges of Old Madras 1640–1800*, 3 vols. (London: John Murray, 1913), 3:475.

31. Evidence of Sir Thomas Strange, former Chief Justice of the Supreme Court at Madras, before the Select Committee of the House of Lords on 11 May, 1830; House of Commons, Vol. VI of 1830, Paper No. 646, p. 261.
32. Henry Dodwell, *Report on the Madras Records* (Madras: Government Press, n.d.), pp. 74–5.
33. In Bombay Norton had acquired a notorious reputation for demanding exorbitant fees (five times greater than normal in England) and for making a mockery of the proceedings at the court. P. V. Vachha, *Famous Judges, Lawyers and Cases of Bombay During the British Period* (Bombay: N. M. Tripathi, 1961), p. 111.
34. Pamela G. Price, 'Resources and Rule in Zamindari South India, 1802–1903: Sivagangai and Ramnad as Kingdoms under the Raj', Ph.D. Dissertation, University of Wisconsin–Madison, 1979.
35. Srivatsava, *Development*, p. 178.
36. Clarke, *The Regulations*, p. 746.
37. Evidence before the Select Committee of the House of Lords on 18 March 1853; House of Commons, Vol. XXXI of 1852–3, Paper No. 627, p. 317, (added emphasis).
38. Evidence before the Select Committee of the House of Commons on 18 April 1853; House of Commons, Vol. XXVII of 1852–3, Paper No. 426, pp. 292–3.
39. Evidence of Henry Lushington, Bengal Civil Service, before the Select Committee of the House of Lords on 26 April 1853; House of Commons, Vol. XXXI of 1852–3, Paper No. 627, p. 518.
40. Evidence of J. P. Willoughby, p. 317.
41. John Bruce Norton, *The Administration of Justice in Southern India* (Madras: Pharoah, 1853), pp. 80–4.
42. *The Madras Times*, 1 October 1858.
43. Madras Native Association, *Report of the Proceedings at the Presentation of an Address to John Bruce Norton, Esq.* (Madras: Scottish Press, 1860), p. 81.
44. Srivatsava, *Development*, pp. 182–4.
45. Letter from N. B. E. Baillie to the Chairman of the Court of Directors, dated 21 February 1848; Judicial Consultations, Vol. 420, dated 18 July 1848, No. 14. Baillie's experience in India as an attorney in the Supreme Court at Calcutta and, later, as a Government Pleader of Bengal proved invaluable in assessing the growth and treatment of the legal profession.
46. Ibid., para. 2.
47. Ibid.
48. Ibid.
49. Ibid., para. 6.
50. Ibid., para. 11.
51. Ibid. See, Srivatsava, *Development*, pp. 32, 35–8 and Paul, 'Stages and Actors in the Drama of India Law: The Dismissal Proceedings of Munsif Vedanayagam Pillai (1826–1889)'.
52. Letter from N. B. E. Baillie to the Chairman of the Court of Directors, dated 21 February 1848; Judicial Consultations, Vol. 420, dated 18 July 1848, No. 14.
53. Letter from J. Davidson to H. Montgomery, dated 27 April 1848; Judicial Consultations, Vol. 550, dated 22 May 1849, No. 18.
54. Ibid.

55. William Plubridge Williams (comp.), *The Acts of the Legislative Council of India relating to the Madras Presidency for 1848 to 1858* (Madras: Scottish Press, 1859), p. 172.
56. *The Daily Times and Spectator*, 1 June 1960.
57. Srivatsava, *Development*, p. 184.
58. The following individuals gave evidence before the two separate Committees of the Parliament. From Bengal, N. B. E. Baillie, C. H. Cameron, F. J. Halliday, J. A. F. Hawkins and J. C. Marshman; from Bombay, Sir Erskine Perry and J. P. Willoughby, and from Madras, Sir Edward Gambier, George Norton and C. E. Trevelyan.
59. Evidence of Richard Clarke, Madras Civil Service, before the Select Committee of the House of Lords on 11 March 1830; House of Commons, Vol. VI of 1830, Paper No. 646, p. 93.
60. Letter from the Board of Superintendence, College of Fort St. George, to the Governor in Council, dated 28 February 1816; Public Consultations, Vol. 436, dated 23 April 1816, Nos. 19–20.
61. Ibid., para. 9. It is not clear how the government responded to this suggestion because the records are not easily accessible from the Tamil Nadu Archives. Nonetheless, had the government adopted this measure they would undoubtedly have secured the services of men who stood above the rest of pleaders, both in the knowledge of personal law and of the regulations.
62. Ibid., paras. 9–12.
63. Ibid., para. 8.
64. Campbell, *Code of Regulations*, 2:323.
65. Letter from the Board of Superintendence, College of Fort St. George, to the Governor in Council, dated 25 June 1821; Public Consultations, Vol. 488, dated 17 July 1821, Nos. 11–12.
66. Letter from the Acting Secretary of the College Board to the Chief Secretary to the Government, dated 29 June 1822; Public Consultations, Vol. 498, dated 12 July 1822, Nos. 31–32.
67. Letter from the Secretary to the Board of the College and for Public Instruction to the Chief Secretary to Government, dated 14 August 1827; Public Consultations, Vol. 552, dated 14 August 1827, Nos. 23–24 (emphasis added).
68. Ibid.
69. Julia Charlotte Maitland, *Letters from Madras during the Years 1836–1839* (London: John Murray, 1843), p. 86.
70. See, the Petition from T. Narrain Sastre to the Board for the College and for Public Instruction, dated 11 May 1835; Public Consultations, Vol. 636, dated 26 May 1835, No. 13.
71. See, University of Madras, *History of Higher Education in South India*, Centenary Commemmoration of the University of Madras 1857–1957, 2 vols. (Madras: Associated Printers, 1957), 2:7–9; see also, Suntharalingam, *Politics and Nationalist Awakening*, pp. 58–66.
72. A. D. Campbell, *The Regulations for the Internal Government of the Madras Territories* (Madras: J. B. Pharoah, 1843), p. 587.
73. V. N. Srinivasa Rao, 'The Origin and Story of the Law College', *Lawyer* 13:1 (February 1968): 23–7.
74. Evidence of George Norton before the Select Committee of the House of

Lords on 6 June 1853; House of Commons, Vol. XXXII of 1852–53, Paper No. 627, Part I, p. 95.
75. R. Suntharalingam, *Politics and Nationalist Awakening*, p. 64.
76. A son of David Norton, one of the Judges of the Sadr Adalat in the 1830s, J. B. Norton had been practising at the Supreme Court as a barrister for twelve years in Madras. C. E. Buckland, *A Dictionary of Indian Biography* (London: 1906); reprint ed. (Varanasi: Indological Book House, 1971), p. 318.
77. John Bruce Norton, *An Inaugural Lecture on the Study of Law and General Jurisprudence* (Madras: Pharoah, 1855), p. 1.
78. Ibid.
79. Ibid., p. 8.
80. Ibid., p. 18.
81. Ibid., p. 12.
82. Prior to the commencement of law classes or immediately thereafter no text books were available except the work compiled by C. R. Baynes, entitled *The Civil Law of the Madras Presidency as Contained in the Existing Regulations and Acts* (Madras: Pharoah, 1852). Later, two more volumes appeared in the market: Samuel R. Dawes, *A Catechism of the Law Governing Procedure in the East India Company's Civil Court in the Presidency of Ft. St. George, Criminal law of the Madras Presidency as contained in the existing Regulations and Acts* (Madras: Pharoah, 1858), and John Bruce Norton, *The Law of Evidence applicable to the Courts of the East India Company, explained in a course of lectures delivered by J. B. Norton* (Madras: Pharoah, 1858).
83. A. J. Arbuthnot, Director of Public Instruction, to the Chief Secretary to the Government, dated Madras 15 October 1858; House of Commons, Vol. LII, Paper No. 49, p. 12.
84. *The Madras Daily Times*, 20 April 1859.
85. The examination consisted of two parts, the written and oral. Candidates answered questions prepared by the Sadr Adalat on the Regulations, Rules of Practice, Hindu and Muslim Law of inheritance, gift, will, sale and mortgage. As part of the written examination, candidates had to listen to a previously decided suit that the Sheristadar read out loud, omitting only the judgement. They had to write down their opinion 'on the points at issue between the parties and the manner in which the suit ought to be decided agreeably to the Regulations and the law of the parties'. The oral examination tested the knowledge of the candidates on the 'Regulation and Acts . . . the constitution, extent of jurisdiction, powers and course of procedure of the Civil Courts'. Dawes, *A Catechism*, pp. 93–4. Sir T. Muthuswamy Iyer who was the first Indian appointed to the Madras High Court in 1878, took this 'Pleader's Test' in 1856 along with seven other candidates. Only he, Raghunatha Rao and S. Vedanayagam Pillai had passed the test. G. Parameswaran Pillai, *Representative Indians* (London: George Routledge, 1897), p. 161.
86. It appears from the annual report of the Presidency College for 1860 that there was 'Certificate in Law' programme besides the Bachelor in Law degree course. The first graduate in Law was one M. Moorgesam who completed his studies in the same year. See, *The Daily Times and Spectator*, 1 May 1860. See also, Parameswaran Pillai, *Representative Indians*, pp. 193–207 and Suntharalingam, 'Madras Native Association', pp. 237–8.

Notes 211

87. Suntharalingam, *Politics and Nationalist Awakening*, p. 109.
88. Norton, *Administration of Justice*, p. 4.
89. John Bruce Norton, *A Letter to Robert Lowe . . . on the Condition and Requirements of the Presidency of Madras* (Madras: Pharoah, 1854), p. 27.
90. See. Baillie's letter to the Chairman of the Court of Directors, dated 21 February 1848 and the evidence of Sir Erskine Perry from Bombay, before the Select Committee of the House of Lords on 17 March 1853; House of Commons, Vol. XXXI of 1852–3, Paper No. 627, p. 261. Sir Erskine's testimony was 'I received a pamphlet yesterday from a trustworthy gentleman, Mr. Norton, of the Madras Bar, which gives a list of examples of the extreme ignorance in judicial matter displayed by the Company's Judges, which quite condemn the system. My testimony from Bombay is to the same effect; I lived on terms of great intimacy with the Civil Service in India, and I had great opportunities of knowing what they think of it, and they also generally condemn it . . . [I]t is indispensable to get professionally educated men to fill the judicial office.'
91. William Holloway, *Notes on Madras Judicial Administration* (Madras: Higginbotham, 1853); C. R. Baynes, *A Plea for the Madras Judges upon the Charges Preferred against them by J. B. Norton, Esq.* (Madras: Higginbotham, 1853), and *A Rejoinder to Mr. Norton's Reply upon case of the Madras Judges* (Madras: Higginbotham, 1853); and T. A. Anstruther, *Some Instances of the Administration of Justice in Southern India* (Madras: Oriental Press, 1853).
92. *The Madras Daily Times*, 3 June 1859.
93. *The Daily Times and Spectator*, 1 February 1860.
94. John Bruce Norton, *Reply to a Madras Civilian's Defense of the Mofussil Courts in India* (London: Stevens and Norton, 1853) and, *A Letter to Charles Robert Baynes, Esq., Civil and Sessions Judge of Madura: Containing A Reply to His "Plea"* (Madras: Pharoah, 1853).
95. See, J. D. M. Derrett, 'J. H. Nelson: A Forgotten Administrator-Historian', in *Historians of India, Pakistan and Ceylon*, edited by C. H. Philips (London: Oxford University Press, 1961), pp. 354–72.
96. *The Madras Times*, 7 July 1861 reported that Sir Charles Wood would have 'effected the consolidation of these Courts as far back as . . . 1853, only . . . he then considered it necessary that certain forms of procedure should be put in force to enable the consolidated Courts to do the business of both Courts.' See, *The Madras Times*, 1 September and 6 December 1858; See also, 'Report on the Amalgamation of Supreme and Sudder Courts (Madras)', House of Commons, Vol. 52, Paper No. 199, pp. 1–90.
97. Madras Native Association, *Report*, pp. 81–2.
98. Suntharalingam, *Politics and Nationalist Awakening*, p. 51.
99. *The Madras Times*, 24 February 1859.
100. V. C. Gopalratnam, *A Century Completed—A History of the Madras High Court 1862–1962* (Madras: Law Journal Office, 1962), p. 268.
101. Some of these instances were to bid farewell to the departing Chief Justice or the Governor, to bring about changes in the existing rules of the Supreme Court, and to protest against the imposition of various taxes on the professions. See, *The Madras Times*, 11 February 1859; *The Daily Times and Spectator*, 21 June 1860 and 12 August 1859, and *The Madras Daily Times*, 27 September 1859.

Chapter 2: RULES OF THE HIGH COURT

1. HCAR, No. 6360, dated 7 January 1864.
2. B. S. Baliga, 'Sir Charles Trevelyan, Governor of Madras (1859–1860)', in *Studies in Madras Administration*, 2 vols. (Madras: Government of Madras, 1960), 1:340.
3. 'Report on the Amalgamation of Supreme and Sudder Courts (Madras)', Parliamentary Papers, House of Commons, vol. 52 of 1860, Paper No. 199, p. 3. Of these four men both Morehead and Strange were judges of the Sadr Adalat, Smyth was the advocate general in the Supreme Court and Norton was a barrister. See, *The Madras Times and Spectator*, 15 August 1860 for criticisms on the recommendations of the Committee. It said, 'The interests of every class have been duly considered, excepting those of the unfortunate suitors. Barristers, Attorneys, Vakeels, and Civil Servants have all had their several advocates, but that most important class of all, the unhappy Suitors, are only allowed to as parties generally endowed with strong instinctive tendencies to perjury, forgery, and contempt of court, who must be constantly restrained and kept under by the despotic arm of judicial power.'
4. T. L. Strange, *Letter to the Government of Fort Saint George on Judicial Reform* (Madras: The Society for Promoting Christian Knowledge, 1860).
5. Baliga, 'Sir Charles Trevelyan', p. 346; see also, GOM, Judicial Department, G.O. No. 109, dated 30 January 1860.
6. Strange preferred the total removal of the double-agency system and combining the functions of a barrister and attorney in a single individual. See, *Letter to the Government*, pp. 66–7.
7. Minute by W. A. Morehead, 'Report on the Amalgamation of Supreme and Sudder Courts (Madras)', p. 28.
8. Ibid. The two forms of practice refer only to the separation of roles between barristers and attorneys in the Supreme Court and there was no distinction between barristers, attorneys and pleaders at the Sadr Adalat. The pleaders as a group had never been allowed in the Supreme Court.
9. Ibid., pp. 37–9.
10. Ibid., p. 45.
11. Baliga, 'Sir Charles Trevelyan', p. 346. See also, GOM, Judicial Department, G.O. No. 109, dated 30 January 1860 (emphasis added).
12. Francis T. Piggott, ed., *The Imperial Statutes Applicable to the Colonies*, 2 vols. (London: Williams Clowes, 1904), 2:136–9; M. P. Jain, *Outlines of Indian Legal History*, 2nd ed. (Bombay: N. M. Tripathy, 1966), pp. 407–15; S. Biligiri Iyengar, (comp.), *Rules of the High Court of Madras on its Original Side . . . with Statutes and Charters of the Supreme Court* (Madras: The Scottish Press, 1887), pp. 17–22. See also, *The Madras Times*, 31 May 1861 for a commentary on the High Court Bill before the Parliament.
13. John Shaw, *The Charters of the High Court of Judicature at Madras, and of the Courts which preceded it, From 1687 to 1865* (Madras: The Government Press, 1888), pp. 130–9; See also, *Historical Account of Courts at Madras* (n.p., n.d.), pp. 43–4.
14. Ibid., p. 130.
15. Ibid., p. 132.

16. John Shaw, *Charters of the High Court*, p. 132.
17. *Historical Account of Courts*, p. 46, (emphasis added).
18. Ibid., p. 45.
19. John Shaw, 'The Predecessors of the Madras High Court', Part II, *Madras Journal of Literature and Science* (1881): 152.
20. *Historical Account*, p. 53, Rule 11.
21. Ibid., Rules 7 through 9.
22. Chief and Deputy interpreters in Tamil and Telugu were C. Krishnaswamy Iyer and P. Parthasarathy. For Persian and Hindustani Syeed Shah Ally Saib was employed. John Shaw, 'The Predecessors of the High Court', pp. 156–7.
23. Rules 6 through 9 of 1863.
24. HCAR, Circular No. 3253, dated 6 November 1884.
25. C. D. Maclean, *Standing Information Regarding Official Administration of the Madras Presidency* (Madras: The Government Press, 1879), p. 163, on the duties of the government pleader.
26. GOM, Judicial Department, G.O. No. 1593, dated 26 September 1862 (emphasis added).
27. HCAR, No. 1927, dated 22 November 1862.
28. Ibid., No. 992, dated 7 October 1862.
29. Ibid.
30. The earlier petition of the vakils, dated 14 December 1863, contains the names of seven individuals together with their professional and academic experience, who had been allowed to practise only on the Appellate Side. They were: T. Teroomalacharyar; V. Ramasamy Iyengar, six years' standing, retired Munsif's diploma, and attended law lectures for two years; W. Caromal Marcelles, about five years' standing, retired Munsif's and Pleader's diploma, attended law lectures for two years; V. Ranga Charry, four years' standing, held certificate of a passed student of the law class, attended law lectures for four years; W. Sloan four years' standing, retired Munsif's diploma, attended law lectures for three years; P. Rangiah Naidu, about four years' standing, attended law lectures, passed a satisfactory examination in Equity, Law of Evidence, etc., held a certificate of proficiency from the Principal and Law Professor, and H. N. Brockman.
31. *The Madras Times*, 23 August 1865.
32. HCAR, No. 6360, dated 7 January 1864.
33. HCAR, No. 368, dated 1 February 1876.
34. Suntharalingam, *Politics and Nationalist Awakening*, p. 137; and Arnold, *The Congress in Tamilnad*, p. 16.
35. *The Madras Times*, 23 August 1865.
36. Ibid., 17 November 1879. See, *ILR-MS* I (1876): 24–39. Justice Holloway originally made this proposition, which afterwards became a rule of practice in the High Court.
37. *The Madras Times*, 16 November 1871.
38. Ibid., see, G. F. M. Buckee, 'An Examination', p. 10; *The Madras Times*, 17 December 1879, and *The Hindu*, 8 September 1894.
39. They were advocates, attorneys, vakils, pleaders and mukhtars.
40. Bisvesvar Mukherji, *The Legal Practitioners' Act* (Calcutta: R. Cambray & Co., 1903), pp. 50–3.

41. HCAR, No. 806, 13 March 1895. He styled himself as a 'High Court Vakil of Travancore, First Grade Pleader of Tanjore, Madura [and] Tinnevelly Districts and [a] Pensioner . . . of the Madras Government from the Educational Service'.
42. Ibid.
43. HCAR, No. 2117, August 1892; No. 806, 13 March 1895; No. 377, 25 February 1897; No. 768, 7 April 1897; Nos. 178 and 178A, 14 and 25 February 1907.
44. Vakils' Association Minutes (hereafter VAM), 15 November 1906.
45. HCAR, No. 182, 23 January 1918. The notification of the High Court, published on 22 December 1916, contained the following general information on the qualification and admission of vakils. It said,

> Every candidate for admission as a vakil of the High Court shall be required to satisfy the court:
>
> (1) either that he passed the examination for the degree of Bachelor of Laws of the University of Madras in or before 1899, or that he has passed the examination for that degree since January 1899 and . . . has also passed the examination in the Law of Practice and Procedure, Civil and Criminal, . . . or that he has taken the degree of Bachelor of Laws of the University of Allahabad or the degree of Bachelor of Laws of the University of Calcutta, and,
>
> (2) that after passing the examination for one of the said degrees he has either served a regular apprenticeship to an advocate, Vakil or Attorney of the High Court under a contract in writing as provided by these rules or actually practised as a Pleader in the Court of a District or Subordinate Judge in the Madras Presidency or in the Chief Court of Mysore, or in the High Court of Travancore or in the Chief Court of Cochin or in the Court of the Judicial Commissioner of Coorg or in the Court of the Commissioner of Coorg for a period of five years immediately preceding the date of his application, or, where the period for which he has actually practised as a Pleader falls short of five years, presided as a Judge of a Civil Court in the Madras Presidency for the period required to make up the deficiency, and,
>
> (3) that he is of good moral character.

46. HCAR, No. 2016, 12 November 1917.
47. HCAR, No. 1590, 15 December 1911.
48. HCAR, No. 2016, 12 November 1917.
49. Ibid. See., S. Chandrasekhar, *The Nagarathar of South India, An Essay and a Bibliography on the Nagarathars in India and South-East Asia* (Madras: Macmillan, 1980) for comprehensive information on the Nattukkottai Chettiyar community.
50. He had argued before the Chief Court several times as a vakil of the Madras High Court.
51. HCAR, No. 2016, 12 November 1917. Minutes of Justice K. Srinivasa Iyengar, dated 2 July 1917 (emphasis added).
52. Abdur Rahim, W. B. Ayling, C. G. Spencer, V. M. Coutts-Trotter, J. H. Bakewell and W. W. Phillips.
53. HCAR, No. 182, 23 January 1918.

Notes   215

54. University of Madras, *History of Higher Education in South India*, 1:14, footnote No. 2. A select passage quoted from the Hartog Committee Report clearly indicates, 'Education was in no small measure influenced by the desire of Indian parents to send their boys to the University mainly because a University degree has hitherto been regarded as a passport to the safe career of Government employment, and to the great lottery of the legal profession with its rich prizes.' See, House of Commons, 'Interim report of the Indian Statutory Commission (Review of growth of education in British India by the Auxiliary Committee appointed by the Commission)' 1929–30, Vol. X, Cd. 3407 and Mabel Hartog, *P. J. Hartog: A Memoir by his Wife* (London: Constable, 1949).
55. This theme will be fully discussed in a later chapter.
56. HCAR, Nos. 1469 and 1470, 11 September 1922. This document deals with the reciprocal arrangement between different High Courts in permitting Advocates and Vakils from one area to appear in another. While the Bombay High Court was unwilling to modify its 'well settled' practice, the other courts agreed in principle to admit practitioners from elsewhere even though the High Courts of Calcutta and Allahabad did not wish to bind themselves to a formal rule.

Chapter 3: BARRISTER-ATTORNEY COALITION

1. Letter from C. E. Trevelyan to Edward Ryan, dated Madras, 7 June 1859. Trevelyan Papers, vol. d. 129, p. 77, located at Bodleian Library. I am grateful to Professor Frykenberg for permitting me to have access to this document from his personal collection.
2. *The Madras Mail*, 1 April 1878.
3. Dodwell, *Report*, pp. 74–5.
4. Arjun Appadurai, *Worship and Conflict Under Colonial Rule: A South Indian Case* (New Delhi: Orient Longman, 1981), and Carol A. Breckenridge, 'The Sri Minakshi Sundaresvarar Temple: Worship and Endowments in South India, 1833–1925,' Ph.D. Dissertation, University of Wisconsin-Madison, 1976.
5. *The Daily Times and Spectator*, 26 June 1860.
6. Rules 3 and 4 of the High Court, dated 1 October 1863.
7. *The Madras Times*, 21 January 1864.
8. Stokes' letter to the Judges of the High Court, dated 25 September 1863; HCAR, No. 4771, dated 19 December 1863, (emphasis added).
9. Ibid., C. F. Chamier's letter to T. Sydney Smyth, dated 19 December 1863 (emphasis added).
10. Ibid.
11. It is interesting to observe that many English names appear along with several Indian names of vakils in the High Court admission rolls. See, *The Madras High Court 1862–1962: Centenary Volume* (Madras: The High Court, 1962), photographic reproduction.
12. These issues will be discussed fully in subsequent pages.
13. The members present at the meeting were J. B. Norton, J. D. Mayne, S. Branson, T. M. Busteed, P. O'Sullivan and J. Miller; the first meeting was held on 14 March 1865 and the second on 16 December 1871.

14. See, Minutes of the Bar, dated 16 December 1871, 7 October 1875, 24 March 1879, 26 July 1882, and 16 February 1883.
15. See, Appendix I for a complete list of rules of practice and fees.
16. *The Madras Times*, 3 February 1872 and 3 August 1877.
17. Minutes of the Bar, dated 7 and 30 January 1877. See, Sloan, *Practice of the Mofussil Courts or Hand Book of Reference for the Judge and Pleader*, second edition (Madras: Higginbotham, 1868), pp. ii–iii for rules on fees allowed.
18. Ibid., 28 March 1878.
19. *The Madras Mail*, 1 April 1878.
20. Ibid.
21. Ibid.
22. Ibid., 5 April 1878.
23. Minutes of the Bar, dated 24 March 1879.
24. Ibid., dated 7 January 1877.
25. Ibid., dated 18 December 1879.
26. Ibid., and John J. Paul, 'Authority and Professional Control of the Subordinate Legal Profession in the Madras Presidency during the Late Nineteenth Century', in *Law and Social Transformation*, edited by Yogendra Malik and Dhirendra Vajpeyi (Leiden: E. J. Brill, 1990).
27. See, *The Madras Mail*, 25 and 28 March 1882 for a reproduction of the relevant sections of the Legal Practitioners' Act of 1879 and the new rules formulated by the High Court in accordance with the provisions of the Act.
28. Ibid.
29. They are: Gray's Inn, Inner Temple, Lincoln's Inn and Middle Temple.
30. *The Madras Mail*, 8 March 1882. The total expense was about £150 and the dinners cost about £1 a term.
31. *The Madras Times*, 13 July 1864.
32. Ibid., 11 September 1869.
33. *The Madras Mail*, 14 February 1879, (emphasis added).
34. Ibid., 22 February 1879.
35. Minutes of the Bar, 7 July 1881.
36. These were the offices of the Government Pleader, Taxing Officer at the High Court, Assistant Secretary to the Government under the Legislative Department, Administrator General, and Professor of Law at the Presidency College. Maclean, *Standing Information*, pp. 162–8. Maclean explains the different responsibilities of these officers under the government.
37. GOM, Legislative Department, No. 1619, dated 13 October 1866; See, Minutes of the Bar, 7 April 1881 for the names of barristers who held these positions, and *The Madras Mail*, 9 April 1879.
38. *The Madras Times*, 27 September and 20 October 1864.
39. Ibid., 14 November 1864.
40. Minutes of the Bar, 28 January 1887.
41. See, *The Madras Times*, 27 June 1876.
42. Some of these appointments were: Chief Justiceship, Advocate Generalship, Public Prosecutorships, Clerk of the Crown and the Registrar of the High Court.
43. See, *The Madras Times*, 8 and 13 April 1872; 27 June 1876; *The Madras Mail*, 15 and 23 January 1879; 9 April 1880, and *The Hindu*, 23 July 1889 for discussions on appointments to these offices.

44. *The Madras Times*, 13 April 1872 (emphasis added).
45. See, *The Madras Times*, 25 March 1880.
46. See, John D. Mayne, *Commentaries on the Indian Penal Code (Act XLV of 1860)*, 8th ed., (Madras: Higginbotham, 1874); John Bruce Norton, *Topics of Jurisprudence or Aids to the Office of the Indian Judge* (Madras: Higginbotham, 1862); G. S. Grove, *A Treatise on the Hindu Law of Inheritance* (Madras: Higginbotham, 1868); Whitley Stokes, ed., *Hindu Law Books* (Madras: Higginbotham, 1865); H. S. Cunningham, *A Digest of Hindu Law as Administered in the Courts of the Madras Presidency* (Madras: Higginbotham, 1877); R. B. Michell, *Digest of the Indian Law Reports for the Year 1876* (Madras: Higginbotham, 1879); F. Normandy, *Digest of High Court Reports* (Madras: Higginbotham, 1880), and Whitley Stokes and others, eds., *Reports of Cases Decided in the High Court of Madras in 1862–1875*, 8 vols. (Madras: Higginbotham, 1864–76).
47. See, *The Madras Jurist, A Journal and Law Reports for all India 1866–76*, 11 vols. (Madras: C. Foster, 1866–76); *The Madras Law Reporter*, reported by a vakil and edited by Spring Branson (Madras: The Mail Press, 1877) and *The Indian Jurist*, 17 vols. (Madras: C. Foster, 1877–93).
48. *The Madras Times*, 30 June 1875.
49. Ibid. 5 April 1876. See also, *The Madras Times*, 11 August 1869.
50. Ibid.
51. Ibid., 25 August 1871.
52. *The Madras Jurist*, 7:4 (April 1872): 121–3.
53. *The Madras Times*, 25 August 1871.
54. John Miller, a well known barrister, was approached by V. Bhashyam Iyengar who later became a great lawyer, Advocate General and a Judge of the High Court, to be admitted as his apprentice. The barrister demanded that a fee of one thousand rupees must be paid for the privilege and when the applicants promised to pay the sum in two instalments, some at the beginning and the rest at the completion of the course, not only did the barrister refuse to accept any such arrangement but sharply asked who would pay the rest if the applicant were to die during the period of apprenticeship which lasted for about a year. Ke. Cuntararakavan, *Sar Vi. Pashyam Aiyankar* [Sir V. Bhashyam Iyengar] (Mayilapur: Intiya Pirintin Orks, 1943), p. 11; see also, by the same author, *Rai Pahatur Pi. Anantacarlu* [Rai Bahadur P. Anandacharlu] (Cennai: Allaiyans Kampani, 1943) pp. 9–11 (in Tamil).
55. See the evidence of Sir Thomas Strange in Chapter 1. See also, E. B. V. Christian, *A Short History of Solicitors* (London: Reeves and Turner, 1896) and Brian Abel-Smith and Robert Stevens, *Lawyers and the Courts: A Sociological Study of the English Legal System* (Cambridge, MA: Harvard University Press, 1967), pp. 53–76, for background information on the development of attorneys as part of the legal profession in England.
56. Shaw, 'The Predecessors', p. 152. See also, *The Madras Times*, 10 April 1872.
57. *The Madras Times*, 25 October 1866.
58. A Parliamentary bill passed during 1830–1 prohibited clerks of the Supreme Court judges from practising as attorneys. The bill said 'no person being a clerk to any Judge of either of the said Supreme Courts, shall, during the time that he shall act as such, be capable of being admitted or of acting as an attorney or solicitor; and in case any such person shall be guilty of a breach of this

enactment, the person so offending shall be forthwith removed from his office of clerk, and shall be incapable for ever thereafter of holding that or any office in any court of justice.' There were obvious reasons for this enactment. First, it was possible that some clerks might have tried to influence the decisions of the judges under whom they had been employed. Closely attached to the machinery of the court as well as the presiding judges, the clerks had unique advantages over the rest of the functionaries of the court; these advantages were exploited whenever the clerks also acted for their clients. Second, the clerks might also have used their special privileges and close contacts with judges as grounds for extorting high fees from their clients. House of Commons, Vol. I of 1830–1, Paper No. 265, pp. 433–5.

59. Strange, *Letter to the Government*, pp. xxxix.
60. *The Madras Times*, 23 September 1861.
61. Shaw, 'The Charters', p. 132.
62. *The Madras Times*, 27 June 1876.
63. Rule 11, Rules of Practice, dated 1 October 1863. See, Sloan, *Rules*, pp. 374–8.
64. Ibid., Rules 12 through 16.
65. P. Anandacharlu, *The Madras Bar and How to Improve It* (Madras: K. R. Press, 1883), p. 5.
66. *The Madras Times*, 27 June 1876. Barristers thought that appearing in chamber and pleading as counsel at the final hearing of cases on the original side were innovations of the High Court and contrary to and beyond the scope of the Charter.
67. *The Madras Times*, 2 August 1871 and 30 October 1879.
68. *The Madras Times*, 23 February 1872.
69. Rule 10, Rules and Orders relating to Advocates, Vakils, and Attorneys and the taxations and allowances of Costs, dated 5 July 1866; See Sloan. *Rules*, pp. 349–52.
70. *The Manchester Guardian*, 28 February 1865, reprinted in *The Madras Times*, 7 April 1865. See also, T. L. Strange, *Letter to the Government*, pp. 66–7.
71. C. V. Sundarum Sastri, *Remarks on the Bill of Cost of Attorneys*, Part 1 (Madras: The Irish Press, 1893), p. 1.
72. Ibid.
73. *The Madras Times*, 7 March 1863. See also *The Madras Mail*, 29 November 1878 for an itemized report on the Bill of Costs of Messrs. Barclay and Morgan, the leading attorneys' firm.
74. Ibid., 8 March 1863.
75. Ibid., 7 March 1863.
76. Ibid., 10 March 1863. This rather long poem with five separate stanzas and chorus is only partly reproduced here.
77. Minutes of the Bar, dated 29 July 1882.
78. *The Indian Jurist* 17:1 (January 1893): 32–5. See, Appendix II for the rules passed by the Attorneys Association.
79. K. A. Nilakanta Sastri, ed., *A Great Liberal: Speeches and Writings of Sir P. S. Sivaswami Aiyar* (Bombay: Allied Publishers, 1965), p. 236. The men present were C. Wilson, A. Champion, E. Barclay, T. W. Laing, C. Sadasiva Row, Biligiri Iyengar, R. Branson, W. Branson, T. C. Mellish, E. G. Burlow, G. Rowlandson and James Short. See, Minutes of the Bar, dated 29 July 1882.

80. Lewis McIver, *Imperial Census of 1881: Operations and Results in the Presidency of Madras*, 2 vols. (Madras: The Government Press, 1883), 2:199.
81. Shaw, *The Charters of the High Court, pp. 160.*
82. *The Madras Jurist* 10:11 (November 1875): 403.
83. Rules 2 through 5. Rules and Order of the High Court of Judicature, Vakils and Attorneys, dated 5 July 1866. See, Sloan, *Rules*, pp. 349–52.
84. *The Madras Times*, 15 January 1876.
85. Shaw, 'The Predecessors', p. 153.
86. In the Matter of the Petition of the Attorneys, *ILR-MS I* (1876): 24–39.
87. Ibid., p. 29.
88. Ibid., p. 35.
89. Ibid., p. 39.
90. Civil Suit, No. 200 of 1915, *MLJ-RS* 31 (1916): 698–712.
91. Gopalratnam, *A Century Completed*, pp. 122–5.

Chapter 4: VAKILS' PREPARATION, PRACTICE AND GROWTH

1. Trevelyan to Ryan, dated Madras, 7 June 1859. Trevelyan Papers, vol. d. 129, p. 77 (emphasis added).
2. Ki Cantiracekaran, *Vi. Kirushnasvami Aiyar* [V. Krishnaswami Iyer] (Cennai: Kalaimakal Kariyalayam, 1945), p. 78 (in Tamil).
3. HCAR, No. 6360, 7 January 1864, and GOM, Judicial Department, No. 10, 5 January 1864.
4. K. P. S. Menon, *C. Sankaran Nair* (New Delhi: Government of India, 1967), pp. 14–15.
5. *Sasilekha*, 24 February 1903 (RNP). See, HCAR, No. 416, 16 January 1894 and No. 1503, May 1895 for examples of vakils who had enrolled as advocates after completing their graduate degrees.
6. Ibid.
7. Minutes of the Bar, 27 April 1898. See, Srinivasa Rao, 'The Origins and Growth', pp. 101–6.
8. See, Rules 7 and 8 of 1 October 1863. S. Biligiri Iyengar, *Rules of the High Court*, p. 156.
9. K. V. Krishnaswami Iyer, 'The Course of Apprenticeship', *MLJ-JS* 38 (January 1920): 8. This paper was read during the Madras Lawyers' Conference in December of 1919. See, *Professional Conduct and Advocacy*, 3rd ed. (Madras: Oxford University Press, 1953), by the same author.
10. HCAR, Circular No. 299, 2 February 1891; Minutes of Justice H. H. Shephard, dated 10 January 1891.
11. Ibid., Rule 7.
12. Ibid., Rule 8 read 'Before any person shall be admitted as a Vakil, he shall sign and fill with the Registrar . . . an affidavit stating the amount and nature of work done by him during the period of his service under the following heads, viz:

   a. No. of plaints prepared
   b. No. of written statement prepared

     c. No. of memoranda of appeal drafted
     d. No. of memoranda of objections drafted
     e. No. of brief prepared under instruction from clients
     f. No. of cases in which notes of arguments have been drawn up
     g. No. of cases in which notes have been taken in court.'

13. At this time, the curriculum was divided into two major sections: First examination in Law (F.L.) and Bachelor in Law (B.L.). The former included such subjects as Jurisprudence, Roman Law, The Law of Contracts and the Law of Torts, while the latter covered Theory and Law of Property, Hindu and Muslim Law, Indian Constitutional Law, The Law of Evidence, and Civil and Criminal Procedure including the Law of Limitation. See, *History of Higher Education in South India*, p. 105.

14. Ke. Cantiracekaran, *Vi. Kirushnasvami Aiyar*, p. 73–88.

15. Rule 8. HCAR, Nos. 1000 and 1007, 19 August 1910. The judges requested Justice P. R. Sundara Iyer, a long term friend of Justice V. Krishnaswami Iyer, to deliver the lectures for 1911 and 1912; these lectures were later published. P. R. Sundara Iyer, *Professional Ethics* (Madras: P. R. Rama Iyer, 1918). According to the available sources, the following delivered subsequent lectures: C. E. Odgers 1913 and 1914; R. Sadagopachariar 1915; T. R. Ramachandra Iyer 1916; V. V. Srinivasa Iyengar 1917–1918; C. P. Ramaswami Iyer 1919–1920; H. D. Cornish 1921–1922; V. Mockett 1923–1924, and C. V. Anantakrishna Iyer 1925. See also, HCAR, No. 1057, 18 July 1914; No. 1166, 16 July 1919 and No. 1586, 28 August 1925.

16. *MLJ-JS* 38 (January 1920): 6.

17. Ibid., p. 9.

18. Ibid., pp. 16–18.

19. For example, when in 1867 T. Rama Rao, who had been an interpreter at the High Court, sought admission as a vakil, the barristers decided to oppose his enrolment. They contended that the 'compulsory attendance as an Interpreter was not an attendance under the rules to qualify him for admission'. C. Sankaran Nair, *Autobiography of Sir C. Sankaran Nair* (Madras: K. P. Parvathi Amma, 1966), pp. 15–16.

20. Ke. Cantiracekaran, *Rai Pakatur Pi. Anantacarlu*, p. 11 and *Sar Vi. Pashyam Aiyankar*, pp. 11–12.

21. For example, in the case of P. S. Sivaswami Iyer and V. Krishnaswami Iyer it was R. Balaji Rao, a Maratha Brahman and a family friend from Tanjore, under whom they apprenticed; S. Kasturi Ranga Iyengar was an apprentice under V. Bhashyam Iyengar; C. V. Kumaraswami Sastri served his term under his own father C. V. Sundaram Sastri. V. Ryru Nambiar and A. Narayana Nambiar, both from Malabar, were apprenticed under C. Sankaran Nair. Alphonso J. Lobo from Canara was an apprentice under K. Narain Rao who also hailed from that region. See, Chandrasekharan, *P. S. Sivaswami Aiyer*, p. 17; V. K. Narasimhan, *Kasturi Ranga Iyengar*, p. 11; HCAR, No. 591, 6 March 1893; *The Hindu*, 27 April 1889; 25 March 1890 and 14 April 1894.

22. Personal interview with V. K. T. Chari, former Advocate General, on 24 April 1982. See, Madhavan Nair, *Sir C. Sankaran Nair*, p. 25, for a description of Sankaran Nair's daily activities.

23. HCAR, No. 766, 3 May 1922. Letter from E. W. Legh, Revenue Secretary, to

F. G. Butler, Registrar, High Court, dated 27 February 1922. See, GOM, Revenue Department, No. 720, 7 May 1923.
24. Justices W. B. Ayling, Abdur Rahim and C. G. Spencer offered no opinion. Justice W. W. Phillips had 'no strong opinion' while the rest, Justices C. V. Kumaraswami Sastri, V. M. Coutts-Trotter, C. Krishnan, V. Ramesam, M. Venkatasubba Rao and M. D. Devadoss expressed a rather strong protest.
25. HCAR, No. 766, 3 May 1923; Minutes by the Chief Justice Coutts-Trotter, dated 7 March 1922. Basheer Ahmed Sayeed, who later became a Judge in the High Court, experienced considerable difficulties around this time in coming up with the fee for his enrolment. In fact, his enrolment was delayed by a year on account of lack of funds. Basheer Ahmed Sayeed, *My Life, A Struggle: An Autobiography*, (Madras: The Academy of Islamic Research, 1983), p. 20.
26. GOM, Revenue Department, No. 896, 15 May 1922. See also, No. 720, 7 May 1923 for a petition from apprentices in law submitted to Khan Bahadur Habibullah, Revenue Member of the Council, against the proposal to increase the enrolment fee.
27. HCAR, No. 374, 11 February 1924. Rule 12.
28. See, *MLJ-JS* 9:3 (March 1899): 122–3. See also, HCAR, No. 1285, 22 July 1925; No. 711, 27 September 1940 and No. 742, 1 October 1941 for further changes in enrolment rules.
29. *The Hindu*, 25 and 27 April 1889; 25 March 1890; 25 April and 22 December 1892.
30. Ke. Cantiracekaran, *Vi. Kirushnasvami Aiyar*, p. 38.
31. C. Sankaran Nair, *Autobiography*, p. 14.
32. *MWN-JS* 1 (August 1910): 86.
33. W. S. Krishnaswami Nayudu, *My Memoirs* (Madras: Author, 1977), pp. 56–7.
34. *The Madras Law Review* 1 (November 1932–March 1933): 104.
35. Cantiracekaran, *Vi. Kirushnasvami Aiyar*, p. 81.
36. *The Madras Mail*, 17 November 1879.
37. Ibid., 6 December 1878.
38. Ibid.
39. Ibid., 7 December 1878.
40. Ibid.
41. Ibid.
42. Ibid., 12 December 1878. The *Times'* views were summarized by the *Mail* in this issue.
43. Ibid.
44. Ibid. These issues would serve as the basis for demanding the creation of an All-India Bar Council during the 1920s.
45. Ibid. (emphasis added).
46. Ibid. (emphasis added).
47. This individual appears to be John Shaw whose name appears among those attorneys who had previously petitioned to the High Court in 1874 regarding the exclusion of vakils from the Original Side. He was also the author of the *Charters of the High Courts and the Courts Which Preceded It*.
48. *The Madras Mail*, 13 December 1878.
49. Ibid.
50. Cited in *The Madras Times*, 30 December 1878.

51. See, *Karnataka Prakasika*, 17 March 1890 and *Mysore Vrittanta Bodhini*, 22 March 1890 (RNP).
52. *The Hindu*, 30 October 1889 and 2 November 1889.
53. *The Madras High Court 1862–1962, Centenary Volume*, p. 39.
54. *The Hindu*, 11 November 1889.
55. Ibid.
56. This theme will be discussed more fully in Chapter 6.
57. Anandacharlu, *The Madras Bar*, p. ii. See also, from the same author, *Our Marriage Laws and How to Reform Them* (Madras: Scottish Press, 1883) and *Our Courts of Law and How to Improve Them* (Madras: K. R. Press, 1882).
58. Ibid., p. i.
59. See the excellent essay written by R. Ragunatha Rao, 'A knowledge of Sanscrit for Lawyers and Judges', *The Hindu*, 5 November 1892.
60. Anandacharlu, *The Madras Bar*, pp. 2–29.
61. Ibid., pp. 29–47.
62. Biligiri Iyengar, *Rules of the High Court*, pp. 169–72. In 1885 an elaborate series of rules related to attorneys were passed; these rules laid down several specific requirements on the part of candidates who wished to enrol themselves as attorneys.
63. *The Madras Mail*, 9 April 1879; *Tarangai Nesan*, 5 October 1889, and *Kerala Patrika*, 30 September 1889 (RNP).
64. *The Hindu*, 16 July 1889 and 29 January 1890; *The Madras Mail*, 9 April 1879; *Kerala Patrika*, 28 and 31 July 1889 (RNP). The first vakil appointed to the Governor's Council was V. Sadagopacharlu in 1862 but his untimely death in 1863 created a vacancy in that position. It was not until 1880 that other vakils occupied such position. *The Madras Times*, 22 August 1863; Gopalratnam, *A Century Completed*, p. 264.
65. From the Government of India's point of view, however, his appointment was made reluctantly because of his sympathies with the aspirations of Indians to enter into the upper echelons of bureaucracy through Civil Service. *British Attitude Towards the Employment of Indians in Civil Service: Report of the Public Service Commission (1886–1887).* Headed by Sir Charles U. Aitchison, Critical Introduction by Bradford Spangenberg (Delhi: Concept Publishing Company, 1977), p. xxiv. G. Parameswaram Pillai, *Representative Indians* (London: George Routledge, 1897), pp. 209–17 provides a brief biographical sketch on Ramaswami Mudaliar.
66. The criteria that the High Court adopted for selecting vakils who could attend the events are not known. Baliga, 'Sir Charles Trevelyan', p. 343; Raleigh Trevelyan, *The Golden Oriole* (New York: Viking, 1987), p. 333, and HCAR, No. 5965, 28 November 1865. The vakils who had been considered eligible to receive invitations to government public balls were: Karaunakara Manavan, Srirangapatnam Parthasaratahy Iyengar, Vembakkam Rajagopalacharlu, Vembakkam Rangachariar, Palavay Rangaiyah Naidu, William Sloan, Tirumala Srinivasachariyar, Srirangapatnaum Tirumalachariyar, Havaly Venkatapathy Rao. It is not clear from the records whether William Sloan was European or Eurasian.
67. Ke. Cuntararakavan, *Sar Vi. Pashyam Aiyankar*, pp. 16 and 27. See, R. Suntharalingam, *Politics and Nationalist Awakening*, pp. 197–207.

68. Suntharalingam, *Politics and Nationalist Awakening*, Appendix, pp. 352–5.
69. Vakils' Association Minutes, 4 and 6 December 1889 (hereafter VAM); *The Hindu*, 8 November 1889 and F. W. Dillon, *From An Indian Bar Room: Sketches, Talks and Tales* (Calcutta: Butterworth, 1920), pp. 1–16.
70. W. R. Cornish, *Report on the Census of the Madras Presidency 1871*, 2 vols. (Madras: The Government Press, 1874), 1:181; *Census of the Town of Madras, 1871* (Madras: The Fort St. George Press, 1873), p. 91, and Lewis McIver, *Imperial Census of 1881, Operative and Results in the Presidency of Madras*, 2 vols. (Madras: The Government Press, 1883), 2:199. Two different figures for vakils are given in the 1881 Report: the tables show that 59 practised in the city alone but the summary statements mention that 83 vakils practised throughout the Presidency. The tables in Misra's book are also somewhat conflicting with the information of the Census Records; he seems to have relied solely on the *Thacker's Indian Directory* for the total enrolment of advocates and vakils in the Madras High Court. According to this *Directory*, there were 65 advocates and 181 vakils who had been enrolled in the High Court between 1870 and 1890. See, Misra, *Indian Middle Classes*, p. 328.
71. H. A. Stuart, *Census of India, 1891*, 28 vols. (Calcutta: The Government of India Press, 1893), 13:346.
72. *The Reports on the Administration of Civil and Criminal Justice in the Presidency of Madras, 1879 and 1880* (Madras: The Scottish Press, 1880 and 1881) and the *Report on the Administration of Civil Justice in the Presidency of Madras, 1881–1908*, 28 vols. (Madras: The Scottish Press, 1882–1909). The figures in Table 1 are based on these reports.
73. *Report of the Indian Education Commission* (Calcutta: Government Printing, 1883), p. 281.
74. Ibid., p. 301.
75. HCAR, No. 1986, dated 5 September 1882. This table is based on the names that appear in the list prepared by the High Court for the Imperial Education Commission. See, Suntharalingam, *Politics and Nationalist Awakening*, Appendix, for additional names of vakils who had graduated from the Madras University prior to 1871 and had been practising as High Court vakils.
76. The most recent survey on the profession conducted by the Bar Council of India reveals the opposite trend. That is, the majority of lawyers are from Backward Classes. N. R. Madhava Menon, S. Rama Rao, and S. Sudarsen, 'Legal Profession in Tamil Nadu', *Indian Bar Review* 10:4 (1983): 574.
77. R. E. Frykenberg, *Guntur District 1788–1848: A History of Local Influence and Central Authority in South India* (Oxford: Clarendon Press, 1965), p. 84.
78. See, *The Hindu*, 27 October and 7 November 1892 for discussion on the advancement of Native Christians against stiff competitions from Brahmans.
79. The Vellalar Christians were: John Arivanandam Pillai, S. Nevins Pillai, P. M. Jaga Rao Pillai, and C. Chelliah Pillai; the names such as A. G. Coellio, A. T. Ambrose, V. M. Fernandes and J. L. DeRosario refer to Goan and Malabar origins. See, *The Hindu*, 7 September 1984 for a brief sketch on P. M. Jaga Rao Pillai.
80. It appears that some members of the Muslim community were only interested in the government appointments and were yet to realize the utility of taking advantage of other possible avenues then open to them. Added to this were

such factors as the total numerical strength of Muslims in the Presidency as opposed to certain parts of Northern India and the spread of Western education among them, which seemed to have influenced their career choices. See, *The Madras Mail*, 13 May 1882.

Chapter 5: LIMITATIONS IN VAKILS' PRACTICE

1. HCAR, No. 2353, 16 December 1916.
2. F. T. Piggot, *The Imperial Statutes*, 1:145.
3. G. Krishnaswami Ayyar and Chakrapani Achari v. T. V. Swaminatha Ayyar, Original Side Appeal No. 6 of 1924, *ILR-MS* 48 (1925): 344.
4. V. C. Gopalratnam, *A Century Completed*, p. 129.
5. *ILR-MS* 48 (1925):357.
6. Ibid.
7. 'Pleading in the Insolvency Courts', *MLJ-JS* 6 (December 1896):473–377.
8. *ILR-MS* 48 (1925): 358 (emphasis added).
9. VAM, 11 July 1923. The resolution was moved by S. Panchapagesa Sastriar who along with G. Krishnaswami Iyer, K. V. Sesha Iyengar and the two joint-secretaries was nominated to form a committee to 'draw up the covering letter to be sent' to the judges.
10. HCAR, No. 1836, 25 October 1923. Letter from the Secretaries, The Madras Vakils' Association, to the Registrar, High Court, dated 23 July 1923.
11. Ibid., Letter from the Registrar, High Court, to the Vakils' Association, dated 25 October 1923.
12. Ibid., Notes prepared by G. S. White, dated 14 August 1923 (emphasis added).
13. The judges who took this view were Sir Walter Schwabe, C. G. Odgers, M. D. Devadoss, E. H. Wallace and D. G. Waller. Although Justice Coutts-Trotter supported the view of the majority, he did not hesitate to point out that 'the position [of vakils] is admittedly, perhaps unjustly, anomalous, because we cannot legislate'. Ibid., Minutes by Justice Coutts-Trotter, dated 3 September 1923.
14. *High Court Centenary Volume*, p. 50.
15. C. V. Kumaraswami Sastri, M. Venkatasubba Rao, C. Krishnan, and V. Ramesam. The minutes of Kumaraswami Sastri written on 16 September 1923 serve as the best example of the arguments adduced by these dissenting judges.
16. HCAR, No. 1836, 11 October 1923. Minutes of Justice Venkatasubba Rao, dated 1 October 1923.
17. VAM, 9 November 1923.
18. HCAR, No. 1878, 10 October 1924. The letter addressed to the Registrar read, 'In passing Section 121 . . . the legislature was only anxious not to arrogate to itself the function of determining the classes of persons on whom the right of audience may be conferred in regard to insolvency matters. . . . To impute to the legislature a deliberate intention of excluding a certain class of practitioners would be opposed to all canons of construction especially when that has the effect of interfering, as if by a side wind, with the powers of the High Court under the Letters Patent. . . . The Association begs to point out that it was not the intention of the Legislature to perpetuate the anomaly of Vakils being permitted to appear in Insolvency Appeals and not in the Original Court.'

19. *ILR-MS* 48 (1925):332.
20. Insolvency Petition No. 392 of 1923, dated 15 January 1924. T. R. Venkatarama Sastri, Nugent Grant, and Sidney Smith represented the associations of vakils, attorneys and advocates. See, VAM, 4 January 1924.
21. The Full Bench consisted of C. G. Spencer, Officiating Chief Justice, and Justices M. D. Devadoss and V. V. Srinivasa Iyengar.
22. *ILR-MS* 48 (1925):360. This observation was made by Justice V. V. Srinivasa Iyengar in his judgment.
23. Ibid., p. 361 (emphasis added).
24. Ibid., pp. 331–68 and *ILR-MS* 52 (1929):92–105.
25. *ILR-MS* 52 (1929):92
26. Ibid., p. 104.
27. Justice Bhashyam Iyengar used the Tamil phrases *malikai katai* and *javulik katai*, that is retail grocery and textile stores, to describe the nature of some vakils' involvement in trade. See, HCAR, No. 289, 21 March 1902. Minutes of Justice Bhashyam Iyengar, dated 15 March 1902.
28. HCAR, No. 486, 13 March 1899. See, *The Civil Rules of Practice*, pp. 117–19.
29. GOM, Judicial Department, No. 1279, 17 May 1916. Letter from R. H. Courtney, Judicial Department, No. 114–B–1, dated 22 January 1916 to the Chief Justice, Madras High Court.
30. HCAR, No. 1618, 28 August 1916. See, *MWN-JS* 17 (October 1926):105–6.
31. See below for further elucidation on this point.
32. *MWN-JS* 17:33 (October 1926):106.
33. Ibid.
34. Ibid.
35. *MWN-JS* 17:36 (November 1926):119.
36. Ibid., pp. 119–121.
37. Ibid., p. 120.
38. Ibid.
39. Horatio H. Shephard, S. Subramania Iyer, James A. Davies, Ralph S. Benson, and Hungerford T. Boddam.
40. HCAR, No. 1618, 28 August 1916 and No. 1126, 14 December 1904. The rule was first dropped from the Original Side Rules in 1905 and from the Appellate Side in 1915. See, *Rules of the High Court of Judicature—Madras, Appellate Side*, p. 13.
41. HCAR, No. 1618, 28 August 1916. See, the copy of the minutes of the Judges on the application from R. Sriramulu Sastri seeking permission to continue his involvement with the Portland Cement Factory, in addition to his professional duties.
42. Ibid. The minutes of Justice Davies, dated 9 December 1899. Justices Shephard and Subramania Iyer also supported this view.
43. Ibid. The minutes of the Chief Justice Arnold White, dated 2 December 1899 (emphasis added). See, D. Duman, *The English and Colonial Bars*, pp. 143–68 for a discussion on the involvement of barristers and solicitors in England with trade or business outside of their profession.
44. Ibid. The minutes of Justice H. D. Boddam, dated 12 December 1899.
45. Ibid. The minutes of Justice Coutts-Trotter, dated 8 March 1916.
46. See, *MLJ-JS* 9:3 (March 1899):120–2. The editorial primarily dwelt on these two points by maintaining that the rule was both 'illegal and undesirable'.

47. HCAR, No. 2353, 16 December 1916. This document deals with an application submitted by N. Krishnaswami Iyengar, Bar Association, Kumbakonam, to the High Court, requesting a clear definition of the terms 'trade or business'. The Judges discussed the feasibility of modifying the rule but decided against it on the pretext that the same rule had already been altered only a few months before. In the course of the discussion, Justice Abdur Rahim made certain observations on 9 November 1916, which best illustrate how some of them were thinking.
48. HCAR, No. 1618, 28 August 1916. Notes written by the Assistant Registrar, dated 23 December 1899.
49. HCAR, No. 1041, 20 July 1899. See, HCAR, No. 400, 26 March 1911 in which E. S. Subramania Pattamaly, High Court Vakil, was permitted to continue as the President of 'The Friends Association Press' and as the Vice-President of the 'Sri Krishna Vilasa Nidhi'.
50. See, GOM, Revenue Department, No. 15, 4 January 1916 which records the names of different types of cooperative societies. There were six major categories:
    a. Central Societies, Central and District Banks;
    b. Central Societies—Unions;
    c. Non-Agricultural Societies—Credit Societies;
    d. Non-Agricultural Societies, Societies for production fund;
    e. Agricultural Societies—Credit Societies;
    f. Agricultural Societies—Forms of Co-operatives.

    It is not clear what distinctions existed between these societies or how differently they functioned from one another. Besides, there were joint-stock companies such as the Indian Bank, the Mylapore Permanent Fund, the Tanjore Permanent Fund and several other Life Insurance Companies. The economic history of the Madras Presidency written from the point of collective development of co-operative and commercial banking institutions still remains an unfinished task for the historian. Christopher J. Baker, *The Politics of South India 1920–1937* (Cambridge: Cambridge University Press, 1976), pp. 184–92.
51. HCAR, No. 303, 7 February 1919. S. Guruswami Chetti was given permission on the condition that he should not practise during the period he was engaged in trade. He seems to have violated his agreement, for which he was suspended from his profession. See, HCAR, No. 1010, 27 April 1920.
52. HCAR, No. 292, 21 March 1902. After a great deal of discussion the judges decided to permit P. Anandacharlu to assume the proprietorship of Vaijayanti Press for which, as he put it, he had 'sunk a large sum of money'.
53. HCAR, No. 386, 18 April 1905; No. 53, 23 April 1908, and No. 298, 25 February 1910 in which the judges approved the publication of *The Hindu*, a daily newspaper, *The Liberal*, a weekly newspaper and *The Madras Weekly Notes*. See, HCAR, No. 252, 18 February 1913 which deals with the publication of *Mercantile Law Journal*.
54. HCAR, No. 1126, 14 December 1904.
55. HCAR, No. 1388, 5 August 1916. Harihara Iyer, a High Court vakil at Madura obtained the sanction to report the proceedings of the Twenty-Second Madras Provincial Conference for a remuneration of Rs 300. However, he was discouraged from such activities in the future.

56. HCAR, No. 1263, 19 August 1922.
57. HCAR, No. 628, 9 May 1910 contains a copy of the Government Order, Revenue Department, No. 1670, 2 December 1909, dealing with the correspondence on the growth of these societies. The government sent a copy of this correspondence to all district collectors with a request that they might watch the working of such societies in their respective headquarters. HCAR, No. 2353, 16 December 1916. Minutes by K. Srinivasa Iyengar, dated 27 November 1916.
58. See, GOM, Judicial Department, No. 1411, 10 August 1907. The government had to pay a sum of Rs 17,250 to C. Sankaran Nair, Advocate General, for conducting the prosecution of the Calcutta Provident Institutions before the Joint-Magistrate, Rajamundery.
59. HCAR, No. 1618, 28 August 1916. Copy of the minutes of Justice H. T. Boddam, dated 12 December 1899, and No. 507, 18 February 1926 and No. 42, 12 May 1931. HCAR, No. 140, 18 February 1927 provides a classic example of abuse of privileges.
60. HCAR, Nos. 1010 and 1011, 27 April 1920 deal with the suspension of S. Guruswami Chetti. After obtaining the sanction of the High Court to do business in 'foodstuffs', he continued in the trade beyond the period originally specified. The judges viewed this as a breach of promise and suspended him with an order that he should immediately vacate his chambers in the High Court. On a different occasion, V. Rangaswami Iyengar approached the High Court for permission to accept the position as Secretary of 'The Asiatic Government Life and Marriage Assurance Company, Ltd.' as he got 'very little income' from his profession and was unable to maintain himself. He, therefore, accepted the probationary offer and was about to move to Mysore. His application was not even circulated among the judges as was normally done. Instead, the Registrar sought the orders from the Chief Justice Coutts-Trotter whether to accord permission or suspend the applicant on account of his failure to submit an application prior to his accepting the temporary position. The Chief Justice, who had consistently opposed lawyers' practice of extraprofessional engagements, simply wrote 'yes', which meant unconditional and immediate suspension. HCAR, No. 332, 30 January 1925.
61. HCAR, No. 289, 21 March 1902. Letter addressed to the Registrar, High Court, dated 13 March 1902.
62. Ibid. Minutes of Justice H. D. Boddam, dated 18 March 1902 (emphasis added).
63. John J. Paul, 'New Frontiers in the Colonial Judicial Administration: Its Laws and Lawyers', paper presented at the International Conference on 'South Asia and World Capitalism', held at the Tufts University (Medford, MA), 12–14 December 1986.
64. *Indian Review* 21 (1920):411.
65. Buckee, 'Allahabad High Court', p. 267.
66. CID Confidential Reports, 1907 which discusses the anti-British meetings behind the closed doors of the bar room in Guntur.

Chapter 6: LEADERS AND PRIVILEGES

1. *Speeches and Writings of Sir T. Muthuswamy Aiyar*, with an introductory Memoir by F. Rowlandson (Madras: The Lawrence Asylum Press, 1895), p. 3.
2. Sir T. Muthuswamy Iyer never practiced law either in Madras or anywhere else as some had thought. C. E. Buckland, *Dictionary of Indian Biography* (London: Swan Sonnenschein, 1906; reprint ed., Varanasi: Indological Books, 1971), p. 9.
3. In April 1885, when P. S. Sivaswami Iyer became a High Court vakil, S. Gopalachariar was the secretary of the association. On the eve of his appointment as a sub-judge, K. P. Sankara Menon took over the responsibilities until the association became effete. Nilakanta Sastri, *A Great Liberal*, pp. 252, 271–2; see, Ki. Cantiracekaran, *Vi. Kirushnasvami Aiyar*, pp. 80–1 and *The Hindu*, 19 September 1894.
4. VAM, 1 March 1889.
5. Ibid. The committee consisted of K. P. Visvanatha Iyer, V. Krishnaswami Iyer, P. R. Sundara Iyer, C. V. Sundaram Sastri, M. Venkataramiah Chetty and K. P. Sankara Menon.
6. VAM, 1 March and 15 April 1889. See, Appendix III for the original rules passed at this meeting.
7. Sankaran Nair and Rozario.
8. *Advocates' Association, Madras (Founded in 1889)*, Golden Jubilee Souvenir 1939 (Madras: Advocates' Association, 1939), p. xlv.
9. Ibid., pp. xlv–xlvi.
10. Ibid.
11. Whereas Bhashyam Iyengar, Sankaran Nair, Sivaswami Iyer, Rozario and Srinivasa Iyengar held the office of the Advocate General, Subramania Iyer, Bhashyam Iyengar and Sankaran Nair were appointed as judges of the High Court. Sivaswami Iyer was later appointed to the Governor's Executive Council. *The Madras High Court 1862–1962: Centenary Volume* (Madras: The Editorial Committee, 1962), pp. 68 and 76.
12. Sankara Menon, Venkatasubbaramiah, Masilamani Pillai, Gopalaswami Mudaliar, Sankaran Nair, Venkataramiah Chetty and Ethiraja Mudaliar.
13. The cases of Sivaswami Iyer, Sankaran Nair and Srinivasa Iyengar lend support to this view.
14. Subramania Iyer, Bhashyam Iyengar, Sundara Iyer, Sivaswami Iyer and Krishnaswami Iyer.
15. These aspects will be discussed more thoroughly in subsequent pages.
16. VAM, 21 October 1889.
17. Based on observations of the records between 1889 and 1908. See, Nilakanta Sastri, *A Great Liberal*, p. 272 and Ki. Cantiracekaran, *Vi. Kirushnasvami Aiyar*, pp. 80–5.
18. VAM, 15 April 1889. Rules XIII, IX and XI.
19. A peon was hired for the salary of Rs 5 a month, VAM, 18 July 1889 and 6 May 1891; a clerk was added later, VAM, 31 March 1890 and 10 September 1891. His initial payment is not known but it was raised to Rs 7 and still later to Rs 8. VAM, 8 November 1889. A bookcase was purchased and the floor was carpeted. VAM, 8 and 21 November 1889; 29 July 1890. A timepiece was bought, VAM, 3 March 1890.

20. VAM, 18 July 1889; 4 December 1889 and 3 March 1890.
21. Ibid., 10 September 1889; 21 October 1889; 5 March 1891; 20 August 1891; 10 September 1891; 8 September 1892; 21 October 1892; 10 February 1893; 7 September 1894.
22. Ibid., 15 April 1889.
23. According to available sources, in Lahore also the president was unanimously elected or appointed. Rustam Shorabji Sidhwa, *The Lahore High Court and Its Principal Bar* (Lahore: Author, n.d.), p. 93. See, VAM, 8 September 1890; 17 July 1891; 4 March 1892; 18 July 1893; 4 May 1894; 22 October 1895; 23 August 1897; 21 April 1899; 5 August 1901; 25 September 1902; 3 September 1906; 24 April 1907; and 13 March 1908.
24. VAM, 8 September 1890; 17 July 1891; 23 August 1897; and 21 April 1899.
25. Both Sivaswami Iyer and Kasturi Ranga Iyengar completed their terms of apprenticeship under R. Balaji Rao and V. Bhashyam Iyengar. K. Chandrasekharan, *P. S. Sivaswami Aiyar* (New Delhi: Publications Division, Government of India, 1969), p. 17 and V. K. Narasimhan, *Kasturi Ranga Iyengar* (New Delhi: Publications Division, Government of India, 1963), p. 11.
26. Narasimhan, *Kasturi Ranga Iyengar*, p. 21.
27. See, R. Suntharalingam, *Politics and Nationalist Awakening*, chapters 2 and 3.
28. D. A. Washbrook, *The Emergence of Provincial Politics: The Madras Presidency 1870–1920* (Cambridge: Cambridge University Press, 1976), pp. 215–60.
29. Narasimhan, *Kasturi Ranga Iyengar*, p. 24.
30. VAM, 5 August 1901. There is a discrepancy between the total number of members present at this meeting and the number of votes cast. There were only 38 members present but the total number of votes recorded was 39.
31. Ibid., 25 September 1902.
32. Ibid.
33. VAM, 3 September 1906. The president-elect was V. Bhashyam Iyengar who had already held that office 1895–1901. Although P. R. Sundara Iyer became the secretary, some members proposed both L. A. Govindaraghava Iyengar and V. C. Desikachariar to that position but they withdrew their nomination in consideration to Sundara Iyer's seniority and experience. C. P. Ramaswami Iyer got elected as an 'after ballot' joint-secretary. The managing committee members were: V. Krishnaswami Iyer (37 votes), T. V. Seshagiri Iyer (35 votes), P. S. Sivaswami Iyer (35 votes), C. P. Ramaswami Iyer (17 votes), T. Ethiraja Mudaliar (13 votes) and L. A. Govindaraghava Iyengar (13 votes). The name of the seventh individual is not decipherable from the records.
34. VAM, 15 April 1889 and 8 February 1897.
35. Ibid., 21 October 1889 and 15 April 1889.
36. Ibid., 30 October 1895.
37. *MWN-JS* 1 (1910):9.
38. During the first decade of the twentieth century, membership rose to over 100, and, by 1918, it reached 300. In the 1920s, membership climbed to nearly 400. In his presidential address Sivaswami Iyer noted that according to the annual list of Advocates of the Madras Bar Council there were 3790 practitioners enrolled under the Bar Council Act, 1926. About 1600 of them were practising in Madras alone and 610 of these were members of the Vakils' Association. *Advocates' Association*, Golden Jubilee Souvenir, p. iii; *Appendix to the Report*

of the Committee Appointed to Consider the Racial Distinctions in Criminal Procedure Applicable to Indians and Non-Indians (Simla: Government Central Press, 1923), p. 244, and Nilakanta Sastri, *A Great Liberal*, p. 276.
39. VAM, 10 September 1889.
40. Ibid., 21 October 1889.
41. Ibid., 7 March 1890.
42. Ibid., Annual Report, 30 April 1890.
43. Ibid., Annual Report, 31 March 1902.
44. Ibid., 5 March 1891.
45. The resolution of 17 July 1891 lends credence to this view. It reads, 'That this meeting observes with deep regret that eleven (11) members are in arrears with respect to ordinary subscription *over a year* and that 7 (seven) members have not paid *any portion* of their library subscription though books have been sent for and debts incurred in anticipation of their paying the same and authorizes the Secretary to give them notice calling upon the necessity of the Association being compelled to take unpleasant steps.'
46. Ibid., 20 August 1891.
47. A. T. Ambrose, P. R. Gopalacharlu, K. Lakshmana Chetty, P. Krishnaswami Pillai, S. Gurusami Chetti, K. A. Achyuta Menon and C. Krishnaswami Row.
48. VAM, 2 September 1892. See, Ibid., 8 September 1892; 21 October 1892; 10 February 1983 and 7 September 1894.
49. See, Ibid., Annual Reports, 31 March 1902 and 31 March 1903. In 1902 and 1903, four and eleven members, respectively, were removed from the Association for non-payment of monthly subscription.
50. *Advocates' Association*, Golden Jubilee Souvenir, p. iii.
51. VAM, 15 April 1889.
52. Dillon, *From An Indian Bar Room*, p. 5.
53. Nilakanta Sastri, *A Great Liberal*, p. 253.
54. Ibid.
55. VAM, 18 July 1889.
56. Ibid., 4 and 6 December 1889.
57. HCAR, No. 2953, 5 December 1889. See, HCAR, No. 134, 20 January 1916; No. 1868, 22 August 1919, and No. 1539, 11 August 1921 which deal with the question of dress worn by vakils.
58. *The Hindu*, 8 November 1889 and *Sathia Varthamani*, 15 November 1889 (RNP).
59. *The High Court of Calcutta: Centenary Souvenir 1862–1962* (Calcutta: High Court, 1962), p. 83 and Calcutta Bar Association, *Centenary Souvenir 1862–1962* (Calcutta: The International Press, 1962), p. 20. The Calcutta rule said that 'on and after the 1st June 1907 vakils of the High Court when appearing in court will be required to wear a blue gown of the prescribed shade, of the cut and shape of a B.A. gown. The wearing of a head-dress will be optional from the said date.'
60. VAM, 3 March 1890.
61. *Andraprakasika*, 13 September 1905 (RNP).
62. HCAR, Circular No. 299, 2 February 1891; Minutes of Justice Shephard, dated 10 January 1891 (emphasis added).
63. Ibid., Minutes of Justice Muthuswami Iyer, dated 12 January 1891. A few years

later, however, the *MLJ* criticized the rules of 1891, which the journal thought did not 'prepare the student either on his moral or intellectual side for success in his career at the bar'. See, 'The Legal Profession in Madras', *MLJ-JS* 4 (May and June 1896):175.
64. VAM, 13 July 1903.
65. See, the Notice of P. Percival, Registrar of the University of Madras, dated 13 November 1965 in *The Madras Jurist*, 1 (1866):41. In 1896 the *MLJ* commented that 'the Bachelor of Laws examination covers a sufficiently large number of legal subjects and requires in the student a good knowledge of the several subjects. It seems unwise and a waste of useful energy that a candidate for the M.L. examination should bring up the same subjects with some addition.' *MLJ-JS* 4 (May and June 1896):174; HCAR, Circular No. 299, 2 February 1891 and No. 416, 16 January 1894, and No. 1503, 14 May 1895 serve as examples of vakils who had become advocates. Two of such individuals were Joseph Satya Nadar, B.A., M.L., and M. K. Vaidyanatha Iyer, M.L.
66. VAM, 18 October 1895.
67. Nilakanta Sastri, *A Great Liberal*, p. 273.
68. VAM, 28 February 1902.
69. HCAR, No. 182, 23 January 1918. At this time the High Court decided to relax this requirement by reducing the term to 12 months instead of 18 months.
70. This was the Madras Chamber of Commerce.
71. See, *The Indian Jurist*, 17 (January 1893):32–5.
72. For example, The Theosophical Society and the Madras Mahajana Sabha catered to the religious and political interests of people. In the 1860s The Cosmopolitan Club was started for social and recreational purposes among Europeans and Indians but as the European members withdrew their support during the 1880s it virtually fell under the control of Indians. See, *The Cosmopolitan Club*, Platinum Jubilee Souvenir 1873–1954 (Madras: Premier Press, 1954).
73. James W. Hurst, *The Growth of American Law—The Law Makers* (Boston: Little Brown and Company, 1950), p. 285.
74. VAM, 15 April 1889.
75. HCAR, No. 465, 16 February 1892.
76. VAM, 24 January 1890. The Managing Committee resolved to purchase several complete sets of law reports and books on this date. They were, *The Bengal Law Reports, Moore's Indian Appeals, The Madras High Court Reports, The Bombay High Court Reports, The North-Western Frontier High Court Reports, Statutes Relating to India*, Acts of the Government of India, *The Madras Code, Ramachendraier's Limitation Act and Small Cause Court Act*, and *Stokes' Hindu Law Books*.
77. Ibid., 13 September 1889 and 5 March 1891 and *Advocates Association*, Golden Jubilee Souvenir, p. iv. See, The Advocates' Association, *Catalogue, March 1950* (Madras: Ravi Printers, 1950), for a complete listing of books housed in the library in 1950. It is very difficult, however, to trace several books listed in the catalogue.
78. Ibid., 10 February 1893.
79. *Index to the Proceedings and Letters of the High Court—Appellate Side, Madras, for the year 1885* (Madras: Scottish Press, 1886), p. 165; VAM, 21 October 1889; and Nilakanta Sastri, *A Great Liberal*, p. 272.

80. Ibid.
81. See, V. C. Gopalratnam, *A Century Completed*, pp. 115–20 for a brief account of the opening of the present High Court Buildings on 12 July 1892, and *The Madras High Court 1862–1962, Centenary Volume*, pp. 30–1.
82. VAM, 31 March 1890; 8 September 1890; 5 May 1894 and 4 February 1896. GOM, Judicial Department, No. 1154, 22 June 1892; HCAR, No. 2542, 4 November 1890; No. 4652, 22 September 1892; Nos. 348 and 640, 4 and 16 February 1893. *The Hindu*, 6 January 1891 and 14 October 1892.
83. *The Hindu*, 6 January 1891.
84. HCAR, No. 640, 16 February 1893. Four vakils—S. Gopalaswamy Iyengar and A. Rajagopala Iyer, and M. E. Srirangachariar and T. V. Seshagiri Iyer—jointly held two chambers, while there were six vakils who occupied two chambers each. They were: C. V. Sundaram Sastri, K. P. Viswanatha Iyer, C. Sankaran Nair, P. V. Krishnaswami Chetti, V. Bhashyam Iyengar, and P. Anandacharlu. The name of a Muslim vakil also figures in the list of occupants. Between 1871 and 1881 no Muslim became a vakil and the first Muslim vakil was was Ahmed Hossain, M.A., B.L.; he completed his apprenticeship under Eardley Norton. *The Hindu*, 5 and 25 March 1890.
85. By September 1900 the Vakils' Association even had a telephone. VAM, 19 March and 3 September 1900.
86. *The Hindu*, 16–17 and 19 November and 4 December 1891; *Tarangai Nesan*, 5 October 1889. The *Vettikkodiyon*, 30 May 1891, however, objected to appointing only the High Court vakils to the Bench, recommending elevation of members from the subordinate judiciary. See, *Swadesamitran*, 10 July and 14 October 1897, and 2 August 1906; *Sasilekha*, 15 August 1899 (RNP); VAM, 3 and 8 February 1897; and, Ke. Cantiracekaran, *Sar Vī Pashyam Aiyankar*, p. 34; *The Hindu*, 29 January 1890 and 7 January 1892; *Tarangai Nesan*, 5 October 1889 (RNP).
87. VAM, 31 March 1902 and 31 March 1903.
88. Ibid., 8 February 1897. The managing committee members' attitude seems to support this view. As the Association was considering 'a social entertainment' in honour of V. Bhashyam Iyengar on the eve of his appointment as the acting advocate general, the first time ever that a vakil held this office since 1802, other vakils showed interest in the event. The managing committee, however, resolved 'that under circumstances the entertainment will only be by the Madras Vakils' Association'.
89. *West Coast*, 27 June 1914 (RNP).
90. Ibid.(emphasis added). See, *Swadesamitran*, 2 August 1906 and *The Hindu*, 6 July 1910 for similar criticisms.
91. *The Law Weekly-Journal Section* 1 (August 1914):111. See, *MWN-JS* 1 (1910):44.
92. From the information gathered from legal journals such as the *LW*, *MLJ*, *MWN* and *The Madras Law Times*, it is possible to arrange chronologically the order of such gatherings. Between 1904 and 1919 vakils assembled regularly each year and thereafter they seem to have met only in every other year until 1927 when they abruptly discontinued the tradition.
93. An estimated crowd of four hundred vakils attended the Eighteenth Annual Gathering in 1923. *MWN-JS* 14 (19123):17–18.

94. When P. R. Sundara Iyer was the host he arranged for S. Srinivasa Iyengar to read a paper entitled 'The Law Reform and Law' which was later published. Next year, K. Srinivasa Iyengar read a paper on 'The Study of the Growth and Development of Hindu Law'. See, *TMLT-JS*, 6 (1909):110–20 and 7 (1910):149–52; *MWN-JS*, 1 (1910):59–62 and *MWN-JS* 20 (1910):175–80. See, the papers read by T. V. Seshagiri Iyer and P. Nagabhushanam in *MWN-JS* 4 (1913):111–16 and *LW-JS* 6 (October 1917):32–42. See also, *MLS-JS* 20 (1910):199–201 for a speech by P. S. Sivaswami Iyer.
95. The address delivered by T. V. Seshagiri Iyer lends credence to this view. *MWN-JS* 4 (1913):111–16. See, *LW-JS* 8 (November 1918):38.
96. *LW-JS* 10 (December 1919):65. See, *MWN-JS* 10 (1919):199–200; and *Advocates' Association*, Golden Jubilee Souvenir, p. xlvii. The *LW* welcomed the resolution but the *MWN* disapproved the steps taken by the Association. The editorial said, 'We strongly deprecate any attempt to make litigation a more ruinous affair in this poor country than it is already, by asking for two sets of vakils' fees in every regular appeal.'
97. *LW-JS* 10 (December 1919):65.
98. *MWN-JS* 4 (August 1914):112.
99. *LW-JS* 1 (August 1914):112; 8 (November 1918):38 and 10 (June 1919):64.
100. M. K. Venkateswara Iyer, *True Brahminism in Life and Law* (Madras: Madras Law Journal Press, 1928), pp. 12–13.
101. *LW-JS* 56 (1943):25. Sir C. P. Ramaswami Iyer was then the Dewan of Travancore. In his letter to the president of the association dated 18 August 1943, he offered a sum of Rs 35,000 towards the fund.
102. From 1913 the members of the Madras Bar Association also met together for what they called the 'Bar Dinner'. The District Court Vakils' Association at Chingleput began to have its annual meetings from 1914 onwards. Usually a Madras vakil presided over or delivered special lectures during these meetings.

Chapter 7: COMPETING VOICES

1. *Advocates' Association*, Golden Jubilee Souvenir, p. iv.
2. Ibid.
3. *MWN-JS* 3 (March 1893):65.
4. See, Chapter 3, pp. 71–3 and Chapter 4, pp. 89–94. See also, *The Hindu*, 20 and 30 January 1890 (dismissal of an attorney); 11 March 1890 (desertion of client by barrister); *Mysore Vrittanta Bodhini*, 22 March 1890 (RNP).
5. See, Chapter 4.
6. Clause 10 of the Letters Patent 1865 and Section 13 of the Legal Practitioners' Act, 1879.
7. The four original Inns of Court or the Bar Council, established in 1894, had the jurisdict n over barristers, while the Incorporated Law Society, which had been in existence since 1825, dealt with solicitors or attorneys. See, Duman, *The English and Colonial Bars*, pp. 37–40 and 66–71; Larson, *The Rise of Professionalism*, pp. 85–6 and Abel-Smith and Stevens, *Lawyers and the Courts*, pp. 53–76.
8. *The Hindu*, 2 and 11 November 1889 and *MLJ-JS* 20 (April 1910):167.

9. *MLJ-JS* 3 (March 1893):66.
10. Ibid., p. 67.
11. VAM, 1 September 1896. On this occasion, the Association appointed a committee consisting of V. Bhashyam Iyengar, C. R. Pattabhirama Iyer, P. S. Sivaswami Iyer and V. Krishnaswami Iyer to look into the alleged misconduct of a vakil and prepare a report.
12. Ibid., 7 September 1894. From the records it is not clear what criticisms were hurled against Raghavendra Row by the local press.
13. GOM, Judicial Department, No. 395, 20 March 1909. This is one of the many fascinating documents, which throws a great deal of additional information on the dynamics of interdepartmental correspondence between the Court of Wards, the Revenue and Judicial Departments on the one hand, and between the Madras government and the High Court, on the other.
14. Ibid. Letter from A. Tottehnham, Under Secretary, Courts of Wards to the Secretary, Revenue Department, dated 12 September 1908.
15. Ibid.
16. Section 20 of the rules relating to district court pleaders said that 'Except when specially authorized by the court, or by consent of the party, a pleader who has advised in connection with the institution of a suit, appeal or other proceedings, or has drawn pleading in connection with any such matter, or has, during the progress of any suit, appeal or other proceeding acted for a party for whom he has advised, drawn pleadings or acted, [may not provide] his services, appear in suit, appeal or other proceedings, or in any appeal, or application for revision arising or in any matter connected therewith for any person, whose interest is opposed to that of his former client.' *The Rules of Practice (Moffusil)*, 3rd. improved edition (Madras: V. S. N. Chari, 1933), p. 10. GOM, Judicial Department, No. 395, 20 March 1909. Letter from the Joint-Secretary, the Vakils' Association, to the Secretary of the Court of Wards, dated 5 August 1908.
17. Ibid. See, Abel-Smith and Stevens, *Lawyers and the Courts*, pp. 221-2.
18. Ibid.
19. The reported cases of 'In the matter of—A High Court Vakil', 'In re Mr G. Krishnaswami Aiyar, a Vakil of the High Court', and 'In the matter of a Vakil of the High Court', are examples of instances in which leading vakils attended the proceedings. See, *TMLT-Report* 6 (1909):329-33; *MLJ-Report* 22:6 (1912):276-84; *ILR-MS* 40 (1917):69-77, and HCAR, No. 1527, 29 August 1916. In the cases cited above P. R. Sundara Iyer, L. A. Govindaraghava Iyer, and V. Ramesam represented the Association.
20. *MLJ-JS* 20:8 (April 1910):167-8.
21. C. P. Ramaswami Iyer, 'The Making of a Lawyer', *Lawyer* 1:1 (October 1955): 13, and Edwin S. Montagu, *An Indian Diary*, edited by Venetia Montagu (London: William Heinemann, 1930), p. 123. During his tour in India in 1917-18, the Secretary of State for India visited Madras and met with C. P. Ramaswami Iyer. Montagu later recorded, 'After lunch we had Ramaswami Aiyar, who is one of the cleverest men I have ever met in my life. He would do brilliantly at the English Bar.'
22. Between 23 November 1891 and 16 February 1892.
23. GOM, Judicial Department, No. 355, 25 February 1892. See, *The Hindu*, 19,

26, and 27 November and 14 December 1891 for views of different newspapers from different parts of India. See also, *Swadesamitran*, 20 November 1891 and *Karnataka Prakashika*, 23 November 1891 (RNP).
24. *The Hindu*, 19 November 1891.
25. VAM, 21 November 1891.
26. *The Hindu*, 31 March 1894.
27. VAM, 17 September 1895; 4 and 26 February 1896. See, GOM, Judicial Department, No. 2373, 18 November 1895. The senior law reporter had been a barrister, while the office of the deputy registrar seems to have been held either by a civilian or a barrister.
28. *MWN-JS* 7 (March 1897):91.
29. Barristers throughout India protested his appointment; their protest intensified the animositity between barristers and vakils in Madras. The controversy involving the question of correct interpretation of law and the rulers' need to uphold established conventions cannot be adequately dealt with in this section. However, this episode set the stage on which the Association's actions could be explained.
30. VAM, 14 April 1897. S. Kasturi Ranga Iyengar, C. R. Pattabhirama Iyer, C. Ramachandra Rao Sahib, Ryru Nambiar and V. Krishnaswami Iyer were appointed to draw up the memorial. The Association had previously resolved to give a 'social entertainment' honouring the appointment of Bhashyam Iyengar and an elaborate committee made up of nine members was appointed for that purpose. See, VAM, 3 February 1897.
31. *Madras High Court 1862–1962*, pp. 39–40 and 69.
32. See, *Manorama*, 28 January 1895 (RNP).
33. S. Subramania Iyer on 23 May permanently filled the vacancy caused by the death of Sir T. Muthuswamy Iyer. VAM, 15 October 1895 and GOM, Judicial Department, No. 2373, 18 November 1895. See, *The Andraprakasika*, 1 February 1899; *Swadesamitran*, 20 March 1899 and *Sasilekha*, 21 March 1899 (RNP).
34. GOM, Judicial Department, No. 371, 9 March 1900.
35. See, GOM, Judicial Department, No. 404, 6 March 1889.
36. Ibid., No. 371, 9 March 1900.
37. Letter from the Chief Secretary, Government of Madras, to the Secretary, Home Department, Government of India, No. 820, dated 16 June 1900 (emphasis added). See, GOM, Judicial Department, Nos. 819–20, 16 June 1900.
38. *Indian Review* 1 (1900):234; *MLJ-JS* 10 (February 1900):116–17; *Manorama*, 4 June 1900 and *Swadesamitran*, 26 January 1900 (RNP).
39. Further investigation needs to be undertaken on this theme.
40. See, Edward H. Levi, *An Introduction to Legal Reasoning* (Chicago: The University of Chicago Press, 1963) for an excellent treatment on the process of interpretation and application of various American Constitutional provisions to different legal issues.
41. Gandhi, *Lawyers and Touts*, p. 28 for a summary of opposing viewpoints.
42. Ibid., p. 27. See, Dodwell, *The Nabobs of Madras*, pp. 148–63 for an account on the condition and the quality of legal practitioners in the eighteenth century.
43. See, Chapter 1, pp. 40–1.

44. See, VAM, 1 September 1890; 21 and 26 August 1891 (on the improvement of the Small Cause Court); 26 August 1891 and 16 February 1892 (on the establishment of the City Civil Court); 26 March 1891 (on rules of qualification of apprentices); 25 January 1892; 28 January and 8 August 1893; 5 May 1894; 1 September 1896; 31 July 1899; 6 October 1899; 3 September and 12 November 1900 (on topics relating to the High Court rules and practices); 24 January 1895; 26 November 1897 and 28 February 1901 (on the Codes of Civil and Criminal Procedure); 15 October 1895 and 26 January 1896 (on legislation against law touts); and 28 November 1897, and 23 October 1907 (on Sedition, Criminal Procedure, Post Office and Stamp Act Bills).
45. Lala Lajpat Rai, *Autobiographical Writings*, edited by Vijaya Chandra Joshi (New Delhi: Servants of the People Society, 1963). See, Kenneth W. Jones, *Arya Dharm: Hindu Consciousness in the 19th-century Punjab* (Berkeley: University of California Press, c. 1976) for an analysis of the Arya Samaj which became a formidable social and political resistant movement in Punjab.
46. GOM, Public Department, No. 638, 8 August 1907 (Confidential). See, Ibid., No. 552, 30 June 1910.
47. Ibid., Letter from Sir Harold Stuart, Home Department (Public), Government of India to the Chief Secretary to the Government of Madras, No. 1852, dated Simla, 22 July 1907.
48. VAM, 23 October 1907. It is instructing to note that V. Krishnaswami Iyer, himself a moderate in politics, seems to have had doubts about the efficacy of the Bill.
49. It was later repealed in 1911 on account of the more elaborate Indian Press Act, 1910.
50. *The Hindu*, 25 and 30 October 1907.
51. See, 'The Madras High Court Vakils' Association and the Public Service Commission Report', *MWN-JS* 9 (April 1918):91–9; 'Memorandum of the Madras High Court Vakils' Association', *MWN-JS* 10 (February 1919):45–8 and 'Memorandum of the . . . Association on the "Bill further to amend the Criminal Procedure Code, 1898" '. *MWN-JS* 9 (August 1918):117–23.
52. Sir C. Sankaran Nair (1901–6) and J. L. Rozario (1915–17).
53. Washbrook, *The Emergence of Provincial Politics*, pp. 219–20. He cites several examples of such brahman mobility from Madura, North Arcot, Tanjore and Trichinopoly districts. This process is still taking place as areas beyond Adyar and Tambaram are integrated to form a greater Metropolitan Madras. Susan Lewandowski, *Migration and Ethnicity in Urban India: Kerala Migrants in the City of Madras, 1870–1970* (New Delhi: Manohar, 1980), Chapter II.
54. W. S. Krishnaswami Nayudu, *My Memoirs* (Madras: Author, 1977), p. 12.
55. *MWN-JS* 18 (September 1927):82. See, Madhavan Nair, *Sir C. Sankaran Nair*, p. 19 where the author questions the credibility of this statement. It is pointless to argue one way or another except to recognize that these suburbs of Madras were the centres where many High Court vakils lived.
56. Nilakanta Sastri, *A Great Liberal*, p. 254.
57. Personal interview on 3 May 1983.
58. Ibid.
59. I am grateful to Dr A. Ramaswami for this information during a formal

conversation on 1 March 1982. See, Washbrook, *The Emergence of Provincial Politics*, p. 284.
60. Washbrook, *Emergence of Provincial Politics*, p. 285.
61. See, Raj Kumar, *Annie Besant's Rise to Power in Indian Politics (1914–1917)* (New Delhi: Concept Publishing Company, 1981).
62. Eugene F. Irschick, *Politics and Social Conflict in South India: The Non-Brahman Movement and Tamil Separatism, 1916–1929* (Berkeley: University of California Press, 1969), pp. 115–16 and Pamela G. Price, 'Ideology and Ethnicity under British Imperial Rule: "Brahmans", Lawyers and Kin-Caste Rules in Madras Presidency', *Modern Asian Studies* 23:1 (1989):151–77.
63. He was a 'leading Original Side lawyer' under whom W. S. Krishnaswami Nayudu completed his apprenticeship. *My Memoirs*, pp. 31–4. In 1910 Ethiraja Mudaliar hosted the seventh annual gathering of vakils. On such occasions, the hosts took advantage of the opportunity to display their lavish hospitality and basked in the compliments of fellow-vakils. As a leading non-brahman advocate, he was twice recommended by the non-brahman press for a seat on the High Court bench and once to the office of the Advocate General. See, *Non-Brahman*, 17 December 1916; *The Justice*, 29 April 1920 and *Dravidian*, 25 February 1920 (RNP). The Madras government considered his nomination to a judgeship of the Small Cause Court and for some reason rejected him. GOM, Home (Judicial) Department, No. 1277, 21 May 1920.
64. He considered himself to be the 'drummer-boy' of the Justice Party. K. M. Balasubramaniam, *South Indian Celebrities*, vol. 1, (Madras: Author, 1934), pp. 15–28.
65. Ibid., pp. 1–14 and S. P. Sen, ed., *Dictionary of National Biography*, 4 vols. (Calcutta: Institute of Historical Studies, 1972), 1:305–7.
66. He was a leading attorney and a partner in 'Messrs. Short, Bewes & Company, an European firm of Solicitors of long standing reputation'. By 1924, he had enrolled himself as an advocate of the High Court and was 'practically the standing counsel' for the above mentioned firm. W. S. Krishnaswami Nayudu, *My Memoirs*, pp. 52–9.
67. It is not clear when this Association was actually formed nor is it known when it became defunct. The records connected with the Association are believed to be with Mr O. T. Radhakrishnan, Advocate, High Court, who is a son of O. Thanikachalam Chetty.
68. GOM, Home (Judicial) Department, No. 1277, 21 May 1920. Letter from A. Ramaswami Mudaliar, Secretary of the Association, to the Chief Secretary to the Government of Madras, dated 8 May 1920.
69. Ibid. Under-Secretary's note.
70. GOM, Law General, No. 983, 2 August 1921. On 1 April 1921, Thanikachalam Chetty moved a resolution which he successfully manoeuvred to get it approved by the Council. The resolution contained two very important recommendations. First, it stressed that future appointments to judicial offices should be made directly from the bar. Second, 'Such recruitment for the next five years should be made from amongst non-Brahmin Hindus, Christians and Muhammedans, so as to secure a due representation of all the different communities in the Judicial Service.'
71. I acknowledge my gratitude to Dr R. Krishnaswami, son of A. Ramaswami

Mudaliar who was a Secretary of the Non-Brahmin Lawyers Association, for this information. The interview was conducted on 28 February 1983.
72. See, *LW-JS* 10 (December 1919):60–63; *MWN-JS* 38:1 (January 1920):1–4 and *MLJ-JS* 11 (February 1920):19–25.
73. *LW-JS* 10 (December 1919):61.
74. See, *MLJ-JS* 38:4 (January 1920):5–18; 38:5 (February 1920):43–58 and 38:6 (March 1920):73–87.
75. *Indian Review* 21 (February 1920), p. 128. See, 'The Presidential Address by S. Srinivasa Iyengar, Advocate General', *MWN-JS* 38:4 (January 1920):23–28.
76. Ibid.
77. *MWN-JS* (February 1, 1920):128.
78. *LW-JS* 13 (February 1921):22; GOM, Public Department, No. 370, 2 June 1920.
79. GOM, Public Department, No. 370, 2 June 1920.
80. GOM, Home (Judicial) Department No. 1277, 21 May 1920.
81. GOM, Public Department, No. 370, 2 June 1920.
82. House of Commons, Cd. 8382, Vol. VII of 1916, Paper No. 87.

Chapter 8: WINDS OF CHANGE

1. C. P. Ramaswami Aiyar, *Presidential Address. . .All India Vakils' Conference* (Madras: Vasantha Press, 1921), p. 2.
2. *Report of the All-India Vakils' Conference*, held at Allahabad on 26 and 27 March 1921 (Allahabad: The Indian Press, 1921); Calcutta Bar Association, *Centenary Souvenir 1862–1962* (Calcutta: The Centenary Celebration Committee, 1962), pp. 38 and 39; *Legislative Assembly Debates*, 12 September 1922, Vol. 3, No. 6 and GOM, Law General, No. 254, 23 January 1923.
3. *New India*, 8 December 1920, and Ramaswami Aiyar, *Presidential Address*, p. 3.
4. During the debates consequent on the resolution to create an Indian bar, J. F. Bryant, an Assembly member, remarked, 'I have not troubled to ask the Government for statistics of the relative numbers of vakils and barristers in this House but you may take it from me, that *the disparity is very great indeed*. The barristers are hopelessly out-numbered. That altruistic instinct which invariably induced us to protect the weak at the expense of the strong will induce us to go to the help of the barristers on this occasion and rescue them from the dilemma in which they find themselves.' *Legislative Assembly Debates*, 12 September 1922, Vol. 3, No. 6 and GOM, Law General, No. 254, 23 January 1923.
5. *Report of the All-India Vakils' Conference*, p. 24.
6. Ibid., Appendix I, p. 1, and Ramaswami Aiyar, *Presidential Address*, p. 3.
7. Jerold S. Auerbach, *Unequal Justice: Lawyers and Social Change in Modern America* (New York: Oxford University Press, 1976), p. 295.
8. H. S. F. Halsbury, *The Complete Statutes of England*, 22 vols. (London: Butterworth, 1929–31):10:79.
9. Cornelia Sorabji, *India Calling: The Memories of Cornelia Sorabji*, reprint edition (London: Nisbet, 1935), p. 30.
10. Ibid., p. 66. *Stridhan* means a woman's personal property in Hindu Law.
11. *The London Times*, 26 September 1902 and *Indian Review* 3 (November

1902):603. See, Harriot Dufferin, 'The National Association for Supplying Female Medical Aid to the Women of India', *The Asiatic Quarterly Review* 1 (April 1886):257–74 and W. W. Hunter, 'A Female Medical Profession for India', *Contemporary Review* 56 (August 1889):207–15 for the incorporation of women within the context of medical care under the colonial rule.
12. *Madras Legal Companion* 2 (August 1903):53–8 and (October–November 1903):63–8. This is a reprint of the paper entitled 'Miss Cornelia Sorabji's Scheme of Legal Relief for Pardahnashis in India', and read by Shah Din at a meeting of the Punjab Law Society, held on 28 May 1903.
13. *The Law Digest and Recorder*, New Series, 2:7 (July 1903):137. See, *Indian Review* 4 (March 1903):177–8; (April 1903):217–18 and (June 1903):401.
14. *Indian Review* 5 (July 1904):573.
15. Allahabad High Court, *Centenary: High Court of Judicature at Allahabad 1866–1966*, I:234; *ILR-Calcutta Series* 44 (1916):290 and *The Indian Law Quarterly* 3:2 (1916):91–3.
16. *Legislative Assembly Debates*, 20 September 1922.
17. *ILR-Patna Series* 1 (1921):104 and *Centenary: High Court of Judicature at Allahabad*, Vol. 1, p. 235 and HCAR, No. 1263, 11 July 1921.
18. Sorabji, *India Calling*, p. 284; *Centenary: High Court of Judicature at Allahabad*, I:235 and Wachha, *Famous Judges*, p. 121. In addition to completing the requirements for a degree of B.C.L. she had passed the LL.B. examination in Bombay.
19. G. A. Natesan, *Sir Hari Singh Gour: His Life and Work* (Madras: Author, 1927), p. 49–54 and Sen, *Dictionary of National Biography*, 2:90–2.
20. GOM, Law General, Letter No. 1059, 20 April 1922.
21. Ibid., Notes of the Assistant Secretary, dated 5 April 1922.
22. GOM, Law General, Letter No. 1059, 20 April 1922.
23. Ibid.
24. Ibid.
25. Ibid., Letter addressed to the Secretary to the Government of India, Home Department, dated 20 April 1922.
26. *Legislative Assembly Debates*, 20 September 1922.
27. Act No. XXIII of 1923. *A Collection of the Acts of the Indian Legislature and of the Governor General for the year 1923* (New Delhi: Government Central Press, 1924).
28. See, *The High Court at Calcutta*, p. 83 and Wachha, *Famous Judges*, pp. 120–1.
29. GOM, Law General, No. 1839, 25 May 1928. Letter addressed to the Private Secretary to the Governor, dated 17 February 1928.
30. Ibid. Letter from W. B. Brander, Chief Secretary to the Government of Burma, to the Chief Secretary, Government of Madras, dated 6 March 1928.
31. Ibid. Letter from A. C. Happell, Registrar, to the Chief Secretary, Government of Madras, dated 6 March 1928.
32. B. B. Misra, *The Indian Middle Classes*, p. 327. See, Unemployment Committee, *Report on the Question of unemployment among the Educated Middle Classes* (Madras:1927) and Unemployment Committee, United Provinces, *Report* (Allahabad: 1936). See also, HCAR, No. 1027, 30 December 1937 for the views of the Judges, Madras High Court, on the recommendations of the Unemployment Committee, United Provinces, headed by T. B. Sapru.

33. *Indian Review* 29 (July 1928):731. Ironically, her father, Justice Devadoss, seemed to have had a change of mind. In 1922, he had sided with Justice Ayling and opposed the proposal for removing the gender disqualification as being 'uncalled for and premature'.
34. Madhava Menon, *The Legal Profession*, p. 128. See, Eleanor McDougall, *Lamps in the Wind: South Indian College Women and their Problems* (London: Livingstone Press, 1940) and S. Muthulakshmi Reddy, *Autobiography* (Madras: MLJ Press, 1964) for examples of women who pursued advanced degrees in liberal arts and professional education. These two volumes quite vividly bring out the social prejudices and personal limitations that women had to overcome in achieving their goals.
35. *Legislative Assembly Debates*, Vol. 1, No. 6, dated 24 February 1921. See, GOM, Law General, Nos. 2173–4, 12 December 1921; and HCAR, No. 2067, 14 October 1921.
36. *Report of the All-India Bar Committee* (New Delhi: The President's Press, 1953), p. 14.
37. Ibid.
38. Ibid.
39. *Reports of the Indian Bar Committee 1923–1924* (New Delhi: 1925), p. 25 and *Indian Review* 25 (January 1924):75. See, *MWN-JS* 15 (February 1924):12–14 for views of Sir Lewis Coward and Sir Charles Mallet.
40. *Legislative Assembly Debates*, 1921. Vol. 1, No. 6 and Minutes of the Bar, 27 April 1898. See, Srinivasa Rao, 'The Origins and Growth', pp. 101–6.
41. *Legislative Assembly Debates*, 21 February 1921.
42. Ibid.
43. Ibid.
44. Ibid.
45. Letter from H. Tonkinson, Additional Deputy Secretary to the Government of India, Home (Judicial) Department, dated Simla, 9 May 1921; GOM, Law General, Nos. 2173–4, 12 December 1921. The letter raised six different questions dealing with the powers of the legislature, organization of a council of legal education, disciplinary power of the council, changes in the existing laws, the desirability of maintaining or abolishing the double-agency throughout India and the impact of the Indian bar on students who would subsequently proceed to England to be called to the bar.
46. *Legislative Assembly Debates*, 12 September 1922, Vol. 3, No. 6 contained in GOM, Law General, No. 254, 23 January 1923.
47. Ibid.
48. Ibid.
49. *MWN-JS* 14 (October 1923):79.
50. Sir E. M. des C. Chamier, Justice V. M. Coutts-Trotter, S. R. Das and Colonel Sir Henry Stanyon; Justice D. F. Mulla, T. Rangachariar and S. S. Patkar; H. P. Duval and J. H. Wise; and M. M. Chatterji.
51. *Report of the Indian Bar Committee*, p. 1.
52. Ibid.
53. *The Times*, Educational Supplement, 29 October 1923, and *MWN-JS* 14 (November 1923):107–10.
54. See, GOM, Law General, No. 9, 3 January 1924 for information on the

correspondence between the bar committee and the local government regarding arrangements to facilitate the interviews of select candidates. See also, A. Krishnaswami Iyer, 'Unification of the Indian Bar', *MLJ-JS* 45:23 (December 1923):107–17 for the views of one individual who was examined by the Bar Committee, and Watrap S. Subramania Aiyar, 'Indian Bar Committee', *LW-JS* 18:22 (December 1923):71–86 and *Report of the Indian Bar Committee*, p. 13. The Committee visited Bombay, Madras, Calcutta, Allahabad, Rangoon, Lahore and Delhi, but sent copies of a questionnaire to Karachi, Lucknow and Nagpur eliciting the views of practitioners from these places.

55. *Report of the Indian Bar Committee*, p. 13.
56. Ibid., pp. 23–4.
57. GOM, Law General, No. 254, 23 January 1923; Minutes of Justice M. Venkatasubba Rao. See, GOM, Law General, No. 1955, 14 June 1926.
58. HCAR, No. 2067, 14 October 1921. In his minutes, Justice W. W. Phillips, a civilian, recorded that 'The dual agency is on many grounds to be preferred to the single legal advisor, but is undoubtedly more expensive and if insisted on in all cases, would deprive many poor litigants in this country of their right to resort to the courts for justice. The Vakil System, i.e., the conjunction of solicitor and counsel in one person, has proved satisfactory, but this result has been in large measure to the fact that barristers . . . have, consciously or unconsciously, set up a high standard of legal morality, which has reacted upon the rest of the legal profession.' See, GOM, Law General, Nos. 2173–4, 12 December 1921.
59. See, GOM, Law General, No. 2003, 23 December 1924. This file contains exhaustive information on the responses from various local bodies on the issues raised by the bar committee.
60. HCAR, No. 2473, 25 November 1926.
61. Ibid.
62. The Committee consisted of A. P. Muddiman, L. Graham, K. Ahmad, T. Rangachariar, Raj Narain, Md. Yakub, K. C. Neogy, H. S. Gour, S. C. Ghose and P. S. Sivaswami Iyer. Except for Muddiman, Graham and Yakub, the rest of the members wrote their separate minutes of dissent. This shows that their Report which has later submitted to the legislature lacked unanimous approval.
63. HCAR, No. 2473, 25 November 1926.
64. Ibid. See also the comments of K. C. Neogy on this point.
65. Ibid. In moving the amendment K. Ahmad observed that 'I fear that people even in this Assembly throw mud at others, both inside and outside. That has been the character of our Indian Legislature and the Indian people and the politics of this country.' Rajat K. Ray, 'Political Change in British India', *The Indian Economic and Social History Review* 14:4 (1977):495–6.
66. Ibid.
67. Ibid.
68. GOM, Judicial Department, No. 1844, 4 December 1902 (Confidential). Minutes of H. W. Winterbotham, dated 19 November 1902. See, *Legislative Council Debates*, Vol. 17, 1924, p. 987. C. P. Ramaswami Iyer, the Law Member, referred to the Hastings-Impey controversy in his answer to a question on the practice of appointment of District Munsifs by the High Court.
69. Between 1880 and 1915 no barrister was ever proved guilty of professional

misconduct in Madras and the High Court seemed to have refrained from instituting proceedings against barristers. Complaints of misconduct were usually reported to the Benchers of the Inn in England. In the defamation case of Sullivan v. Norton, reported in *ILR-MS* 10 (1887):28–38, the High Court decided that 'An advocate in India cannot be proceeded against civilly or criminally for words uttered in his office as advocate.' In 1916, however, the High Court assumed a rather unusual attitude against K. N. Gopaul, Bar-at-Law. Not only did the judges think that the High Court had 'full powers' under the letters patent to proceed against barristers for professional misconduct but also ordered the removal of his name from the list of advocates. A copy of their order was later forwarded to the Benchers of the Middle Temple. HCAR, No. 1263, 17 July 1916.

70. GOM, Law General, No. 1955, 14 June 1926.
71. Ibid., *Indian Bar Committee Report*, p. 22 and *All India Bar Committee Report*, p. 18.
72. On 2 November 1924 *The Hindu* reported that on one occasion Sir Alexander Muddiman, the Chairman of the Reforms Enquiry Committee in 1924, had contemptuously referred to Sir P. S. Sivaswami Iyer, a member of the same committee, as a 'two rupee pleader'.
73. *Report of the All-India Bar Committee*, p. 19; HCAR, No. 849, 22 October 1928 and Sapru, *Encyclopaedia*, p. 225.
74. Ibid., p. 18; *Indian Bar Committee Report*, p. 23 and *ILR-MS* 52 (1929):92–105.
75. HCAR, No. 845, 22 October 1928.
76. Ibid., Minutes of Justice H. O. C. Beasley, dated 26 November 1928.
77. In 1921, 1924 and 1926.
78. Exceptions to the general attitude of the majority in 1921 were Justices Coutts-Trotter and Spencer, who felt that the bar councils should have power 'to certain extent very much like the benches [sic] of the Inns of Court'. GOM, Law General, Nos. 2173 and 2174, 12 December 1921.
79. GOM, Law General, No. 2003, 23 December 1924; Letter from the Registrar to the Secretary to the Government of Madras, Law General Department, dated 28 August 1924.
80. Justices C. V. Kumaraswami Sastri, V. Ramesam, M. Venkatasubba Rao and V. V. Srinivasa Iyengar.
81. GOM, Law General, No. 1955, 6 June 1926; Letter from S. Wadsworth, Registrar, to the Secretary to the Government of Madras, Law General Department, dated 6 May 1926.
82. The Resolutions of the Madras Bar Association, dated 10 September 1924 and 12 May 1926; GOM, Law General, No. 2003, 23 December 1924, and No. 1955, 6 June 1926.
83. *Handbook of Information on the Administration of the Presidency of Madras* (Madras: Government Press, 1928), pp. 21–5.
84. *The Madras High Court 1862–1962*, Centenary Volume, pp. 70 and 80. He was called to the Bar by the Middle Temple in 1903 and became the Advocate General between 15 February 1923 and 9 March 1924.
85. GOM, Law General, Nos. 2173 and 2174, 12 December 1921; Memorandum No. 2191 B-2, dated 2 June 1921 from the advocate general.
86. Ibid., Minutes of Sir K. Srinivasa Iyengar, dated 5 November 1921 and GOM,

Law General, No. 2003, 23 December 1924; Minutes by C. P. Ramaswami Iyer, dated 5 December 1924.
87. HCAR, No. 845, 22 October 1928 and *LW-JS* 27 (May 1928):28–34.
88. *MWN-JS* 19 (October 15, 1928):54 and *LW-JS* 28:14 (October 1928): iii.
89. HCAR, No. 845, 22 October 1928. This file contains several clippings of newspaper editorials and correspondences on the subject but the file does not provide any information on the names of the dailies from which the articles had been cut out.
90. *MWN-JS* 19 (29 August 1928):43.
91. HCAR, No. 845, 22 October 1928. Rule 2 of the High Court Rules for the constitution of the Bar Council.
92. *LW-JS* 28:14 (October 1928):ii.
93. *MWN-JS* 19:26 (October 1928):44.
94. Ibid., 19:24 (August 1928):36.
95. HCAR, No. 847, 22 October 1928.
96. S. Srinivasa Iyengar (1917–20, 1934–9) and T. R. Ramachandra Iyer (1921–34); S. Srinivasa Iyengar (1911–12, 1915–16), T. R. Ramachandra Iyer (1912–14) and T. R. Venkatarama Sastri (1920–1); and T. R. Venkatarama Sastri (1908–11) and K. Bhashyam Iyengar (1921–4).
97. *LW-JS* 28:14 (October 1928):ii.
98. Ibid.

CONCLUSION

1. Misra, *The Indian Middle Classes*, p. 164.
2. Orby Mootham, *The East India Company's Sadar Courts, 1801–1834* (Bombay: N. M. Tripathy, 1983), p. 92.
3. See, Chapter 1, note 2.
4. Marc Galanter, *Competing Equalities: Law and the Backward Classes in India* (Berkeley: University of California Press, c. 1984), p. 18.
5. Mootham, *The East India Company's Sadar Courts*, p. 93.
6. K. N. Venkatasubba Sastri, *The Munro System of British Statesmanship in India* (Mysore: University of Mysore, 1939), p. 231.
7. Peter Penner and Richard D. MacLean, eds., *The Rebel Bureaucrat: Frederick John Shore (1799–1837) as Critic of William Bentinck's India* (Delhi: Chanakya Publications, 1983), p. 251.
8. R. E. Frykenberg, 'Modern Education in South India, 1784–1854: Its Roots and Its Role as a Vehicle of Integration under Company Raj', *The American Historical Review* 91:1 (February 1986):65.
9. N. S. Chandrasekhara, *Dewan Rangacharlu* (Delhi: Publication Division, Government of India, 1968), p. 16.
10. See, *The Indian Jurist* 17 (September 1893):468–71 for a brief biographical sketch on Holloway.
11. See, A. D. Webb, 'Charles Edward Trevelyan in India: A Study of the Channels of Influence Employed by a Covenanted Civil Servant in the Translation of Personal Ideas into Official Policy', *South Asia* NS 6:2 (November 1983):15–23.
12. *The Indian Jurist* (April 1891):210.

13. Gary B. Nash, 'The Philadelphia Bench and Bar, 1800–1861', *Comparative Studies in Society and History* 7 (1964–5):206–7.
14. K. C. Markandan, *Madras Legislative Council: Its Constitution and Working Between 1861 and 1909* (Delhi: S. Chand, 1964), pp. 84–199. A perusal of the appendices in this volume reveals that many vakils, both from the city and from the districts, were members of the Legislative Council.
15. K. S. Ramaswami Sastri, *The Future of the Brahmin* (Madras: Cooperative Printing Works, 1935), p. 11.
16. Works by Eugene Irschick, S. Saraswathi, D. A. Washbrook, C. J. Baker, D. Arnold, K. Nambi Arooran, E. S. Vissvanathan and many others deal with different aspect of this controversy. See, G. A. Oddie, 'The State of the Art', *South India*, p. 177.
17. C. Ramachendrier, *Collection of the Decisions of the High Courts and the Privy Council on the Hindu Law of Marriage and the Effects of Apostacy After Marriage* (Madras: Scottish Press, 1891), pp. 12–13 and K. S. Ramaswami Sastri, *Professor K. Sundararama Aiyar: His Life and Works* (Srirangam: Sri Vani Vilas Press, n.d.), pp. 79–80.
18. K. S. Ramaswami Sastri, *The Future of the Brahmin*, p. 11 and Edgar Thurston, *Castes and Tribes of Southern India*, Assisted by K. Rangachari, 7 vols. (Madras: Government Press, 1909):1:337 and 341.
19. U. Ve. Caminataiyar, *En Carittiram* [My History] (Tiruvanmiyur: Taktar U. Ve. Caminataiyar Nul Nilayam, 1982). A fascinating account of a Tamil literateur, whose life was entirely devoted to retrieving, editing, and publishing the classical texts in Tamil, his autobiography contains rich cultural information on that part of Tamil society which was only marginally affected by English education during the second half of the nineteenth century.
20. R. Suntharalingam, *Politics and Nationalist Awakening*, pp. 18–19.
21. C. V. Viswanatha Sastri, *Biography of a Grandfather and His Grandson* (Madras: Author, 1939), p. 47; M. P. Duraiswamy, *Memories of Sir T. Muthusami Ayyars, the First Indian Judge of the High Court of Madras* (Tanjore: Kalyanasundaram Power Press, 1911), p. 268; S. C. Srinivasa Chariar, comp., *Political Opinions of Raja Sir T. Madhava Row, K.C.S.I.* (Madras: Ripon Press, 1890), pp. 114–16; and Tiru. Vi. Kaliyanacuntaranar, *Tiru. Vi. Ka. Valkkaik Kurippukal* [Tiru. Vi. Ka. Memoirs], 2 vols. (Tirunelveli: Saiva Siddhanta Works Publishing Society, 1969), 1:347.
22. A.P.S., 'South Indian Snobs', *The Indian Review* 10:38 (August 1904):193. See, *Books That Have Influenced Me: Symposium* (Madras: G. A. Natesan, 1947), with contributions by many eminent lawyers and intellectuals in Madras.
23. For studies on brahman communities in other parts of Indis, see Frank F. Conlon, *A Caste in a Changing World: the Chitrapur Saraswat Brahmans, 1700–1935* (Berkeley: University of California Press, c. 1977); Christine E. Dobbin, *Urban Leadership in Western India: Politics and Communities in Bombay City, 1840–1885* (London: Oxford University Press, 1972); D. D. Karve, Trans., *The New Brahmans: Five Maharastrian Families* (Berkeley: University of California Press, 1963); and Henriette M. Sender, *The Kashmiri Pandits: A Study of Cultural Choice in North India up to 1930* (New Delhi: Oxford University Press, 1989).
24. *The Hindu*, 4 October 1982.

BIBLIOGRAPHY

I. MANUSCRIPTS

High Court of Judicature, Madras. Administrative Records, 1862–1928.
High Court Vakils' Association. Minutes. 1889–1908 and 1921–8.
Madras Bar Association. Minutes. 1865–1900.
Records from the Tamil Nadu Archives. Madras. 1812–1928.
    Criminal Investigation Department.
    Education Department.
    History of Freedom Movement Files.
    Judicial Consultations.
    Judicial Department.
    Law (General) Department.
    Legislative Department.
    Public Consultations.
    Public Department.
    Revenue Department.
Sir C. E. Trevelyan's Private Papers. Vol. d. 129. Bodleian Library, Oxford.

II. PRINTED SOURCES

A. Cited Decisions

'In the Matter of the Petition of the Attorneys'. *ILR-MS* 1 (1876): 24–39.
'In the Matter of the Petition of Parthasaradi'. *ILR-MS* 8 (1885): 14–15.
Jagapati Mudaliar v. Ekambara Mudaliar. Civil Revision Petition, No. 99 of 1897. December 15, 1897. *ILR-MS* 21 (1897): 274–7.
'In the matter of—A Vakil of the High Court'. *TMLT-R* 6 (1909): 329–33.
'In re. Mr. G. Krishnaswami Iyer, a Vakil of the High Court'. *MLJ-R* 22 (1912): 276–84.
Civil Suit. No. 200 of 1915. *MLJ-R* 31 (1916): 698–712.
'In the Matter of a Vakil of the High Court'. *ILR-MS* 40 (1917): 69–77.
Thenal Ammal v. Sokkammal. Second Appeal. No. 1755 of 1914. 11 April 1917. *ILR-MS* 41 (1918): 233–6.
G. Krishnaswamy Ayyar and Chakrapani Achari v. T. V. Swaminatha Iyer. Original Side Appeal. No. 6 of 1924. *ILR-MS* 48 (1925): 331–68.
'In re. The Powers of the Advocates under the Indian Bar Councils Act on the Insolvent Side of the High Court'. *ILR-MS* 52 (1929): 92–105.

B. Parliamentary Papers

House of Commons. Vol. VI of 1830. Paper No. 646.
House of Commons. Vol. I of 1830–1. Paper No. 265.
House of Commons. Vol. IX of 1831–2. Paper No. 735.
House of Commons. Vol. XII of 1832. Paper No. 735.
House of Commons. Vol. XXVII of 1852–3. Paper No. 426.
House of Commons. Vol. XXXI of 1852–3. Paper No. 627.
House of Commons. Vol. LII of 1858. Paper No. 49.
House of Commons. Cd. 8382. Vol. VII of 1916, Paper No. 87.
House of Commons. Cd. 203. Vol. IV of 1919. Paper No. 81.

C. Acts of the Governor General or Viceroy

Act XXVII of 1836.
Act I of 1846.
Act XXXVIII of 1850.
Act XXX of 1853.
Act I of 1879 (Indian Stamp Act).
Act XVIII of 1879 (Legal Practitioners' Act).
Act XXIII of 1923 (Legal Practitioners' Amendment Act).

D. Regulations of the Government of Fort St. George

Regulation X of 1802.
Regulation XIV of 1816.
Regulation V of 1817.
Regulation IV of 1832.

E. Debates

Legislative Assembly Debates. 1921–4.
Legislative Council Debates, 1924.

F. Reports

British Attitude Towards the Employment of Indians in Civil Service: Report of the Public Service Commission (1886–1887), Headed by Sir Charles U. Aitchison. Critical Introduction by Bradford Spangenberg. Delhi: Concept Publishing Company, 1977.
Madras Native Newspaper Reports.
Report of the All-India Bar Committee. New Delhi: The President's Press, 1953.
Report of the All-India Vakils' Conference. Held at Allahabad on 26th and 27th March, 1921. Allahabad: The Indian Press, 1921.
Report of the Indian Bar Committee 1923–1924. (Chamier's Committee Report) New Delhi, 1925.

Report of the Indian Education Commission. Calcutta: Government Printing, 1883.
The Reports on the Administration of Civil and Criminal Justice in the Presidency of Madras, 1879 and 1880. 2 vols. Madras: The Scottish Press, 1880 and 1881.
The Report on the Administration of Civil Justice in the Presidency of Madras, 1881–1908. 28 vols. Madras: The Scottish Press, 1882–1909.

G. Newspapers

The Daily Times.
The Hindu.
The London Times.
The Madras Daily Times.
The Madras Times.
The Madras Mail.
The New India.

H. Journals and Law Reports

The High Court Reports.
The Indian Jurist.
The Indian Law Journal.
The Indian Law Quarterly.
The Indian Law Reports—Allahabad Series.
The Indian Law Reports—Calcutta Series.
The Indian Law Reports—Madras Series.
The Indian Law Reports—Patna Series.
The Indian Review.
The Law Recorder and Digest.
The Law Weekly.
The Madras Jurist.
The Madras Law Journal.
The Madras Law Review.
The Madras Law Times.
The Madras Review.
The Madras Weekly Notes.

I. Monographs

Abel-Smith, Brian., and Robert Stevens. *Lawyers and the Courts: A Sociological Study of the English Legal System*. Cambridge, MA: Harvard University Press, 1967.

Advocates' Association, Madras. *Advocates' Association, Madras (Founded in 1889)*. Golden Jubilee Souvenir 1939. Madras: Advocates' Association, 1939.

Anandacharlu, P. *The Madras Bar and How to Improve It*. Madras: K. R. Press, 1893.

Anstruther, T. A. *Some Instance of the Administration of Justice in Southern India*. Madras: Oriental Press, 1853.

Appadurai, Arjun. *Worship and Conflict Under Colonial Rule: A South Indian Case*. New Delhi: Orient Longman, 1981.

Appendix to the Report of the Committee Appointed to Consider the Racial Distinctions in Criminal Procedure Applicable to Indians and Non-Indians. Simla: Government Central Press, 1923.

Arnold, David. *The Congress in Tamilnad: Nationalistic Politics in South India 1919–1937*. London: Curzon Press 1977.

Auerback, Jerold S. *Unequal Justice: Lawyers and Social Change in Modern America*. New York: Oxford University Press, 1976.

Baker, Christopher J. *An Indian Rural Economy, 1880–1955: The Tamilnad Countryside*. Oxford: Clarendon Press, 1984.

——— *The Politics of South India 1920–1937*. Cambridge: Cambridge University Press, 1976.

Balasubramaniam, K. M. *South Indian Celebrities*. 2 vols. Madras: Author, 1934.

Baliga, B. S. *Studies in Madras Administration*. 2 vols. Madras: Government of Madras, 1960.

Bar Association, Calcutta. *Centenary Souvenir 1862–1962*. Calcutta: The International Press, 1962.

Baynes, Charles R. *The Civil Law of the Madras Presidency as Contained in the Existing Regulations and Acts*. Madras: Pharoah, 1852.

——— *A Plea for the Madras Judges upon the Charges Preferred against them by J. B. Norton, Esq*. Madras: Higginbotham, 1853.

Biligiri Iyengar, S., comp. *Rules of the High Court of Madras on its Original Side . . . with Statutes and Charters of the Supreme Court*. Madras: The Scottish Press, 1887.

Buckland, C. E. *A Dictionary of Indian Biography*. London: Swan Sonnenschein, 1906; reprint ed. Varanasi: Indological Books, 1971.

Calcutta Bar Association. *Centenary Souvenir 1862–1962*. Calcutta: The Centenary Celebration Committee, 1962.

Campbell, A. D. *Code of Regulations for the Internal Government of the Madras Territories, From A.D. 1802 to A.D. 1834*, 3 vols. Madras: Fort St. George Press, n.d.

——— *The Regulations for the Internal Government of the Madras Territories*. Madras: J. B. Pharoah, 1843.

Centenary Celebrations of the District & Sessions Court, Chingleput, 1880–1980. Chingleput: Bar Association, 1980.

Chandrasekhara, N. S. *Dewan Rangacharlu*. New Delhi: Publications Division, Government of India, 1968.

Chandrasekharan, K. *P. S. Sivaswami Aiyer*. New Delhi: Publications Division, Government of India, 1969.

Clark, Richard., comp. *The Regulations of the Government of Fort. St. George in force at the end of 1847*. London: J. & H. Cox, 1848.
A Collection of the Acts of the Indian Legislature and of the Governor General for the year 1923. New Delhi: Government Central Press, 1924.
Cornish, W. R. *Report on the Census of the Madras Presidency 1871*. 2 vols. Madras: The Government Press, 1874.
——— *Census of the Town of Madras, 1871*. Madras: The Fort St. George Press, 1873.
The Cosmopolitan Club, Platinum Jubilee Souvenir 1873–1954. Madras: Premier Press, 1954.
Dias, C. J., R. Luckham, D. O. Lynch and J. C. N. Paul, eds. *Lawyers in the Third World: Comparative and Developmental Perspectives*. Uppsala: Scandinavian Institute of African Studies, 1981.
Dawes, Samuel R. *A Catechism of the Law Governing Procedure in the East India Company's Civil Court in the Presidency of Ft. St. George in Original Suits*. Madras: Higginbotham, 1857.
Derrett, J. D. M. *Religion, Law and the State in India*. London: Faber and Faber, 1968.
Dillon, F. W. *From An Indian Bar Room: Sketches, Talks and Tales*. Calcutta: Butterworth, 1920.
Dodwell, Henry. *Report on the Madras Records*. Madras: Government Press, n.d.
Duman, Daniel. *The English and Colonial Bars in the Nineteenth Century*. London: Croom Helm, 1983.
Duraiswamy, M. P. *Memories of Sir T. Muthusami Ayyars, the First Indian Judge of the High Court of Madras*. Tanjore: Kalyanasundaram Power Press, 1911.
Dutt-Majumdar, Nirmalendu. *Conduct of Advocates & Legal Profession: Short History*. Calcutta: Eastern Law House, 1974.
Frykenberg, R. E. *Guntur District 1788–1848: A History of Local Influence and Central Authority in South India*. Oxford: Clarendon Press, 1965.
Frykenberg, R. E. and Pauline Kolenda, eds. *Studies of South India: an Anthology of Recent Research and Scholarship*. Madras: New Era Publications, 1985.
Galanter, Marc. *Competing Equalities: Law and the Backward Classes in India*. Berkeley: University of California Press, 1984.
Gandhi, J. S. *Lawyers and Touts: A Study in the Sociology of Legal Profession*. Delhi: Hindustan Publishing Corporation, 1982.
Gandhi, M. K. *The Law and The Lawyers*. Edited by S. B. Kher. Ahemedabad: Navajivan Publishing House, 1962.
Gopalratnam, V. C. *A Century Completed—A History of the Madras High Court 1862–1962*. Madras: Law Journal Office, 1962.
Halsbury, H. S. G. *The Complete Statutes of England*. 22 vols. London: Butterworth, 1929–1931.

Handbook of Information on the Administration of the Presidency of Madras. Madras: Government Press, 1928.

Hardgrave, Robert L. *The Dravidian Movement.* Bombay: Popular Prakashan, 1965.

High Court of Judicature, Allahabad. *Centenary—High Court of Judicature at Allahabad 1866–1966.* 2 vols. Allahabad. Centenary Commemoration Volume Committee, 1966.

High Court of Judicature, Calcutta. *The High Court of Calcutta: Centenary Souvenir 1862–1962.* Calcutta: High Court, 1962.

High Court of Judicature, Madras. *Index to the Proceedings and Letters of the High Court—Appellate Side, Madras, for the year 1885.* Madras: Scottish Press, 1886.

——— *The Madras High Court 1862–1962: Centenary Volume.* Madras: The Editorial Committee, 1962.

——— *Rules of the High Court of Judicature, Madras: Appellate Side.* Madras: The Scottish Press, 1900.

Historical Account of Courts at Madras, n.p., n.d.

Holloway, William. *Notes on Madras Judicial Administration.* Madras: Higginbotham, 1853.

Hurst, James Willard. *The Growth of American Law—The Law Makers.* Boston: Little, Brown, 1950.

Ilbert, Courtenay. *The Government of India: Being A Digest of the Statute Law Relating Thereto.* 3rd ed. Oxford: Clarendon Press, 1915.

Irschick, Eugene F. *Politics and Social Conflict in South India; The Non-Brahman Movement and Tamil Separatism, 1916–1929.* Berkeley: University of California Press, 1969.

Jain, M. P. *Outlines of Indian Legal History.* 2nd ed. Bombay: N. M. Tripathi, 1966.

Jeffery, Roger. *The Politics of Health in India.* Berkeley: University of California Press, 1988.

Katju, Kailasnath. *Reminiscences and Experiments in Advocacy.* Calcutta: University of Calcutta, 1952.

Krishnaswami Iyer, K. V. *Professional Conduct and Advocacy.* 3rd ed. Madras: Oxford University Press, 1953.

Krishnaswami Nayudu, W. S. *My Memoirs*, Madras: Author, 1977.

Kumar, Raj. *Annie Besant's Rise to Power in Indian Politics (1914–1917).* New Delhi: Concept Publishing Company, 1981.

Lajpat Rai, Lala. *Autobiographical Writings.* Edited by Vijaya Chandra Joshi. New Delhi: Servants of the People Society, 1963.

Lewandowski, Susan. *Migration and Ethnicity in Urban India: Kerala Migrants in the City of Madras, 1870–1970.* New Delhi: Manohar, 1980.

Lockyer, Charles. *Account of the Trade in India.* London: 1711. Cited by Kaye, John William. *The Administration of the East India Company*, Reprint ed., Allahabad: Kitab Mahal, 1966.

Love, Henry Davidson. *Vestiges of Old Madras 1640–1800.* 3 vols. London: John Murray, 1913.
Maclean, C. D. *Standing Information Regarding Official Administration of the Madras Presidency.* Madras: The Government Press, 1879.
Madhavan Nair, Chettur. *A Short History of Sir C. Sankaran Nair, C.I.E. (fighter for India's freedom) member of the Viceroy's Executive Council.* Madras: C. Madhavan Nair, [196-].
Madras Native Association. *Report of the Proceedings at the presentation of an Address to John Bruce Norton, Esq.* Madras: Scottish Press, 1860.
[Maitland, Julia Charlotte]. *Letters from Madras during the years 1836–1839.* London: John Murray, 1843.
Markandan, K. C. *Madras Legislative Council: Its Constitution and Workings Between 1861 and 1909.* Delhi: S. Chand, 1964.
McIver, Lewis. *Imperial Census of 1881: Operations and Results in the Presidency of Madras.* 2 vols. Madras: The Government Press, 1883.
McKinstry, Sam W. *The Brokerage Role of Rajasthani Lawyers in Three Districts of Rajasthan, India As Evidenced through Lawyer-Client Relations: Fact or Fiction?* Washington: University of America Press, 1980.
Menon, K. P. S. *C. Sankaran Nair.* New Delhi: Government of India, 1967.
Misra, Bankey Bihari. *The Indian Middle Classes: Their Growth in Modern Times.* London: Oxford University Press, 1961.
Montagu, Edwin S. *An Indian Diary.* Edited by Venetia Montagu. London: William Heinemann, 1930.
Mootham, Orby. *The East India Company's Sadar Courts, 1801–1834.* Bombay: N. M. Tripathy, 1983.
Mukherji, P. *Indian Constitutional Documents.* 2 vols. Calcutta: Thacker, Spink & Co., 1918.
Mukherji, Bisvesvar. *The Legal Practitioners' Act.* Calcutta: R. Cambray, 1903.
Narasimhan, V. K. *Kasturi Ranga Iyengar.* New Delhi: Publications Division, Government of India, 1963.
Natesan, G. A. *Sir Hari Singh Gour: His Life and Work.* Madras: Author, 1927.
Nilakanta Sastri, K. A., ed. *A Great Liberal: Speeches and Writings of Sir P. S. Sivaswami Aiyar.* Bombay: Allied Publishers, 1965.
Norton, John Bruce. *A Letter to Charles Robert Baynes, Esq., Civil and Sessions Judge of Madura: Containing A Reply to His "Plea."* Madras: Pharoah, 1853.
———. *A Letter to Robert Lowe . . . on the Condition and Requirements of the Presidency of Madras.* Madras: Pharoah, 1854.
———. *The Administration of Justice in Southern India.* Madras: Pharoah, 1853.

―――― *An Inaugural Lecture on the Study of Law and General Jurisprudence*. Madras: Pharoah, 1855.

―――― *The Law of Evidence applicable to the Courts of the East India Company, explained in a course of lectures delivered by J. B. Norton*, Madras: Pharoah, 1858.

―――― *Reply to a Madras Civilian's Defence of the Mofussil Courts in India*. London: Stevens and Norton, 1853.

Parameswaran Pillai, G. *Representative Indians*. London: George Routledge, 1897.

Penner, Peter., and Maclean, Richard D.; eds. *The Rebel Bureaucrat: Frederick John Shore (1799–1837) as Critic of William Bentinck's India*. Delhi: Chanakya Publications, 1983.

Philips, C. H., ed. *Handbook of Oriental History*. London: Royal Historical Society, 1951.

Piggott, Francis T., ed. *The Imperial Statutes Applicable to the Colonies*. 2 vols. London: William Clowes, 1904.

Ramachandrier, C. *Collection of the Decisions of the High Courts and the Privy Council on the Hindu Law of Marriage and the Effects of Apostacy After Marriage*. Madras: Scottish Press, 1891.

Ramaswami Iyer, C. P. *Biographical Vistas*. Bombay: Asia Publishing House, 1968.

―――― *Presidential Address . . . All India Vakils' Conference*. Madras: Vasantha Press, 1921.

Ramaswami Sastri, K. S. *The Future of the Brahmin*. Madras: Cooperative Printing Works, 1935.

―――― *Professor K. Sundararama Aiyar: His Life and Works*. Srirangam: Sri Vani Vilas Press, n.d.

Rogers, John D. *Crime, Justice and Society in Colonial Sri Lanka*. London: Curzon Press, 1987.

The Rules of Criminal Practice. 3rd ed. Madras: The Madras Law Journal Office, 1939.

The Rules of Practice (Moffussil). 3rd ed. Madras: V. S. N. Chari, 1933.

Sadasivan, D. *The Growth of Public Opinion in the Madras Presidency (1858–1909)*. Madras: University of Madras, 1974.

Sahay, Pande Nawal Kishor. *A Short History of the Indian Bar*. Patna: Bhaktiniketan, 1931.

Sankaran Nair, C. *Gandhi and Anarchy*. 2nd. ed. Madras: Tagore, 1922.

―――― *Autobiography of Sir C. Sankaran Nair*. Madras: K. P. Parvathi Amma, 1966.

Sapru, Tej Bahadur., ed. *Encyclopaedia of the General Acts and Codes of India*. 10 vols. Calcutta: Butterworth, 1935.

Sarva-deva-vilasa. Edited with critical introduction by V. Raghavan. Adyar: Adyar Library and Research Centre [1958].

Sayeed, Basheer Ahmed. *My Life A Struggle: An Autobiography*. Madras: The Academy of Islamic Research, 1983.

Bibliography 253

Sen, S. P. ed. *Dictionary of National Biography*. 4 vols. Calcutta: Institute of Historical Studies, 1975.

Setalvad, M. C. *The Common Law in India*. Bombay: N. M. Tripathi, 1981.

Shaw, John. *The Charters of the High Court of Judicature at Madras, and of the Courts which preceded it. From 1687 to 1865*. Madras: The Government Press, 1888.

Shukla, J. D. *Indianisation of All-India Services and Its Impact on Administration*. New Delhi: Allied Publishers, 1982.

Sidhwa, Rustam Shorabji. *The Lahore High Court and Its Principal Bar*. Lahore: Author, n.d.

Sloan, William. *Practice of the Mofussil Courts or Hand Book of Reference for the Judge and Pleader*. 2nd ed. Madras: Higginbotham, 1868.

Sorabji, Cornelia. *India Calling: The Memories of Cornelia Sorabji*. Reprint ed. London: Nisbet, 1935.

Speeches and Writings of Sir T. Muthuswamy Aiyar. With an Introductory Memoir by F. Rowlandson. Madras: The Lawrence Asylum Press, 1895.

Srinivasa Chariar, S. C., comp. *Political Opinions of Raja Sir T. Madhava Row, K.C.S.I*. Madras: Ripon Press, 1890.

Srivatsava, Ramesh Chandra. *Development of Judicial System in India Under the East India Company, 1833–1858*. Lucknow: Lucknow Publishing House, 1971.

Strange, T. L. *Letter to the Government of Fort Saint George on Judicial Reform*. Madras: The Society for Promoting Christian Knowledge, 1860.

Stuart, H. A. *Census of India, 1891*. 28 vols. Calcutta: The Government of India Press, 1893.

Sundara Iyer, P. R. *Professional Ethics*. Madras: P. R. Rama Iyer, 1918.

Sundarum Sastri, C. V. *Remarks on the Bill of Cost of Attorneys, Part I*. Madras: The Irish Press, 1893.

Suntharalingam, R. *Politics and Nationalist Awakening in South India, 1852–1891*. Tucson: University of Arizona Press, 1974.

Thurston, Edgar. *Castes and Tribes of Southern India*. Assisted by K. Rangachari. 7 vols. Madras: Government Press, 1909.

Trevelyan, Raleigh. *The Golden Oriole*. New York: Viking, 1987.

Tyabji, Husain B. *Badruddin Tyabji, a biography*. Bombay: Thacker, 1952.

University of Madras. *History of Higher Education in South India. Centenary Commemoration of the University of Madras, 1857–1957*. 2 vols. Madras: Associated Printers, 1957.

Vachha, P. V. *Famous Judges, Lawyers and Cases of Bombay During the British Period*. Bombay: N. M. Tripathi, 1961.

Venkatasubba Sastri, K. N. *The Munro System of British Statesmanship in India*. Mysore: University of Mysore, 1939.

Venkateswara Aiyar, M. K. *True Brahminism in Life and Law.* Madras: Madras Law Journal Press, 1928.
Viswanatha Sastri, V. S. *Biography of a Grandfather and his Grandson.* Madras: Author, 1939.
Washbrook, D. A. *The Emergence of Provincial Politics: The Madras Presidency 1870–1920.* Cambridge: Cambridge University Press, 1976.
Williams, William Plubridge, comp. *The Acts of the Legislative Council of India relating to the Madras Presidency for 1848 to 1858.* Madras: Scottish Press, 1859.

J. Articles

A.P.S. 'South Indian Snobs'. *The Madras Review* 10 (August 1904): 186–193.
Abel, Richard L. 'The Underdevelopment of Legal Profession: A Review Article on Third World Lawyers'. *American Bar Foundation Research Journal* (1982): 871–93.
Derrett, J. D. M. 'J. H. Nelson: A Forgotten Administrator-Historian'. In *Historians of India, Pakistan and Ceylon.* Edited by C. H. Philips, London: Oxford University Press, 1961.
Frykenberg, R. E. 'Modern Education in South India, 1784–1854: Its Roots and Its Role as a Vehicle of Integration under Company Raj'. *The American Historical Review* 91:1 (February 1986): 37–65.
Galanter, Marc. 'An Incomplete Bibliography of the Indian Legal Profession'. *Law and Society Review* 3:2–3 (November 1968–February 1969): 445–62.
────── 'Study of Indian Legal Profession'. *Law and Society Review* 3:2–3 (November 1968–February 1969): 201–17.
Kidder, Robert L. 'Report on the Conference on the Comparative Study of the Legal Profession with Special Reference to India'. *Law and Society Review* 3:2–3 (November 1968–February 1969): 415–44.
────── 'Formal Litigation and Professional Insecurity: Legal Entrepreneurship in South India'. *Law and Society Review* 9:1 (1974): 11–37.
Mendelsohn, Oliver. 'The Pathology of Indian Legal System'. *Modern Asian Studies.* 15:4 (1981): 823–63.
Morrison, Charles. 'Social Organisation at the District Courts: Colleague Relationship among Indian Lawyers'. *Law and Society Review* 3:2–3 (November 1968–February 1969): 251–67.
────── 'Kinship in Professional Relations: A Study of North Indian District Lawyers'. *Comparative Studies in Society and History* 14 (1972): 1–14.
Nash, Gary B. 'The Philadelphia Bench and Bar, 1800–1861'. *Comparative Studies in Society and History* 7 (1964–5): 206–37.

Oommen, T. K. 'The Legal Profession in India: Some Sociological Perspectives'. In *The Legal Profession: A Preliminary Study of the Tamilnadu Bar*. Edited by N. R. Madhava Menon, (New Delhi: Bar Council of India Trust, 1984) pp. 1–46.
Paul, John and Lata Krishnamurty. 'A Tentative Bibliography on Indian Legal Profession (with Special Reference to Tamil Nadu)'. In *The Legal Profession: A Preliminary Study of the Tamilnadu Bar*. Edited by N. R. Madhava Menon (New Delhi: Bar Council of India Trust, 1984) pp. 244–62.
———— 'Removal of the Sex Bar in the Indian Legal Profession: An Historical Note'. *Committee on South Asian Women Bulletin* 4:4 (1986): 21–5.
———— 'Authority and Profession Control of the Subordinate Legal Profession in the Madras Presidency During the Late Nineteenth Century'. In *Law and Social Transformation*. Edited by Yogendra Malik and Dhirendra Vajpeyi. Leiden: Brill, 1989.
Price, Pamela G. 'Ideology and Ethnicity under British Imperial Rule: 'Brahmans, Lawyers and Kin-Caste Rules in Madras Presidency'. *Modern Asian Studies* 23:1 (1989): 151–77.
Ray, Rajat K. 'Political Change in British India'. *The Indian Economic and Social History Review*. 14:4 (October–December 1977): 493–17.
Rowe, Peter. 'Indian Lawyers and Political Modernization: Observations in Four District Towns'. *Law and Society Review* 3:2–3 (November 1968–February 1969): 219–50.
Schmitthener, Samuel. 'A Sketch of the Development of the Legal Profession in India'. *Law and Society Review* 3:2–3 (November 1968–February 1969): 337–82.
Shaw, John. 'The Predecessors of the Madras High Court, Part II'. *Madras Journal of Literature and Science* (1881): 81–157.
Srinivasa Rao, V. N. 'The Growth of the Madras Bar'. *Lawyer* 7:1 (November 1967): 9–13.
———— 'The Origin and Growth of the Legal Profession in Tamil Nadu—A Historical Study From 1640 to 1947'. In *The Legal Profession: A Preliminary Study of the Tamilnadu Bar*, N. R. Madhava Menon, ed. (New Delhi: Bar Council of Indian Trust, 1984), pp. 47–99.
———— 'The Origin and Story of the Law College'. *Lawyer* 13:1 (February 1968): 23–7.
Webb, A. D. 'Charles Edward Trevelyan in India: A Study of the Channels of Influence Employed by a Covenanted Civil Servant in the Translation of Personal Ideas into Official Policy.' *South Asia* NS 6:2 (November 1983): 15–23.

K. Tamil Books

Cellammal, Es. *Annal Civasvami Aiyar* [The Great Sivasvami Iyer]. Madras: Pi. Ji. Pal, [1965].

Caminataiyar, U. Ve. *En Carittiram* [My History]. Tiruvanmiyur: Taktar U. Ve. Caminataiyar Nul Nilayam, 1982.

——— *Ninaivu mancari* [Garland of Memories]. 2 vols. Madras: Kabeer Printing Works, 1957.

Cantiracekaran, Ki. *Vi. Kirushnasvami Aiyar* [V. Krishnaswami Iyer]. Cennai: Kalaimakal Kariyalayam, 1945.

Cuntara Rakavan, Ke., and Ranka Rakavan, Ke. *Tivan Pahatur* [Diwan Bahadhur Srinivasa Raghava Iyengar]. Cennai: Kalamohini Piras, 1956.

——— *Sar Vi. Pashyam Aiyankar* [Sir V. Bhashyam Iyengar]. Mayilapur: Intiya Pirintin Orks, 1943.

——— *Rai Pahatur Pi. Anantacarlu* [Rai Bahadhur P. Anandacharlu]. Cennai: Allaiyans Kampani, 1943.

Kaliyanacuntaranar, Tiru. Vi. *Tiru. Vi. Ka. Valkkaik Kurippukal* [Tiru. Vi. Ka. Memoirs]. 2 vols. Tirunelveli: Saiva Siddhanta Works Publishing Society, 1969.

L. Unpublished Materials

Breckenridge, Carol A. 'The Sri Minaksi Sundaresvarar Temple: Worship and Endowments in South India, 1833–1925'. Ph.D. dissertation. University of Wisconsin-Madison. 1976.

Buckee, G. F. M. 'An Examination of the Development and Structure of the Legal Profession at Allahabad, 1866–1935'. Ph.D. dissertation. School of Oriental and African Studies. London, 1971.

Hume, John C. 'Medicine in the Punjab, 1849–1911'. Ph.D. dissertation, Duke University, 1977.

Meschievitz, Catherine. 'Civil Litigation and Judicial Policy in the Madras Presidency, 1800–1843'. Ph.D. dissertation. University of Wisconsin-Madison, 1986.

Paul, John. 'Stages and Actors in the Drama of Indian Law: The Dismissal Proceedings of Munsif Vedanayagam Pillai (1826–1889)'. Paper read at the Twelfth Annual Conference on South Asia held at the University of Wisconsin-Madison. 4–6 November 1983.

——— 'New Frontiers in the Colonial Judicial Administration: Its Laws and Lawyers'. Paper read at the International Conference on 'South Asia and World Capitalism', held at the Tufts University, Medford, MA. 12–14 December 1986.

——— 'Indigenization of the Western Medical Profession during the Nineteenth Century, with Special Reference to South India'. Paper read at the Sixtieth Annual Meeting of the American Association for the History of Medicine, Philadelphia. 30 April through 3 May 1987.

Price, Pamela G. 'Resources and Rule in Zamindari South India, 1802–1903: Sivagangai and Ramnad As Kingdoms Under the *Raj*'. Ph.D. dissertation, University of Wisconsin-Madison. 1979.

III. INTERVIEWS

Mr. V. K. T. Chari. Former Advocate General of Madras. 24 April 1982.
Dr. R. Krishnaswami. Advocate. Madras. 28 February 1983.
Mr. M. Raja. Secretary. Tamilnadu Legal Aid Board. 2 April 1982.
Dr. A. Ramaswami. Retired Professor. Madras. 1 March 1982.
Mr. Govind Swaminathan. Former Advocate General of Madras. 8 May 1983.

INDEX

Act XXVII of 1836, 34
Act I of 1846, 23, 25, 29, 59, 183
Act XXXVIII of 1850, 25
Act XX of 1853, 25, 29
advocates, 60, 83–4, 102–3, 105–6, 108, 134, 136, 139, 150, 163, 170, 173, 178–80, 184, 186
Advocates' Association, Madras, 5
agraharam, 8
Ahmad, K., 172
All India Bar Council, 80, 83, 190
All-India Bar Committee Report, 165, 190 (*see also Chamier's Committee Report*)
Allahabad, 58
Ananda Bai, B., 162–4
Anandacharlu, P., 8, 81–2, 94–5, 97, 115, 121, 130
Ananthakrishna Iyer, C. V., 180
Anstruther, Alexander, 22
Anstruther, Thomas A., 38
Appellate Side, 4, 5, 7, 45–6, 49, 53, 60–1*, 75, 80, 147, 174, 185
Arbuthnot Firm, 103
arzis, 27
The Atheaneum and Statesman, 77
attorneys, 2, 4, 25, 46–7, 62, 73, 77, 80–1, 89–91, 93, 96, 102–3, 105–6, 108, 130, 132, 134, 137–8, 150, 157, 169–70, 173, 178, 184–7, 191; academic background, 75–6; *ad hoc* meetings, 78; association, 91, 176; 'attorney-vakils', 74; bill of costs, 74, 76–7, 174, 186; Europeans, 95; grievances, 80–1; High Court rules, 74–5; Indians, 95; opposition to vakils, 79–81; pre-High Court practice, 73–4; precedence over pleaders, 74; *see also* High Court, barristers, vakils
Auerback, Jerold S., 158

Bachelor of Law (B.L.), 37, 60, 95, 128
Bachelor in Civil Law (B.C.L.), 159
Baillie, N. B. E., 26, 27, 29
Balaji Rao, R., 82, 88, 127, 140
bankers, 93
Bar Assocation (also the Madras Bar), 5, 7, 62, 64, 78–9, 83, 89, 119, 161, 175–6, 187; conflict among members, 66–9; government patronage, 69–70; resolutions: against vakils, 63; on fees, 63; against giving commissions, 65–6; *see also* Vakils' Association
Barclay, E., 79
barristers, 2, 4, 7, 23–5, 39, 41, 46–7, 59–63, 67–76, 78–80, 83, 86, 89–91, 93, 95, 98, 102, 119, 122–3, 127, 130, 132, 134, 137–8, 140–3, 147, 150, 157–8, 165–72, 174–6, 179, 183, 185–7, 191; admission to Supreme Court, 23–5; barrister-attorney coalition, 7, 59, 185; barrister-judges, 62; barrister-vakils, 49, 51, 61–2; contributions, 70–1; 'eight-term' barristers, 68; position in High Court, 59–62; Indian barristers, 83; practice in Supreme Court, 22–3;

260 *Index*

precedence over attorneys and vakils, 74; public opinion of, 71–3; *see also*, attorneys, High Court, pleaders, Supreme Court, and vakils
Baynes, Charles R., 38
Beasley, H. O. C. (Justice), 174
Benson, Justice, 112
Besant, Annie, 148
Bhashyam Iyengar, K., 135, 180
Bhashyam Iyengar, V., 8, 82, 97, 120, 127, 138, 146; Advocate General, 142; Justice, 115, 120–1, 174
Bittleston, Adam (Justice), 61
Boddam, Justice, 112–13, 115
brahmans, 8, 137, 147, 149, 152, 180, 188–90
Branson, Reddy, 139
Branson, Spring J. H., 69, 142, 186
Bryant, J. B., 166
Buckee, G. F. M., 4–5
Butler, F. G., 175

Calcutta, 58
Ceded Districts, 147
Chamier, E. M. D., 10
Chamier's Committee Report, 169, 175, 177; *see also All-India Bar Committee Report*
Champion, Alfred, 59, 64
Chettiars, Nattukkottai, 56
City Civil Court, 83
Civil and Criminal Procedures Codes, 84–5
Civil and Military Gazette, 93
Clarke, Richard, 21
Co-operative Societies Act (1912), 109
Coimbatore Spinning and Weaving Company, Ltd., 114
Coimbatore Varthaka Vridhi Dharmajana Sangam, 114

College of Fort St. George, 6, 21, 31, 183
Collins, Sir Arthur (Chief Justice), 93–4, 111–12
Court of Wards, 139–40
Court of Directors, 26, 183
Court of the Recorder, 73
Coutts-Trotter, Sir V. M., (Chief Justice) 81, 108, 113, 115, 161, 170, 172, 178

Dale, Clement, 52
Datta, S. K., 171
Davidson, John, 29
Davis, Justice, 111
Desikachari, K. C., 121, 139
Devadoss, Seeta, 164
Devadoss, M. D. (Justice), 104, 106, 175
Devanadhan, V. V., 107
doctors, 71, 92
double-agency, 46, 54, 71, 77, 99, 170, 176, 185, 190
dubashis, 1
Duraiswami Iyer, S., 180
durbar, 56

East India Company, 1, 17, 45, 182, 187
editors, 82–3
Education Commission, 99
Egmore, 124–5, 146, 148
engineering, 35, 37, 99
Ethiraja Mudaliar, T., 121, 149
Eurasians, 21, 75
Evidence Bill, 72

First World War, 158
Fort St. George Gazette, 47
Frere, Hatley (Justice), 61

Galanter, Marc, 1
Ganapathi Iyer, P. R., 121, 150
Gandhian agitation, 3

gomastahs, 66
Gopalaswami Mudaliar, T. V., 121
Gould, John, 81
Gounder, 147
Gour, Hari S., 161, 168
Government of Fort St. George, 29, 148
Government of India, 10, 21, 23, 26, 29, 145, 161, 175
Government of Bengal, 19
Governor General, 34, 53
Grant, Nugent, 180
Gray's Inn, 68, 146
Guha, Regina, 160

Hailey, Sir Malcolm, 168
Haldane, Viscount, 166
Happel, A. C., 163
Hazra, S. B., 160
High Court, of Allahabad, 4, 116, 158, 178
High Court, of Bengal (or Calcutta), 2, 4, 47, 54, 55, 116, 166–7, 170, 172, 178
High Court, of Bombay, 2, 4, 47, 54, 55, 72, 116, 166–7, 170, 172, 178
High Court, of Madras, 2, 4, 6, 47, 54, 56, 60; 1862 Rules, 48–50; 1863 Rules, 50–4; reasons for, 54, 170, 174; views on bar councils, 174–5
High Court, of Travancore, 55–6
The Hindu, 93–4, 133, 141
Hindu Law, 19, 49, 68, 159, 184
Holloway, William (Justice), 38, 45, 54, 61–2, 184
Home Rule Movement, 148
House of Lords, 22

Ibrahim Sahib, Muhammad, 180
Indian Advocates' Act (1961), 2
Indian Bank, 110

Indian Bar Council Act (1926), 2, 14, 107–8, 138, 171; results, 173–4, 177–9; *see also* the Madras Bar Council
Indian Christians, 21, 101
Indian Civil Service Commission, 96
The Indian Jurist, 185
Indian National Congress, 97, 144, 148
Indore, 159
Inner Temple, 164
Inns of Court, London, 67, 129, 166, 175
insolvency court, 83, 166, 174, 186
Insolvency Commissioner, 103
Iyengar (also Sri Vaishanavas), 8, 120, 125, 146; *see also* brahmans
Iyer (also Saivas), 8, 120, 125, 146; *see also* brahmans

Jallianwala Bagh massacre, 145
Jana Upaharam Vridhi, Ltd., 114
journalists, 93, 97
Justice Party, 100, 148

Kasturi Ranga Iyengar, S., 123–4
Kathiawar, 159
Kernan, Justice, 89, 91–3
King's Inn, Ireland, 67
Krishnamachari, K., 120
Krishnan, C. (Justice), 161
Krishnaswami Iyengar, K. S., 180
Krishnaswami Iyer, Alladi, 105, 180
Krishnaswami Iyer, G., 106
Krishnaswami Iyer, V., 8, 103, 121, 123, 133; Justice, 85, 116
Krishnaswami Nayudu, W. S., 88
Kumaraswami Sastri, C. V., 56; Justice, 107–8

Lahore, 58

Index

Lajpat Rai, Lala, 144
Lakshiminarasu Chetty, G., 40
Lal, Nand, 166
Lascelles, F. H., 63–6, 68–9, 79
Law College, Madras, 84, 96;
  Muslim graduates, 101
The Law Digest and Recorder, 159
Lawyers' Conference, Madras, 86, 151–2, 157
The Legal Practitioners' Act (Act XVIII of 1879), 66, 109, 138, 160, 162, 164, 167, 173
The Legal Practitioners' (Women) Act of 1923, 161
Leith, John F., 24
Letters Patent (of 1862), 13, 47, 48, 184; amended (in 1865), 55, 85, 105, 138, 173, 184
Lincoln's Inn, 146
Lockyer, Charles, 12, 17, 182
The London Times, 159, 169
Lord Reading (Viceroy), 157
Lowe, Robert, 38

Mackenzie, G. F., 114
The Madras Bar Council, 174–81; election rules, 177–8; first election, 179–81; views on its formation, 174–7
The Madras Daily Times, 36, 38
The Madras Law Journal, 113, 138, 140
Madras Mahajana Sabha, 97, 124
The Madras Mail, 68, 90–1, 142
Madras Native Association, 40, 97
'Madras system', 6, 38
The Madras Times, 60, 68–70, 72, 74, 77–8, 90–1
Madras University, 55, 138, 163
The Madras Weekly Notes, 110, 151, 179
Madura, 147
Maitland, Julia, 33

Malabar, 146
The Manchester Guardian, 76
Masilamani Pillai, V., 121
Master of Law (M.L.), 60, 83, 129
Mayne, John D., 36, 48, 49, 59, 71, 186
Mayors Court, Madras, 12, 22, 73
medicine, 35, 37, 99, 143
Menon, K. P. M., 180
Middle Temple, 68–9, 146
Misra, B. B., 6, 19
Montagu-Chelmsford Reforms of 1919, 10, 145, 157
Moore, Lewis (Justice), 112, 116
Morehead, William A., 45, 46
Morgan, Sir Walter (Chief Justice), 70, 81
Morgan, Walter, 70
Muddiman, Sir Alexander, 171–2
mufassal, 23
mukhtars, 55, 159
Munro, Sir Thomas, 183
munsifs, 25, 28, 132
Muslim (or Mohomedan) Law, 19, 49, 68
Muthuswamy Iyer, Sir T. (Justice), 119, 128
mutiny, 39, 184
Mylapore, 124–5, 146, 148

Naidu vakil, 147
Nair, T. M., 149
T. Namberumal Chetty, v. M. P. Narasimhachar, 81
Nash, Gary B., 187
'native bar', 40, 47, 71, 119
Neogy, K. C., 167–8
New Delhi, 165, 167
non-brahmans, 137, 180
Non-Brahman Lawyers' Association, 136, 149, 151–2, 188; *see also*, Vakils' Association

Index 263

Non-Cooperation Movement, 145
Norton, Eardley, 66, 83, 166
Norton, George, 6, 34, 35, 59, 183
Norton, John B. (also J. B. and John Bruce), 35, 36, 37, 39, 40, 45, 46, 47, 59, 71, 184, 186

O'Sullivan, Patrick, 59, 66, 81
Oddie, G. A., 10, 11
Odgers, Justice, 175
Oldfield, Justice, 114
Original Side, 4, 5, 7, 49–51, 53–4, 60, 63, 71, 73, 75–6, 79–80, 84, 86, 104, 119, 139–40, 147, 166–7, 170, 172–4, 185–6

Paddison, G. F., 164
Palayapatti, 139
Parliamentary Committee, 22, 24, 30
'pamphlet controversy', 30, 37–9, 184
Parthasarathy Iyengar, C. R., 114
Parthasarathy Iyengar, M. O., 146
Patna, 58
Pattabhirama Iyer, C. R., 121
Phillips, Henry D. (Justice), 61–2
pleaders, 2, 6, 13, 15–33, 39–41, 46, 48, 50–1, 82, 88, 97, 108–12, 114, 116, 128, 132, 137, 150, 157, 169, 182–4; admission to criminal courts, 25; descriptions of Clarke, 21–2; evaluations of Baillie, 26–30; Eurasians and Indian Christians, 21; Hindus and Muslims, 19, 21, 26, 29, 32; leadership, 40; legal training, 31–7; 'officer of the court', 2, 183; 'pamphlet controversy', 37–9; 'private vakils', 37; qualifications of, 19–20; rules of practice: Regulation X of 1802, 18–19; Regulation XIV of 1816, 20–1; Act I of 1846, 23–5; transactions, 25; *see also* vakils.
preaudience, 83, 171–2
Presidency Towns' Insolvency Act of 1909, 103, 105, 107
Presidency College, Madras, 6, 35, 36, 37, 49, 124, 184
Public Service Commission, 70
purdahnashins (or *purdah*), 159, 160

Raghavendra Row, H., 139
Rahim, Abdur (Justice), 102
raja, 17
Rama Rao, T., 40, 81–2, 120, 127, 146
Ramachandra Iyer, K., 121
Ramachandra Iyer, T. R., 116, 120–1, 180
Ramachandra Rao Sahib, C., 121
Ramadas, V., 135
Ramakrishna Iyer, M. R., 121
Ramalingam Chettiar, T. A., 180
Ramanujachari, V., 40
Ramaswami Iyer, Sir C. P., 116, 121, 135, 157–8, 177, 182
Ramaswami Mudaliar, A., 116, 149
Ramaswami Mudaliar, Salem, 96–7
Ramesam, Vepa, 121
Rangachariar, T., 121, 167–8, 170, 172, 180
Rangaiah Naidu, P., 40
Regulation X of 1802, 12, 13, 17, 18, 19, 20, 182
Regulation XXVII of 1814, 19
Regulation XIV of 1816, 20, 34, 182
Regulation V of 1817, 32, 34
Regulation IV of 1832, 21

Index

Ranganatha Sastri, C. V., 97
Rising Sun, 40
Rozario, J. L., 120

Sadagopachari, V., 40, 52, 140
Sadagopachariar, R., 120
Sadasiva Iyer, T. (Justice), 56
sadr amins, 28
Sadr Adalat, 13, 18, 20, 21, 25, 29, 30, 34, 37, 39, 45, 47, 59, 60, 62, 73–4, 82, 183–4
sanad, 20
Sankara Menon, K. P., 120–1
Sankaran Nair, C., 88, 120–1, 123, 146, 149
Sapru, Sir Tej Bahadur, 157, 164, 166–7
Saran, Munshi Iswar, 165, 167–8
Sastri, K. R. S., 121
saucars, 89
Schmitthener, S., 4
Schwabe, Sir Walter (Chief Justice), 105
Scotland, Sir Colley H. (Chief Justice), 48, 54, 61
Secretary of State for India, 9, 47, 142–3
Seditious Meetings Bill, 145
Seshagiri Iyer, T. V., 135; Justice, 56
Sex Disqualification (Removal) Act, of 1919, 158, 160
Shanmugam Chetty, R. K., 149
Shephard, Horatio H., 84, 88; Justice, 111, 128
Sivaswami Iyer, P. S., 8, 87–8, 116, 120–1, 123–5, 127, 129, 146
Small Cause Court, 76, 97–8
Smyth, Sydney T., 45, 46, 61
Sorabji, Cornelia, 159–60
Spencer, Charles G. (Justice), 106
Srinivasa Iyengar, Sir K., 56–7, 121, 135, 177

Srinivasa Iyengar, S., 9–10, 120–1, 157–8, 180; Advocate General, 150
Srinivasa Iyengar, V. V., 106, 163; Justice, 121; *see also*, Vakils' Association
Srinivasa Rao, V. N., 4, 5, 13
Sriramulu Sastri, R. 112
Stokes, Whitley, 60–2, 69
Strange, Sir Thomas, 12, 17, 22, 182
Strange, Thomas L., 45
Subramania Iyer, G., 97
Subramania Iyer, S., 8, 40, 82, 88, 97, 120, 127, 132, 146; Justice, 111, 141
Subramania Sastri, K. R., 123
Sundara Iyer, P. R., 8, 87, 121
Sundarum Sastri, C. V., 77, 121
Suntharalingam, R., 11, 37
Supreme Court, Madras, 6, 12, 23, 24, 39, 46, 48, 50, 51, 59, 62, 73–4, 102–3, 107, 183–4
Swaminatha Iyer, M. A., 55
Swaminathan, Govind, 147

Tamil Nadu Brahmins' Association, 190
Tanjore, 147
Thanikachalam Chettiar, O., 88, 149
Tinnevelly, 146
touts, 63, 66, 73, 89, 95, 161
Trevelyan, Sir Charles E., 6, 45, 47, 59, 82, 96, 184
Trichy, 147
Triplicane, 146
Trivandrum, 55

United India Life Assurance Company, 110

Vaidyanatha Iyer, S., 83
vakalat or *vakalatnamah*, 3, 20, 23, 166

Index

'vakil bar', 109, 110, 122–3, 134, 141
'vakil raj', 172
'vakil-system', 13
vakils, 1, 8, 13, 45, 47–8, 51–2, 61–2, 70–1, 76, 80–1, 147, 150, 158, 163, 165–72, 175–6, 178–9, 182–8, 191; academic preparation, 82–3; admission of candidates outside Madras, 55–7; annual gatherings, 133–6; apprenticeship, 84–5, 128–9; attendance at lectures, 85–6; attire, 127; attorneys' rivalry, 79–91; brahman domination, 120, 137, 146–7; career opportunities, 96–7; criticisms from judges, 89–94; from Pudukkottai, 56–7; enrolment, 86–7; High Court admission rules, 48–54; juniors, 87–9; leadership roles, 97–8; 'less fortunate' vakils, 135; non-brahman vakils, 9, 180; numerical growth, 98–9; senior-junior relations, 134–5; vakil-advocates, 129–30; vakil-judges, 57; *see also*, attorneys, barristers, High Court, Lawyers' Conference, pleaders, 'private vakils', Sadr Adalat, 'native bar', 'vakil bar', 'vakil raj' and 'vakil system'
Vakils' Association, Allahabad, 158
Vakils' Association, Madras High Court, 8–11, 55–7, 89, 93, 95, 97, 102–3, 106, 109–10, 120, 122, 128, 131, 161, 175–6, 180–1, 187, 190; functions: supervision of members, 137–40; representation to authorities, 140–3; advisory role, 143–6; officers: president, 122; secretary, 122; managing committee, 123; elections, 123–5; resolutions: membership, 125; collection of dues, 126–7; vakil-advocates, 128–30; privileges: library, 131; vakils' chambers, 131–2; appointments, 132–3; annual gatherings, 133–6; rival association, 149–53; *see also*, attorneys, Bar Association.
Veeraraghavachariar, M., 97
Venkatachalam Pantulu, C., 180
Venkatarama Sastri, T. R., 121, 180
Venkataramana Rao, P., 180
Venkataramayya, W. L., 133
Venkataramiah Chetty, M., 8, 121
Venkatasubba Rao, M., 105
Venkatasubbaramiah, C., 121
Venkatroyalu Naidu, M., 40
Vincent, Sir William, 161
Visvanatha Iyer, K. P., 121
Viswanatha Sastri, V., 130

Waddy, Cadwallader, 69
Waller, David G., 106
Wallis, Sir John E. P. (Chief Justice), 56–7
Walsh, P. (Justice), 108
The West Coast, 133
White, Sir Arnold C., Advocate General, 112, 142; Chief Justice, 112
Willoughby, John P., 23, 24
Wilson, R., 91
Women's Graduate Union, 161
Women's Indian Association, 161
'Wood's Dispatch', 35

zamindar (and *zamindari*), 17, 23, 139
zenana, 159
zillah, 19